D1130335

Doctors from Hell

First Sentient Publications edition, 2005

Grateful acknowledgment is made for permission to reproduce photographs from the United States Holocaust Memorial Museum, the Museum of the Jimmy Carter Library, and the National Archives and Records Administration.

Cover design by Kim Johansen, Black Dog Design
Book design by Nicholas Cummings

Library of Congress Cataloging-in-Publication Data

Spitz, Vivien.
  Doctors from hell : the horrific account of Nazi experiments on humans / Vivien Spitz.—1st Sentient Publications ed.
    p. cm.
  Includes bibliographical references.
  ISBN 1-59181-032-9
  1. Human experimentation in medicine—Germany—History—20th century. 2. Medical ethics—Germany—History—20th century. 3. Nuremberg Trial of Major German War Criminals, Nuremberg, Germany, 1945-1946. 4. National socialism—Moral and ethical aspects. 5. National socialism and medicine.
  I. Title.
  R853.H8S68 2005
  174.2'8--dc22

                                        2005006021

Printed in the United States of America

10

SENTIENT PUBLICATIONS
A Limited Liability Company
1113 Spruce St.
Boulder, CO 80302
www.sentientpublications.com

Doctors from Hell

The Horrific Account of
Nazi Experiments on Humans

Vivien Spitz

with a new Foreword by Elie Wiesel

SENTIENT PUBLICATIONS, LLC

The Moving Finger writes; and having writ,
Moves on; nor all your Piety nor Wit
Shall lure it back to cancel half a Line,
Nor all your Tears wash out a word of it.

—The Rubaiyat, Omar Khayyam

Dedication

Whoever [shall] save a single life, saves an entire world.

—The Talmud

In genocides there are perpetrators. There are victims. There are silent bystanders. There are rescuers.

This book is dedicated to two rescuers: the late Father Bruno Reynders and Dr. Michel Reynders.

In 1939, a Benedictine monk was on a mission in Frankfurt, Germany. Hearing some commotion in the street, he looked up and, to his horror, he saw an old Jew being harassed, maligned, and brutalized by the passers-by. The monk was Pere Bruno Reynders of Louvain, Belgium. He was outraged by the scene to the point of nausea.

When the Nazis invaded Belgium and began persecuting and deporting Jews, Pere Bruno decided to come to the help of these innocent people and, with the help of his family and many friends, he was able to rescue about 320 Jewish children and a few adults. Among his cooperating relatives was his nephew, Michel, then a young teenager, who assisted him as a messenger and occasional escort.

Always shy and modest, when asked why he put his life at risk to save Jewish children, Pere Bruno said, "because they were human beings in peril, and it was our duty to help save their lives." Michel Reynders never forgot these words and became a doctor, guided by the same principles. He retired in 1995 as a Clinical Professor of the

University of Colorado School of Medicine and lives in Denver, Colorado, with Colette, his wife of forty-four years. They have two sons and four grandsons.

Hippocratic Oath

I swear by Apollo Physician and Asclepius and Hygieia and Panaceia and all the gods and goddesses, making them my witnesses, that I will fulfill according to my ability and judgment this oath and this covenant:

To hold him who has taught me this art as equal to my parents and to live my life in partnership with him, and if he is in need of money to give him a share of mine, and to regard his offspring as equal to my brothers in male lineage and to teach them this art—if they desire to learn it—without fee and covenant; to give a share of precepts and oral instruction and all the other learning to my sons and to the sons of him who has instructed me and to pupils who have signed the covenant and have taken an oath according to the medical law, but no one else.

I will apply dietetic measures for the benefit of the sick according to my ability and judgment; I will keep them from harm and injustice.

I will neither give a deadly drug to anybody who asked for it, nor will I make a suggestion to this effect. Similarly I will not give to a woman an abortive remedy. In purity and holiness I will guard my life and my art.

I will not use the knife, not even on sufferers from stone, but will withdraw in favor of such men as are engaged in this work.

Whatever houses I may visit, I will come for the benefit of the sick, remaining free of all intentional injustice, of all mischief and in particular of sexual relations with both female and male persons, be they free or slaves.

What I may see or hear in the course of the treatment or even outside of the treatment in regard to the life of men, which on no account one must spread abroad, I will keep to myself, holding such things shameful to be spoken about.

If I fulfill this oath and do not violate it, may it be granted to me to enjoy life and art, being honored with fame among all men for all time to come; if I transgress it and swear falsely, may the opposite of all this be my lot.

Contents

Without Conscience

Foreword by
Elie Wiesel

This is one of those stories that invite fear.

Now we know. During the period of the past century that I call Night, medicine was practiced in certain places not to heal but to harm, not to fight off death but to serve it.

In the conflict between Good and Evil during the Second World War, the infamous Nazi doctors played a crucial role. They preceded the torturers and assassins in the science of organized cruelty that we call the Holocaust. There is a Talmudic adage, quite disturbing, that applies to them: *Tov she-barofim le-gehinom*—"The best doctors are destined for hell." The Nazi doctors made hell.

Inspired by Nazi ideology and implemented by its apostles, eugenics and euthanasia in the late 1930s and early 1940s served no social necessity and had no scientific justification. Like a poison, they ultimately contaminated all intellectual activity in Germany. But the doctors were the precursors. How can we explain their betrayal? What made them forget or eclipse the Hippocratic Oath? What gagged their conscience? What happened to their humanity?

In all truth, the medical field was not the only one to subscribe to Hitler's plan. There was the judicial profession. And in some ways, the church. Only the literary world retained its sense of honor: the great writers, for the most part, were exiled. Not only Jews—Thomas Mann and Bertolt Brecht were not Jewish, but they were unable to breathe in the stifling air of the Third Reich. Doctors, on the other hand, mostly stayed—not the Jewish ones, but the others.

We know the facts. The motives as well. One day, Hitler and Himmler's health minister made it known to leaders in the medical field that, according to a secret decision made at the highest level, it was necessary to get rid of "useless mouths"—the insane, the terminally ill, children, and elderly people who were condemned to misfortune by nature and to suffering and fear by God. Few in the German medical profession believed it worthy or good to refuse.

Thus, instead of doing their job, instead of bringing assistance and comfort to the sick people who needed them most, instead of helping the mutilated and the handicapped to live, eat, and hope one more day, one more hour, doctors became their executioners.

In October 1939, several weeks after the beginning of hostilities, Hitler gave the first order concerning the *Gnadentod,* or "charitable death." On the 15th of that month, gas was used for the first time to kill "patients" in Poznán, Poland. But similar centers had already been created in Germany three years earlier. Now, psychiatrists and other doctors collaborated in a professional atmosphere exemplary for its camaraderie and efficiency. In less than two years, 70,000 sick people disappeared into the gas chambers. The *Gnadentod* program was going so well that the head of the Wehrmacht Hospital psychiatric ward, Professor Wurth, worried, "With all the mentally ill being eliminated, who will want to pursue studies in the burgeoning field of psychiatry?" The program was interrupted only when the bishop of Münster, Clemens August Graf von Galen, had the courage to denounce it from his cathedral's pulpit; protest, in other words, came not from the medical profession, but from the church. Finally, public opinion was moved: too many German families were directly affected.

Like the fanatical German theorists, Nazi doctors did their work without any crisis of conscience. They were convinced that by helping Hitler to realize his racial ambitions, they were contributing to the salvation of humanity. The eminent Nazi doctor responsible for "ethical" questions, Rudolf Ramm, did not hesitate to declare that "only an honest and moral person may become a good doctor."

Thus, the doctors who tortured, tormented, and killed men and women in the concentration camps for "medical" reasons had no scruples. Human guinea pigs, prisoners both young and not so young, weakened or still in good health, were subjected to unspeakable suffering and agony in laboratories managed by doctors from the best German families and the most prestigious German universities. As a consequence, after the war, there were survivors of occupied Germany who refused to receive care from German doctors. They were scared. They remembered other doctors—or the same ones—from elsewhere.

In Ravensbrück, Dachau, Buchenwald, and Auschwitz, German scientists operated on their victims without anesthesia in an effort to discover cures for obscure diseases. The researchers let them die of hunger, thirst, cold; they drowned them, amputated their limbs, suffocated them, dissected their still-living bodies to study their behavior and measure their stamina.

At the first trial of doctors before the international court at Nuremberg in 1946, 23 of the accused were charged with having initiated, directed, and organized criminal activities against prisoners. Acting under their authority, a number of well-respected doctors caved in to their orders. How did they turn into assassins?

I personally met only one: Josef Mengele, who was known best not as a doctor but as a criminal and a murderer. Like so many other deportees, I saw him the night of my arrival in Birkenau. I remember the thought that crossed my mind: he looked elegant. I remember his calm voice as he asked me my occupation and age (warned by an inmate, I made myself older). And I recall his fateful gesture that separated the living from the soon-to-be dead. I learned his name only later. Morbid rumors went around about him. Wherever he sprang up, Death spread its shadow. It was known that he was always on the lookout for little twins and children with spinal problems. In the camp for Gypsies, he came across as likeable, warm, and tender toward one particular boy. He had the boy dressed in nice clothes, gave him the best food. This was his favorite prisoner. And on the night the Gypsies were liquidated, the doctor himself led this boy to the gas chamber.

Did I meet other doctors? In my barracks at Buna, some of them supervised the division of those permitted to live from those who were to die. I have described elsewhere the silence that preceded this event: it filled our being. We were afraid to look at one another. As on Yom Kippur evening, I had the feeling that the dead were mixed with the living. As for the doctors, I knew not who they were and have forgotten their faces.

Over the succeeding years, as I studied documents and archives about the Final Solution, I became familiar with the dominant role played by Nazi medicine and science. They were integral to the concentration-camp system and were as guilty as the various branches of Hitler's armed services and police force of the monstrous crimes committed in occupied Europe out of hatred for the Jews and other so-called inferior races and groups. Yet after Germany's defeat, with rare exceptions, criminal doctors calmly returned home to resume normal practices and ordinary life. No one bothered them at home, nothing threatened them. Only on the occasion of the trial of Adolf Eichmann in Jerusalem did German justice suddenly remember their crimes. The police found their addresses in telephone books.

But if an Eichmann shocks us, a Mengele revolts us. Eichmann was a rather ordinary low-life, without education or culture, whereas Mengele spent a number of years at a university. The existence of an Eichmann casts doubt on the nature and mentality of the German people, but the possibility of a Mengele throws into question the very basis of German education and culture. If the former represents Evil at a bureaucratic level, the latter embodies Evil at an intellectual level. Eichmann denied having been anti-Semitic and pleaded not guilty: he was only following orders. But the Nazi doctors? None among them acted under duress—neither those who presided over the nocturnal division of new arrivals, nor those who killed the prisoners in their laboratories. They could have slipped away; they could have said no. Until the end, they considered themselves public servants loyal to

German politics and science. In other words, patriots, devoted researchers. Without too great a stretch, maybe even societal benefactors. Martyrs.

Must one conclude that, since a humane science exists, there was also a science that wasn't humane? I won't even consider racist theorists who tried to treat racism as an exact science. Their vulgar stupidity deserves nothing but disdain. But there were excellent physicians, well-informed chemists, and great surgeons—all racist. How could they seek truth and happiness for human beings at the same time that they hated some of them solely because they belonged to human communities other than their own?

One of the brutal shocks of my adult life came the day I discovered that many of the officers of the *Einsatzgruppen*—the death commandos in Eastern Europe—had received degrees from Germany's best universities. Some held doctorates in literature, others in philosophy, theology, or history. They had spent many years studying, learning the lessons of past generations, yet nothing kept them from killing Jewish children at Babi Yar, in Minsk, Ponàr. Their education provided them with no shield, no shelter from the temptation and seduction of cruelty that people may carry within. Why? This question still haunts me.

It is impossible to study the history of German medicine during the Nazi period in isolation from German education in general. Who or what is to blame for the creation of the assassins in white coats? Was the culprit the anti-Semitic heritage that German theologians and philosophers were dredging up? The harmful effects of propaganda? Perhaps higher education placed too much emphasis on abstract ideas and too little on humanity. I no longer remember which psychiatrist wrote a dissertation demonstrating that the assassins hadn't lost their moral bearings: they knew how to discern Good and Evil; it was the sense of reality that was missing. In their eyes, the victims did not belong to humankind; they were abstractions. The Nazi doctors were able to manipulate their bodies, play with their brains, mutilate their future without remorse; they tortured them in a thousand ways before putting an end to their lives.

Yet inside the concentration camps, among the prisoners, medicine remained a noble profession. More or less everywhere, doctors without instruments or medications tried desperately to relieve the suffering and misfortune of their fellow prisoners, sometimes at the price of their own health or their own lives. I knew several such doctors. For them, each human being represented not an abstract idea but a universe with its secrets, its treasures, its sources of anguish, and its poor possibilities for victory, however fleeting, over Death and its disciples. In an inhumane universe, they had remained humane.

When I think about the Nazi doctors, the medical executioners, I lose hope. To find it again, I think about the others, the victim-doctors; I see again their burning gazes, their ashen faces.

Why did some know how to bring honor to humankind, while others renounced humankind with hatred? It is a question of choice. A choice that even now belongs to us—to uniformed soldiers, but even more so to doctors. The killers could have decided not to kill.

Yet these horrors of medical perversion continued beyond Auschwitz. Traces may be found, for example, in the hellish Stalin and post-Stalin eras. Communist doctors betrayed their brethren. Psychiatrists collaborated with the secret police to torture prisoners.

And how can the recent, shameful torture to which Muslim prisoners were subjected by American soldiers be justified? Shouldn't the prison conditions in Iraq have been condemned by legal professionals and military doctors alike?

Am I naive in believing that medicine is still a noble profession, upholding the highest ethical principles? For the ill, doctors still stand for life. And for us all, hope.

Elie Wiesel
April, 2005

This essay was modified by the author from an essay in his collection *D'où viens-tu?* (Editions du Seuil, 2001) and was translated from the French by Jamie Moore. It was then published in *The New England Journal of Medicine*, who graciously granted permission for its inclusion here.

Foreword by
Fredrick R. Abrams, M.D.

I wish I were writing this as a foreword to a book that simply reminds readers of an aberration that happened once-upon-a-time in Germany over half a century ago, *but in many respects it was not an aberration. I wish* I could report that it was the behavior of only a few misguided individuals that led the scientists and doctors of that country down a perverse path, *but it was not a few.* It was a preponderance of politically co-opted scientists and physician opportunists. The professional group that had the largest percentage of Nazi Party members was medicine. It was not a minority of professional outcasts that approved of sorting civilian prisoners for either work or execution, nor did their fellows ostracize the doctors that carried out atrocious experiments. In fact, it was the doctors that upheld the ethics of medicine that were ostracized. Protesters sometimes shared the fate of the persons whom they were trying to protect.

 I wish I could write that after the trials at Nuremberg, the lessons learned and the international laws and codes that followed had put an end to genocide, torture, and experimentation on unconsenting human beings, *but the laws and codes continue to be flouted.* It is essential to revisit history as Vivien Spitz documented it, contemporaneously. We must remain aware that, despite the veneer of civilization and the outward manifestations of culture and refinement, insidious atavistic impulses remain in every country and no nation has a monopoly on atrocity.

There is good science and there is bad science—in the sense of careful and accurate theory and experimentation. Facts have no dogma and scientific fact-finding benefits society, but no science may be divorced from its human context. When it is, the scene is set for tragedy. Science and ideology are treacherous partners. When an ounce of science is mixed with a ton of zealotry, catastrophic results can be anticipated. This explosive mixture led to the disaster in German scientific activities of medical experimentation and eugenic research. Vivien Spitz provides witness to testimony that reports atrocities performed by professionals whose betrayal of trust is beyond outrageous, because they are members of a profession ostensibly dedicated to human welfare. There have been many theories about how and why this happened in a country considered to be among the most cultured and civilized of its day. What can lay the foundation for the scale of such horrendous behavior?

It serves a demagogue well to set up a scapegoat or a public enemy to unite the populace behind him and by so doing, enable them to overlook incursions on human rights through fear and ignorance. It serves him well to designate a group as *other* and, for that reason, treat them as inferior, subhuman, and ineligible for the protection of the laws of civilized society. Do the Jews, Gypsies, and homosexuals of Hitler's Germany spring to mind as you read this?

Think first of the early history of the United States. Here are examples that speak to unethical medical experimentation long before the Nazi era. In the 1800s in the American south, Dr. Thomas Hamilton of Georgia placed a slave in a pit oven in order to study heat stroke. Dr. Walter Jones of Virginia and several colleagues poured scalding water over sick slaves in an experiment to cure typhoid fever. Consider that Dr. J. Marion Sims perfected an operation on a series of slave women of Alabama that cured a maternal birth injury that untreated, caused continuous flow of urine from the vagina. The "Father of Gynecologic Surgery," Dr. Ephraim McDowell of Kentucky, before successfully removing an ovarian tumor from a white patient, had first operated on four slaves. Dr. Crawford Long of Georgia conducted a controlled demonstration of anesthesia by amputating two fingers from a slave boy—-one with ether and the other without. There is no record that either finger was diseased. In 1856, the *Medical Journal of Virginia* proposed severe sanctions be imposed on a surgeon after investigating the accusation of a slave that his leg had been amputated for an ulcer "just to let the students see the operation." Regardless of medical necessity, the master could permit or prohibit surgery on "property" he owned. The master made no complaint, therefore there was no remedy.[1]

What of eugenics, academic forerunner of the racial purity doctrine that justified abuse of "undesirable elements" of society? The rediscovered findings of Mendel at the turn of the century advanced the ideas of social Darwinism. Evolution was studied widely among nations, but for unprecedented *implementation* of eugenic theory, again you must look to the United States. It was hard to accommodate the institution of slavery to a theology that created humankind in God's image, especially in a nation where all men were created equal. Conventional wisdom that assumed inferiority of the black person and of the mentally deficient was explained by theories of degeneracy—as retrogression from the authentic human, therefore allowing them to be subject to treatment normal humans would not. As the eugenic movement progressed in the United States in the twentieth century, congenital degeneracy was presented in scientific terms as a hereditary disease, along with congenital pauperism, congenital prostitution, and congenital criminality. Beginning in Indiana in 1907, more than half the state legislatures were persuaded to pass laws permitting "involuntary asexualization." They did not distinguish between sterilization and castration. Epilepsy, feeble-mindedness, and insanity were grouped together as indications for sterilization, to avoid future generations with these afflictions.

---

1. Martin S. Pernick Ph.D., "*The Patient's Role in Medical Decision Making: A Social History of Informed Consent in Medical Therapy,*" in *Appendices, Study on the Foundations of Informed Consent,* Volume 3 of *Making Health Care Decisions* (President's Commission for the Study of Ethical Problems in Medicine and Biomedical and Behavioral Research, October 1982).

As the states succumbed to this pseudoscience, Supreme Court Justice Oliver Wendell Holmes added authority in the infamous *Buck v. Bell* Supreme Court decision in 1927. Carrie Buck, the eighteen-year-old illegitimate daughter of an allegedly feeble-minded mother, herself gave birth to a child. Carrie reportedly had the mental age of nine, and her child was alleged to be feeble-minded. (As the child matured, long after the case was closed, the child proved to be quite normal.) The Virginia law permitted involuntary sterilization, and the board of the institution in which Carrie lived recommended it. Schoolteacher and self-anointed "expert" Harry Laughlin was a prolific author and speaker on the subject of eugenics. He was asked to review her records. Without seeing the patient, he stated that she was a member of the "shiftless, ignorant, and worthless class of anti-social whites" and the possibility of her feeble-mindedness being due to non-hereditary causes was "exceptionally remote." Carrie's lawyer, in his prescient brief, noted the peril to society if the sterilization law were upheld, warning:

A reign of doctors will be inaugurated and in the name of science new classes will be added, even races may be brought within the scope of such a regulation and the worst forms of tyranny may be practiced.

It *was* upheld—in the oft-quoted phrase of Justice Holmes, *"three generations of imbeciles are enough."*

In 1932, Harry Laughlin wrote:

Our studies show also that the *compulsory feature* is now soundly established in long practice. They show also that the subject for sterilization does not necessarily have to be an inmate of an institution, but *may be selected with equal legality from the public at large*. It remains to be seen whether the state can extend sterilization to *apparently* normal individuals who have come from exceedingly inferior stocks, judged by the constitutional qualities of their close kin.

How chilling an idea that some authority could pick out people from society at large and sterilize them, not even based on their own shortcomings, but based on "constitutional qualities" discerned in their relatives! Who, you might ask, would do this selecting? As you will see, the answer in Hitler's Germany was to appoint teams of doctors to do so.

Sterilizations in Germany and the conquered countries were sanctioned and enforced by government edict, but in America, governors vetoed several of the state laws and the judiciary reversed others on Constitutional grounds. There has been a determined opposition to the movement from its inception, sometimes based on exposing the appallingly flawed science underpinning eugenic sterilization, sometimes based more fundamentally on human rights, sometimes based on religious teachings. Nevertheless, even after the revelations at Nuremberg, a few states continued eugenic sterilization.[2] As of 1995, Mississippi's law had not been rescinded, allowing for the compulsory sterilization of "the socially inadequate." As recently as 2003, reparations were made to victims of compulsory sterilization in North Carolina. Despite that, people convicted of criminal activity continue to be offered reduced sentences if they agree to sterilization.

It would appear that the Germans lagged behind their American colleagues in *implementing* the eugenic endorsements of doctors and anthropologists. In 1924, Professor F. Lenz chided his German colleagues for falling so far behind America in exploiting genetic knowledge in the interest of racial hygiene. Hitler read the German textbook by E. Bauer, E. Fischer, and F. Lenz, *The Principles of Human Heredity and Race Hygiene*, while he was imprisoned in Landsberg in 1923, and the racial elements were written into *Mein Kampf*. The German eugenic doctrine of *Lebensunwertes Lebens* (lives unworthy to be lived)—described in a book written by a jurist, Professor Binding, and a psychiatrist, Professor Hoche—was never implemented in America. However in Germany a program of racial cleansing under a ruthless political Nazi regime led from compulsory steriliza-

2. Phillip R. Reilly, *The Surgical Solution: A History of Involuntary Sterilization in the United States* (Baltimore, MD: Johns Hopkins University Press, 1991).

tion to murder (euphemistically termed *euthanasia*). Later, when the mass murders were rampant in 1943, Dr Fischer wrote, "It is a rare and special good fortune for a theoretical science to flourish at a time when the prevailing ideology welcomes it, and its findings can immediately serve the policy of the State." He continued as an influential part of the medical establishment after the war. In the introduction of the book *Cleansing the Fatherland*,[3] Christian Pross documents the postwar collusion of the medical establishment in whitewashing many who supported Nazi policy, naming names and noting only a few who were belatedly called to justice. Often the majority, purporting to protect the honor of the German medical profession, ostracized the whistleblowers, who then lost faculty appointments or promotions. Many science archives, rewritten after the war, show conspicuous absence of the history of medicine between 1933 and 1945.

It is easy to see why the Nazis based much of their master race ideology upon American foundations. Sterilization law was passed in Germany in 1933 (twenty-six years after Indiana did so), following careful study of California's law. In 1936, Laughlin (who had written for German journals) and other Americans received honorary degrees from the University of Heidelberg. Eugenics programs in Germany practiced the ideas that were proposed but not undertaken in the U.S. It began after Hitler became Chancellor, with the compulsory sterilization law for "congenital mental defects, schizophrenia, manic-depressive psychosis, hereditary epilepsy and severe alcoholism." In 1937, all German "coloured" children were to be sterilized and—after Drs. Abel, Schade and Fischer provided expert reports—physicians sterilized 300 children. In 1939, Psychiatrists Heyde, Maus, Nitsche, Panze, Pohlisch, Reisch, C, Schneider, Villinger, and Zucker and thirty-nine other physicians screened 250,000 mental patients for seriousness of illness, curability, and genetic factors. Of this group, 75,000 were marked for death. The Chief of the regional SS soon reported he had supervised the shooting of 4,400 Polish mental patients and 2,000

---

3. Götz Aly, Peter Chroust, Christian Pross; *Cleansing the Fatherland: Nazi Medicine and Racial Hygiene*, trans. Belinda Cooper (Baltimore, MD: John Hopkins University Press, 1994).

from a Prussian institution. In 1940, carbon monoxide was the agent of choice, and 70,000 mental patients in German hospitals were reported in meticulously kept records to have been killed, but cause of death was falsified. In 1941, with the invasion of Russia, *Einsatzgruppen* (unique units of soldiers) with the specific mission of murdering Jews, Gypsies, and mental patients, moved with the armies into conquered territories.

In December of 1941, Himmler asked the doctors that had carried out the "euthanasia" to comb the concentration camps for those who were unable to work or were otherwise undesirable, resulting in a vast number of deaths by the poison gas Zyklon B. The same year, Professor Fischer speaks of Jews as "beings of another species." This sort of pronouncement by someone regarded as an authority dehumanizes victims and gives predisposed people permission to act on their most sordid impulses.

Dr. Mennecke, in January of 1942, wrote of a large contingent of doctors and male and female nurses moving to Poland to set up an extermination camp at Chelmno. In December of that year, Dr Hallevorden reported that over the summer he had been able to dissect the brains of 500 feeble-minded patients, and Dr. Schneider opened an institution where "idiots and epileptics" were studied, after which they were killed and their brains examined. Dr Hallevorden continued his work and reported in 1944 that he had 697 brains, including those he dissected himself. His own records show that in 1944 Dr Mengele sent sera from twins he had infected with typhoid, eyes from Gypsies, and internal organs from children to be studied at the anthropology institute. After the war, Dr. Hallevorden admitted that he had provided the extermination camps with containers and fixatives. He reported to an interrogator that he had approached the camp saying, "Look here now boys, if you are going to kill all these people at least take the brains out, so that the material can be utilized." In 1949, he published from the Max Planck Institute (where he remained a department head) the case of a brain disorder of a child born of a mother who had been accidentally injured by carbon monoxide poison. Hallevorden's brain collection was shared for study with the University of Frankfort until 1990, when it was buried in a cemetery in Munich.[4]

No nation compared in scale with the meticulously organized, highly prioritized, deliberate atrocities in Germany between 1933 and 1945. In all, there are official German reports of at least 350,000 sterilizations between 1934 and 1939. The sterilizations stopped because the judges and doctors were busy with the war and because murder had been substituted for sterilization. In addition to the hundreds of thousands of mental patients murdered quickly, there were an estimated eighty thousand mental patients in German and French mental institutions that died of starvation after the "euthanasia" program came to a halt. Millions among the Jews, Gypsies, Slavic slave laborers, homosexuals, and Russian and Polish soldier-prisoners were killed with the help of expert doctors who selected those fit to work and those fit only for experimentation or death.[5]

What has transpired in the world of medicine since the horrifying examples of deviant doctors were exposed—the doctors about whom Vivien Spitz writes? In the aftermath of the war, it was learned that Japanese doctors used Chinese civilians to test germ warfare agents before and during WWII. Unlike the German doctors, they were not prosecuted, so the US could acquire the data for its germ warfare program without disclosing strategic information that would have been presented in a trial.

Despite the notoriety of the behavior and the codes and declarations that resulted, American doctors established studies starting in the 1940s and continuing over three decades, during which American citizens in civilian hospitals were subjected to radiation without their consent, in the interest of learning how to defend the country against atomic war. After these experiments became declassified, President Clinton established the Advisory Commission on Radiation Experiments in 1993 to investigate and suggest compensation for the

---

4. Ibid.
5. Benno Muller-Hill, *Murderous Science: Elimination by Scientific Selection of Jews, Gypsies, and Others in Germany 1933-1945*, trans. George R. Fraser, (Oxford: Oxford University Press, 1984).

surviving subjects. Also exposed were LSD experiments that caused the death of American soldiers, who were experimented upon without their knowledge.

In the 1966 *New England Journal of Medicine,* Dr. Henry Beecher cited twenty-two unethical post-Nuremberg experiments in America, conducted in university, Veteran's Administration, military, and private hospitals. They included experiments in which doctors withheld penicillin—known to prevent rheumatic fever—from cohorts of soldiers who had exudative strep throat. Some soldiers received placebo, some received sulfa, which resulted in more than seventy unnecessary cases of rheumatic heart disease. No consents for experimental treatment had been discussed, much less signed.

Another case report described a poorly researched attempt to create antibodies by injecting malignant melanoma cells of an afflicted girl into her mother in order to see if immune substances could be generated for treatment. The patient died the next day, demonstrating the dubious value of the experiment. The unwarranted risk to the mother, although she consented, eventuated in her death fifteen months later of malignant melanoma.

The most notorious American experiment had begun before the war and was not a part of Dr. Beecher's article. It concerned the failure to treat over four hundred black men for syphilis, *"to observe the natural course of the disease"*—as if centuries of observing the outcomes of syphilis had not clearly demonstrated this. The Tuskeegee study began in 1933. Despite the availability of penicillin, the subjects continued without therapy until 1972. No one protested the study despite several papers that described it in scientific journals. Saddest of all, it was done under the auspices of the U.S. Public Health Service. Not until the second Clinton administration were an apology and reparations offered, too late for many who died or suffered the physical and mental ravages of the disease.

In the book *Medicine Betrayed,* sponsored by the British Medical Association in 1992, a working party investigated and compiled abuses of human rights to which doctors contributed substantially. They reported, for example, psychiatric abuse in the USSR, Romania, and Cuba, where psychiatrists treated political dissidents as mentally ill candidates for institutionalization. In Japan, social and cultural indication, rather than medical, seemed to be the basis for institutionalization when a family member brought disgrace on the family name.

Punitive amputations by doctors under Islamic law were cited. From Chile there were reports of cases in which doctors revived tortured prisoners so political police interrogations could continue. The investigators detailed other specific instances of physician participation in torture in Greece, Kashmir, Argentina, the former East Germany, Brazil, El Salvador, Turkey, Venezuela, Mauritania, Philippines, India, South Africa, Uruguay, and on and on.

What kind of doctor can be involved in these activities? What are the motives of "doctors from hell"? Some German doctors sought the glory of professional distinction among peers through contributing to the welfare of humanity—humanity only as an abstract idea. They were committed to a dispassionate intellectual science that enabled them to seize a socially sanctioned opportunity for human experimentation. Other German doctors claimed they merely continued a practice with which they were familiar—that of healing. For their ideology, the illness was of the body of the state. The disease was an invasion by those of inferior blood that would weaken the "purity" (read "health") of the state. To them it was not unlike the amputation of a gangrenous limb or excising a malignant growth. The doctors obliterated all impulses of compassion and ruthlessly pursued those impulses that were necessary to promote the well-being of the state, with which they identified utterly.

The authors of *Medicine Betrayed* pointed out that the torturers were most often those in a structure with its own culture and mission, such as the military or police force. They were the ones, then and now, "who were following orders." The calculated detachment of bureaucracy played its part as well, for it allowed individuals to disclaim responsibility for any outcomes, because each step of a murderous process was delegated to a different person. One provided the gun. Another obtained the bullets. A third loaded the gun. Yet another rounded up the targets. Someone else far away pulled the trigger, so how could they be at fault?

In his book about the physicians involved,[6] Robert Lifton conceived of the idea of "doubling." This he described as a psychological state that was necessary to avoid mental disintegration under extreme circumstances. Doubling allowed a person to maintain the normal intimacy of human relationships with those in the "real" world while simultaneously allowing themselves to carry on otherwise unthinkable behavior by the same "self" in a parallel world. Several of the involved doctors later committed suicide. Was it because of remorse and guilt or because of fear of the shameful consequences of exposure? Or was it simply the collapse of their ideology, the end of an unrestrained era for them, with no professional future in sight?

Christian Pross[7] comments on the diary of Dr. Voss and the pleasure the doctor derived from the "special bonuses" of war—a professorship at Posen and the crematorium there. He quotes the diary, "How nice it would be if we could drive the whole pack of them [the Poles] through such ovens. Yesterday two wagonloads of Polish ashes were taken away. Outside my office, the robinias are blooming beautifully, just as in Leipzig." The Commandant of Auschwitz, Rudolf Hoss, described in his autobiography the mass murders and the suffering they caused *him*, but he neglected to mention the three carloads of valuables removed from Auschwitz.

We prefer to think of this behavior as so egregious that it merits a novel explanation. Pross, on the other hand, offers an explanation that supports the idea of the "banality of evil" so aptly phrased by Hannah Arendt. "Along with the homeless, the beggars, the inmates of insane asylums and the Jews of the Eastern European ghettos, the German authorities eliminated the visible poor, those people who required 'unnecessary expenditures' during their lifetimes. Their mistreatment and liquidation provided housing, employment, assets and old age pensions for others." The killing of the "useless provided beds for physically wounded soldiers and civilians during all out war by emptying mental hospitals, foster homes, and institutions for the handi-

---

6. Robert Jay Lifton, *The Nazi Doctors: Medical Killing and the Psychology of Genocide* (Basic Books, 1986).
7. *Cleansing the Fatherland.*

capped." The dismissal of Jewish scientists from the Kaiser Wilhelm Consortium provided dozens of openings for professional promotion and opportunities for advancement in addition to usurping the reins and funds of research grants. Few of the many hundreds of associated scientists and doctors objected. On the contrary, they sent an official joint letter to Hitler, pledging specifically to the goals of the Nazi hierarchy.

Add martial music, torchlight parades, and the skill of propagandists to manipulate the emotions, commingling national pride and hatred for a fabricated internal enemy. All that, plus awareness of the egocentric nature of human beings, dispels the need for esoteric theories to explain the behavior of a nation not yet recovered from the humiliating and impoverishing consequences of a lost war. Look to the jobs for individuals created by a new war and the sudden permission to take over the businesses of a disenfranchised segment of the citizenry. See the opportunity to work out the frustrations and disappointments of daily life on the scapegoat provided by governmental authority. Look to the practical benefits to the German state of massive confiscations of wealth and property, elimination of "unproductive eaters," and the profitable economics of slave labor without the necessity of supporting the slaves, who were expendable and in seemingly endless supply.

Vivien Spitz has reminded us graphically that we must constantly be aware of the baser instincts of human beings while we aspire to the nobler. Outward manifestations of piety and righteousness do not protect the citizenry. Each belt buckle that German soldiers wore had embossed upon it *Gott Mit Uns* (God Is with Us). Over the door of the courthouse in the Palace of Justice complex in Nuremberg were engraved the Ten Commandments. The group that established those commandments was precisely the group that was deprived of citizenship, human rights, and even life, under the laws promulgated in the name of that very city—the anti-Jewish Nuremberg Laws of 1935.

Are we at risk here in America? Addressing narrowly only the duties of physicians, there is this caveat. Certainly, doctors are not practicing in the poisonous atmosphere of Hitler's Germany or any other totalitarian government. Yet, even an American doctor may introduce bias, unethical and possibly subconscious, when he or she is asked to think about the *entire population* to be treated, rather than to serve the *individual patient* who is seeking help. It is true that consideration of community and of the greater good is an obligation of citizenship, but there must be limits. Whenever the doctor begins to exclude patients from medical services or uses professional skills against the patient's interest or deviates from a position of individual patient advocacy in therapy or in research, he or she starts down a slippery slope. The law can indicate the minimal duties of a physician and specify the limits, but the future of the profession depends upon the doctor's integrity and adherence to the ethical premises of the profession—and above all, the appreciation of our common humanity.

Fredrick R. Abrams, M.D.
December 28, 2004

Introduction

Each generation of Americans has to face circumstances not of its own choosing, by which its character is measured and its spirit is tested.

—President Jimmy Carter

DR. JULIUS MOSES was a general practitioner in Berlin between 1920 and 1932. He refused to conform to the developing mindset of German physicians who would eventually link theory and practice in medicine to a marriage between science and crimes against humanity.

In 1930 seventy-five children died at the hands of grossly negligent doctors during vaccine injections. Dr. Moses informed the public. Thereafter he contributed to guidelines developed for scientific human experiments passed by the National Health Authority, stressing the individual rights of the patients.

In 1932 Moses warned that in a National Socialist Third Reich the doctors' duty would be to create a "new, noble humanity." He warned further that only those patients who were curable would be treated. The incurably sick would be considered "human ballast," "trash," "valueless," and "unproductive," thus requiring that they be destroyed. His prescient warning would put him in jeopardy.

Dr. Moses was the embodiment of the physician's conscience.

Even after Adolf Hitler and the National Socialist Party came to power in 1933, Moses, a Social Democrat, did not emigrate. In 1942, at age seventy-four, he was sent to the Theresienstadt concentration camp in Czechoslovakia, where he died of starvation shortly thereafter.

On September 15, 1927, the Kaiser Wilhelm Institute of Anthropology, Human Genetics, and Eugenics was opened in Berlin. It was divided into four departments: Anthropology, Genetics, Eugenics, and Experimental Genetic Pathology. A 1931 report stated: "The term 'eugenics' means to establish a connection between the results of the studies in human genetics and practical measures in population policy."

After Hitler came to power in 1933, a Superior Genetic Health Court was established. Thus began the perverse degradation of German medicine and the demonic human experimentation and murder of thousands of innocent people by willing German doctors. Some doctors may have had pangs of conscience, but jumped at the chance to experiment on humans.[1]

The darkest evil of the violent twentieth century resulted in the mass violation of basic human rights and the dignity of life, which was exposed in World War II with the defeat of Nazi Germany by the United States, Britain, France, and the Soviet Union on May 8, 1945.

Basic human rights have historically been violated in many cultures of the world—civilized and uncivilized. Germany was a civilized, modern society that marched into a cesspool of evil with its state-sponsored, planned mass genocide of all of the Jews of Europe, which annihilated six million in its concentration and death camps, sucking into its vortex five million non-Jews as well. This was an event unmatched in human history. Evil was brought before the bar of justice at the Nuremberg war crimes trials, further exposing the depths to which humankind is capable of sinking.

Out of these landmark trials came the establishment of the Nuremberg Code, which sets the guidelines still in use today for medical research involving human beings. Thus a new standard of ethical medical behavior was established for the post-World War II era, an era in which human rights has been given paramount importance.

This document requires, among other things, the voluntary informed consent of the human subject, which protects the right of the individual to control his own body. The code also instructs doctors to weigh the risk against the expected benefit and to avoid unnecessary pain and suffering.

In writing this book, I worked from a condensed transcript of the 11,538-page court reporters' record (which I helped prepare), deemed the "record that will never forget," from our National Archives.

Chapter 1 of *Doctors from Hell* answers the question frequently asked of me: How did you happen to go to Nuremberg to report the medical case of the war crimes trials? Recruited by the U. S. War Department in 1946 at age twenty-two, I endured a terrifying flight over the North Atlantic on a military C-54 with troops going over to relieve war-weary soldiers in Germany.

Chapter 2 covers the International Military Tribunal trial of the major Nazi leaders charged with crimes against humanity and calculated genocide. The case was titled *In the Matter of the United States of America, the French Republic, the United Kingdom of Great Britain and Northern Ireland, and the Union of Soviet Socialist Republics versus Hermann Wilhelm Goering, et al.*

Chapter 3 sets up the twelve Subsequent Proceedings, of which the medical case is the first. These twelve trials were held before American judges in military tribunals. On October 25, 1946, The *United States of America versus Karl Brandt, et al.*, charged twenty doctors and three medical assistants with war crimes and crimes against humanity before Military Tribunal 1. These twenty doctors were not political and military leaders, but highly educated scientists who had taken the Oath of Hippocrates to heal and cure, but were turned into torturers and murderers through their participation in the Nazi regime.

Chapter 4 describes the case of the Nazi doctors, as well as my personal story of difficult and hazardous living in the cold, snowy, bombed-out city of Nuremberg, where there was no heat or hot water anywhere.

In chapter 5 I recount the specifics of high-altitude experiments in which concentration camp inmates were forced into high-altitude chambers and sent to sixty-eight thousand feet without oxygen.

In chapter 6, inmates testify to freezing experiments in which victims were placed in long, narrow tanks of ice water for up to three hours, at which point death occurred.

Chapter 7 gives details of malaria experiments in which twelve hundred inmates, including a large number of Polish Catholic priests, were infected with controlled mosquito bites or injected with malaria-infected blood.

One of the most savage, sadistic, and inhumane experiments—involving bone, muscle, and nerve regeneration and bone transplantation—is covered in chapter 8. Sections of bone, muscles, and nerves, including whole legs taken off at the hips, were removed from inmates to attempt to transplant them to other victims.

Chapter 9 details experiments in which inmates were artificially wounded and infected with mustard gas. Burns appeared and spread over their entire bodies wherever drops contacted the skin. Lungs and organs were eaten away.

Sulfanilamide experiments, described in chapter 10, were conducted on many Polish Catholic priests in Dachau. They were wounded, and the wounds were infected with streptococcus, gas gangrene, and tetanus. Wood shavings and ground glass were forced into the wounds. Sulfa drugs, which would have healed these wounds, were withheld.

In chapter 11, I give an account of the Nazis' sea water experiments. German, Czech, and Polish Gypsies were given no food and forced to drink salty sea water for five to nine days. During my turn in the courtroom, survivor witness Karl Hollenrainer rushed from the witness stand with a knife and attempted to stab Dr. Beiglboeck in the prisoners' dock.

Chapter 12 gives the reader a break from the horror and tells the story of the December 1946 holiday period, my first Christmas away from home. My colleagues and I were given a chance to recuperate from our psychological wounds and try to regain a modicum of normalcy.

In chapter 13, I describe epidemic jaundice experiments on Polish Jews. These inmates suffered untold pain and many deaths.

Sterilization experiments are described in chapter 14. These were conducted on Polish Jews and Russian prisoners of war to develop a suitable method for the sterilization of millions of people by radiation, surgery, and drugs in a state-sponsored, planned, mass genocide of large population groups.

In chapter 15, I cover experiments on German criminals, prisoners of war, and Polish Jews, who were infected by laceration of the skin and the introduction of a typhus culture by contagious lice, or by the intravenous or intramuscular injection of fresh blood containing the typhus virus. These experiments killed 90 percent of the victims.

In chapter 16, the experiments with poison are detailed. Poison bullets were shot into Russian prisoners of war to investigate the effect of poison on humans and to time how fast death occurred. Poison was also secretly administered in food, as the doctors stood behind curtains to watch the reactions.

Incendiary bomb experiments are described in chapter 17. Victims were inflicted with phosphorous from the bombs. Then the wounds were ignited, and the skin burned for up to sixty-eight seconds before the flames were extinguished.

In chapter 18, I relate the particulars of experiments on inmates that involved pus, blood coagulant, and gas.

At one time 112 Jewish inmates were selected for a skeleton collection. They were killed and defleshed. This is described in chapter 19.

Chapter 20 covers the "euthanasia" (murder) program put into operation to cleanse Germany of "useless eaters," covering many categories of the population from well but "undesirable" people to mentally and physically deformed babies, diseased children and adults, the sick, old, and infirm.

In chapter 21, I discuss the code of medical ethics that was a product of this trial and how it was arrived at.

Chapter 22 gives the judgments, sentences, and the final statements of the defendants, and the Nuremberg Code, which covers permissible medical experiments for the future.

In chapters 23 and 24 I briefly describe my post-Nuremberg life back in the United States. This includes my marriage, the birth of two sons, my life as a military wife, and eventually the continuation of my career as a court reporter in courts-martial cases, in the Denver district court, and finally as Chief Reporter in the United States House of Representatives. During this time I faced serious Holocaust deniers four times, which fired me up to put together a lecture on the Nazi doctors' trial, using captured German film, and started me on a twelve-year mission to speak and educate that took me all over the United States and Canada, and to Singapore.

During these years I met the most famous Holocaust survivor, Nobel Laureate Elie Wiesel, and I describe this memorable, overwhelming meeting. And during the 1970s I met a German Bundestag court reporter, Heinz Lorenz, not knowing that he had been Hitler's court reporter in the Berlin bunker at the end.

In 1995 the Steven Spielberg SHOAH Visual History Foundation interviewed me, categorizing me as a "witness to history." As such, I invite you to sit in my front row seat in that Nuremberg courtroom and look into the eyes of these medical perpetrators, only to see evil staring back. I ask you to listen to the guinea pig victims who survived as they describe the indescribable—tortuous and deadly experiments conducted on them without their consent.

I want you, the reader, to realize the infinite capacity for demonic evil and depravity in ordinarily good people with free will who make choices that turn them into unethical, immoral perpetrators with victims at their mercy. What is the culpability of the silent bystander who is indifferent to evil? We are capable of being rescuers; do we have the courage to be rescuers?

The past is prologue—and why are the lessons not being learned?

· 1 ·

October 1946
Westover Air Field, Massachusetts

THE KNOCKS ON the door were at first dull and recessed deep in the dream scenes of my sleep. Then they stopped.

They came again, harder and louder, as though from a steel fist, awakening me from my dream.

"Miss! Miss! Wake up!" Knock, knock, knock! "Miss!"

The sounds were urgent now. Rubbing my eyes in the darkness, I switched on the metal table lamp and looked at the clock. Two a.m.! Two a.m.?

Groggily, I stumbled to the door in my pajamas, opened it, and peered around it. Under the dim, bare light bulb in the ceiling of the narrow hall stood the dark outline of a tall figure.

"Get dressed, Miss. Be prepared to fly at 6:00 a.m. Meet us in the briefing room at 4:00."

"Yes, sir," I mumbled in disbelief and closed the door. The haziness of sleep cobwebs started falling away, leaving stark reality. This is it; I'm going! But this was not supposed to happen for four more days. And I just got in bed an hour ago.

Only two days before, I had experienced my first contact with the U.S. military. I was the only woman passenger among several soldiers when we flew from Selfridge Air Force Base in Detroit to Westover Air Field in Massachusetts.

Upon my arrival at Westover, I had presented my U.S. War Department orders to the major in charge, indicating that I was a civilian contract court reporter assigned to the Office of the Chief of Counsel for War Crimes in Nuremberg, Germany. He looked my papers over and then stared at me with a frown, looking somewhat concerned.

"You're barely twenty-two, ma'am. Do you know where you're going?" The warning tone in his voice was unsettling.

"Yes," I said confidently. "To Nuremberg, Germany, to work on the war trials."

"Do you know what it's like in Nuremberg today? It's only eighteen months after the end of the war! It's a bombed-out city, with unrecovered bodies still in the rubble everywhere. A sour stench carried by the wind. No heat anywhere, except in fireplaces. No hot water for baths. Chlorine pills for drinking water. Nazi terrorists are still hiding in the debris under the bombed-out Walled City. They come out at night to shoot anyone on the street who appears to be American or British or on the Allied payroll—military or civilian! Or occasionally to throw a bomb into facilities used by the Allies."

"I guess I didn't know any of this," I replied, trying to picture the alarming scene he had just painted. Nevertheless, I remembered why I had embarked on this trip and said, "But I just have to go. I'm half German and I cannot believe what I'm seeing on the Movietone newsreels in the theaters about the atrocities the Germans have committed—especially the German doctors. I have to go to see for myself. I'm a court reporter, and the War Department needs court reporters. I want to take these doctors' testimony, watch their faces. I want to hear how they defend these terrible atrocities and experiments on human beings."

Shaking his head, he then provided me with a dog tag ID to hang around my neck and a handful of papers to read and study. Next he asked the sergeant to show me to my billet, the tiny private room where I would be staying. I did not realize my orders indicated a high priority on flights to Germany until he told me so. He said it would probably still be about six days before I would be leaving the base.

I was wearing a warm suit and had my trench coat over my arm, my handbag over my shoulder, and my one suitcase in hand. The sergeant, sensing that I was bewildered, said with kindness in his voice, "Here, let me take that." He carried my suitcase into my temporary room, where I left it to follow him for a guided tour.

We entered a lounge area with comfortable-looking vinyl sofas and chairs. There were coffee tables with magazines and ashtrays; end tables held lamps, and a radio sat on a table on one side of the room along with a coffee service. A soft drink dispenser stood against the wall. Although the new and wondrous invention of a radio with a picture—called television—had been developed in the 1930s, there would be no widespread use of it until about 1948. That was still two years away, so there was no TV set in the lounge that the sergeant showed me.

Pictures of military aircraft of all sizes were on the walls. My curiosity led me to learn more about the Air Force and its warplanes from those walls than I had ever known before. I had good personal reasons now to become more knowledgeable about the planes of the U.S. Air Force, since I would soon be flying on one.

There was the Boeing Flying Fortress precision bomber—so successful in committing Germany to rubble—with its long-range fighter escorts. The B-29 Superfortress—the most advanced airplane developed by the U.S. during World War II, which helped bring about the final defeat of Japan in August 1945. This fighter plane was unique because tons of bombs could be flown at longer distances than ever before, which enabled the U.S. to attack from farther away. The U.S. had about eighty thousand military aircraft at peak strength in May of 1945, at the end of the war. The lounge had dozens of pictures showing the different aircraft used in the wars with Germany and Japan—fighters, transports, and bombers among them.

Then I saw a picture of the plane on which I would be flying to Germany—the Douglas C-54 Skymaster long-range military transport with four propeller-driven engines. I felt more comfortable because of those four engines. My first flight was at Christmas time in

9

1943, after I graduated from Gregg Business College in Chicago, when I flew to Detroit to start my first job in a court reporting agency. That was on American Airlines in a plane with two propeller engines. It was a stormy, frightening flight over Lake Michigan with lightning flashing all around us. I made that flight several times, flying back to Chicago and continuing by train to my home in Woodstock, Illinois.

I knew this flight to Germany would be a long one—many hours over the North Atlantic—and I had a great deal of trepidation about making it safely.

As I walked around the lounge, my attention was diverted from the pictures to the loud jitterbug music of Glenn Miller's "In the Mood," which jumped from a nearby jukebox. Now I felt relaxed, strolling down a memory lane that took me back to the soda joint in Woodstock, where I used to put nickels in the jukebox to play the jitterbug music that my high school friends and I danced to.

The sergeant showed me the location of the briefing room for the flight orientation that I would be going to just before my flight. We entered the mess hall where I would be eating my meals with American soldiers and other civilian employees going overseas. Leaving me back in the lounge with a cautionary warning about not entering secured areas where only military personnel were allowed, the sergeant excused himself.

I found my way back to my billet, unpacked the few clothes I had packed in my suitcase, inspected my army cot, and tried to feel settled in. Yet, I just knew I would not be comfortable in this male-dominated military, about to embark on an adventure that I seemed driven to make.

I could not know that going to Germany would change my life significantly and forever. I was to view film and photographs of atrocities, see the mutilations that were inflicted on victims, watch them testify in tears from the witness stand, and, all the while, record their words. The effect of all this would be to remind me how valuable life is and how blessed I was to have been born in a free, democratic country. From that point on, I would no longer tolerate any bigotry, although I would often be confronted with it after returning to the United States.

When it was time for chow, I found my way to the mess hall. Trying to feel at ease, I picked up my metal tray and got in line for the cafeteria-style food service. I didn't see any other women anywhere!

The atmosphere turned out to be friendly and the GIs in line before and after me were chatty, asking lots of questions. They noted that I was not in military uniform and wanted to know how I happened to be going to Germany. I told them the War Department had recruited me as a civilian court reporter to work on the war trials, which had already started. They were not familiar with the trials. Once we had our food, they invited me to join them at their long table. In our conversation, I learned that they, too, were flying to Germany, to relieve post-war weary occupation forces who would return to the U.S. These were very young soldiers who had not seen any combat.

My dinner companions told me they were having their base Halloween party the next evening and asked if I would like to go. I readily agreed, since I would not be flying out for five more days.

I had to have a costume, of course. They had already put theirs together in their clever, innovative fashion and were eager to help me come up with one. They managed to acquire some large GI pants and an oversized GI shirt, a long cook's apron, and a rag mop top for my wig. Although I was tall and slender, I looked like a hefty military cook when they were done with me. In costume, I felt more relaxed.

The mess hall was decorated for Halloween. Orange and black streamers were strung across the ceiling and large accordion-pleated paper pumpkins hung from them. Black cats, witches, and ghosts peered out from every wall. Big Band dance music of the 1940s resonated from the jukebox, filling the room with every popular song, from the Andrews Sisters' "Rum and Coca-Cola" to "Boogie Woogie Bugle Boy from Company B" to "Symphony" and "Harbor Lights." Young women from Mount Holyoke College nearby in Hadley, Massachusetts, appeared—the first women I had seen anywhere since my arrival. This turned out to be the first big party of my twenty-two years. And what fun it was! What fun!

I got back to my billet and in bed by 1:00 a.m. I had one hour of sleep before the knocks on the door came.

The U.S. War Department Recruitment

Only eighteen months before, on May 8, 1945, the war had ended in Germany. I had been on my first court reporting job in Detroit, having worked with a freelance reporting agency since November 1943. Then one day, a flier from the United States War Department came into our office, recruiting approximately twenty-six high-speed manual and machine shorthand court reporters from all over the country to go to Germany to report the trial of Hermann Wilhelm Goering and twenty-one other major Nazi leaders. Scheduled to start in November 1945, this trial was to be held before an International Military Tribunal composed of four judges and four alternate judges, two from each victorious country: the United States, France, Great Britain, and the Soviet Union. Thereafter, twelve more trials (called the Subsequent Proceedings), including the Nazi doctors' trial, were to be conducted. I wanted the doctors' trial.

Publicity about the impending trials was on the front pages of newspapers all across the country, on our Philco radios, and in the theaters on Movietone newsreels. I applied immediately, wondering if I would be chosen when I had so little experience and so few people were needed.

I waited anxiously in Detroit to hear from the War Department. When I heard, they told me I was too young. I had to be twenty-one and I was only twenty. My heart sank in disappointment. However, I was told that I would be accepted at twenty-one, provided I could pass the U.S. Civil Service examination with a score of two hundred words per minute in shorthand at 95 percent accuracy. The next months were unbearable for me as I tried to grow older as fast as I could!

I was excited the day I that was notified of my acceptance. It came with a lot of paperwork and instructions for getting the necessary physical examination and inoculations, and taking the Civil Service examination. I passed with 98 percent accuracy. Because the reporters for the major Nazi leaders' trial had already been selected, I had to wait about a year to receive my orders, which were for the Subsequent Proceedings. They came near the end of October 1946; I was twenty-two.

Orientation and Boarding the Plane

Now, on November 1, 1946, I was about to get on a plane bound for Paris, then Frankfurt, and finally, Nuremberg. After a quick shower of barely warm water, I repacked my suitcase—just a day and a half after unpacking. The steamer trunk that had carried the belongings of my mother's father and grandparents from Nierberg, Germany to the United States in 1846 was now en route back to Germany one hundred years later, carrying my belongings for an entirely different purpose.

So tired I could barely stand up, I found my way to the briefing room by 4:00 a.m., almost late. All the GIs were there, the sergeant, a captain, and the major. None of us appeared to be very mentally alert, least of all me. I was again the only woman. The flight orientation began with instructions on how to don a parachute and a Mae West life jacket.

The captain, sensing how sleepy I was, shocked me to alertness by asking me to demonstrate what we had just learned. I failed the test miserably. In a good-natured fashion, he buckled me into the cumbersome parachute, with the heavy pack hanging off my bottom. He showed us where the ripcord was and how to pull it should it become necessary to jump from the plane. TO JUMP FROM THE PLANE?! That hit the sleep center of my brain and put me at wide-awake attention. Now I was really beginning to have second thoughts. The captain snap-buckled me into the life jacket. For the next half hour we all practiced putting on and taking off our parachutes and Mae Wests. Fortunately, I had had the good sense to put on wool slacks for this long, cold trip.

After receiving our final boarding instructions, we went back to our billets and gathered our belongings. The GIs had military gear and large backpacks. I had my suitcase, my shoulder bag, and my fleece-lined trench coat. We all climbed up the steps and boarded the Douglas C-54 Skymaster transport.

The main cabin had seats for twenty-six passengers. In the flight compartment, the Air Force pilot and copilot sat side by side and had dual controls. The navigator and radio operator sat behind. Two relief crew members sat in the crew compartment, which had rest bunks, a toilet, a water tank, and stowage for parachutes and life rafts. The main compartment had overhead baggage racks and stowage for four life rafts. In the back were a coatroom, buffet and food storage unit, lavatory, and washroom.

The plane was loaded at 6:00 a.m. in the chilling, wind-whipped, cloudy darkness. My fellow travelers and I were all so tired, only five hours after ending our fun-filled evening, but we were both anxious and excited as the engines started. This is it! We're on our way. After the plane warmed up, we started a long, bumpy roll down the runway before lifting off into the dark November sky, engines roaring.

It was too dark to see anything but the lights below, getting tinier and tinier as we climbed higher into the dark clouds. Barely able to hear each other over the droning roar of the engines, we remained quiet. We were heading north-northeast into the predawn skies on our route over Nova Scotia, Newfoundland, and the tip of Greenland, to land in Iceland—well over 1,500 miles away. The plane's maximum speed was 229 miles per hour at 7,500 feet. Cruising speed was 185 miles per hour at 10,000 feet.

Anxiety about the unknown clutched my mind. But before we ever got over Nova Scotia, I was in a deep sleep. I did not awaken for over eight hours, until our landing at Reykjavik, Iceland—a white island of snow and ice barely three hundred miles wide.

Detained there many hours while the plane was repaired, we waited in the small airport building. Shortly before reboarding for the next leg of our trip, I was introduced to my new seatmate, the wife of the Prime Minister of Iceland. Now there would be two women on board.

Emergency over the North Atlantic

Airborne once again, we headed southeast over the North Atlantic, bound for Paris. Hours into that segment of the flight, beyond the point of return, an emergency developed. We were not told what it was, but we did precisely as instructed without panicking: get the life jackets on and prepare to ditch—in the North Atlantic! What did ditching mean? Into the ice-cold pitching waves of the

North Atlantic? The rafts would be thrown into the water, and we would have to scramble into them? The plane would sink shortly. Our rafts would have to get us away from the plane to keep us from being sucked under into the black canyons of the waves!

Just weeks before, on October 3, 1946, the worst commercial air disaster in history had occurred when a Berlin-bound American Overseas Airlines plane crashed in Newfoundland. Thirty-nine men, women, and children lost their lives, including the crew. These were U.S. War Department employees or families of employees already in Germany.

We spent silent hours in prayer and overwhelming anxiety, sitting in our life jackets, knowing nothing other than that we were still airborne.

I forgot what had driven me to go to Germany as a deep chasm of fear engulfed me. All I could think about was: How did I ever get here? What am I doing here? My life is going to end before it even gets started! And all these soldiers! Some were as young as, or younger than, I was.

In my mind's eye I could vividly see my mother, standing in tears at Selfridge Air Force Base in Detroit only days before, hugging her twenty-two-year-old daughter good-bye, enveloped in fear and hoping I would be safe.

Were we going to get there? What was the problem with the plane? Overwhelming anxiety struck silent panic in my heart. I could see it in the eyes of the GIs, nervously glancing around. We didn't talk. We were paralyzed, terrified. What did ditching mean?

Safe Landing in Paris

Finally we came in over beautiful, green Ireland. We were all so overjoyed at the sight of land that we almost didn't care if we crashed at that point! Removing our clumsy life jackets at last, we began to breathe more easily. Finally, after twenty-two total hours in the air, we landed safely in Paris and then were told the problem had been a fuel shortage!

We were all weary and limp from the long, anxiety-ridden trip. My GI friends and I parted to go to our different destinations. Embassy personnel met the Prime Minister's wife and drove her away in a limousine. Military personnel met me at the plane and drove me to a small hotel near the Champs Elysees and the Arc d'Triomphe.

After a couple of days of walking around Paris, awaiting further orders, I found myself mesmerized by the city. Then the military notified me I was to leave for Frankfurt on a U.S. Army Air Force C-47 Skytrain, a small twin-engine, propeller-driven plane.

Boarding the Douglas C-47 Skytrain for Frankfurt

The three-man crew consisted of a pilot, copilot, and radio operator. There was a baggage compartment, the main cabin, and a lavatory. They called this plane the Gooney Bird.

My seatmate here was an American War Department civilian employee on leave, returning from Paris to his job in Frankfurt. His work involved the registration of graves of U.S. soldiers who had been buried in Europe. He had yards of beautiful French dress fabric for his *Fraulein* girlfriend in Frankfurt. He also had a wife back in the U.S. It was my introduction to one of the many facets of overseas life in military-occupied Germany. After I arrived in Nuremberg, I learned that this double life was quite common.

I was not anxious during this segment of the trip, so I enjoyed looking out the window down to the French countryside. It seemed that every building, large and small, had a beautiful red tile roof—something I had never before seen.

Then suddenly the landscape below changed drastically. We were now flying over Germany, looking down on a bomb-destroyed, black and gray, war-ravaged landscape, dark and foreboding. I could not take my eyes off of the devastation as we came over Frankfurt, a pre-war city of six hundred thousand, now transformed by deserted areas for miles in all directions. Only building skeletons still stood. Empty windows stared back at me.

Landing in Frankfurt, I was met by the military and put up overnight. I encountered the well known, foot-thick German feath-erbed for the first time. The next morning I reported to a major who told me my orders had changed and I was to remain in Frankfurt to report commission and evidentiary hearings there. This was a shock-ing disappointment to me. I did not want to report in Frankfurt, but in Nuremberg. I was stunned.

I quickly gathered my wits and with subdued anger stated, "No, I have a signed contract with the War Department for Nuremberg and I am going to Nuremberg, or you can send me right back to the United States." I surprised myself, taking such a strong stand. This was how-ever, the first time I realized the power inherent in being a U.S. citizen with a War Department contract. Had I been a stateside War Department employee sent to Germany to work, I would not have had such leverage. The major did not argue further. I felt quite proud of myself, standing my ground with such determination.

The Final Anxiety-Ridden Flight

Shortly thereafter, with my orders intact, I left for Nuremberg on another C-47, this time with bucket seats lining the walls on each side of the tiny fuselage. As I remember, four of us were snugly seated on each wall. The military chaplain facing me across the narrow aisle was very somber and did not seem talkative. None of us did.

Over the shoulders of those facing me I could see dark, angry-looking clouds out of the windows. The air was very turbulent, and we could not see anything below. We were bouncing all over the sky. The Air Force pilot at the controls was talking to someone in the cock-pit—the copilot or radio operator—about having to circle through the clouds over Nuremberg to wait for landing instructions. The cockpit door was open, so we could hear everything. He was getting low on fuel too. Then, accompanied by unbridled profanity, he exclaimed, "I'll just go straight down through the clouds, and they'll have to let me land!"

We all heard it, and again there was dead silence. The chaplain across from me, with his eyes closed, had his lips moving in prayer. I was praying too. It was just too soon after our anxiety-ridden North Atlantic threat for me to face another crisis.

As we bumped in circles around the cloudy sky, the pilot finally radioed the control tower, demanding an emergency landing. He shouted, "I can't wait any longer; I'm running out of fuel! I'm coming in!"

We felt the pressure of the rapid descent through the low clouds and then the rough landing. A lot of anxious thoughts crowded my mind as we rolled to a stop. Nobody said a word. At last I had arrived in cold, snowy, bombed-out Nuremberg and was on the ground, safe. It was November 6, 1946.

For the whole trip of over forty-five hundred air miles from Detroit to Nuremberg—thirty-five hours in the air—I never had to ask where to report next. A military officer was always there to check my orders, direct me, put me up in overnight quarters or a hotel, see that I got to places on time, and tell me where to go for meals. I began to sense urgency from the War Department. I was transported quickly, flying all the way, while judges and others of higher or lower rank were traveling by ship for twelve or more days at sea, followed by a train ride from Bremerhaven in north Germany to Nuremberg. Granted, I was young, alone, and female, but it probably had more to do with a need for highly qualified court reporters to start the twelve trials of the Subsequent Proceedings. The first trial was Case No. 1, The Medical Case.

The Nuremberg War Crimes Trials

WORLD WAR II ended in Europe on May 8, 1945, with the total defeat of Adolf Hitler's "Thousand-Year" Third Reich by the Big Four victorious powers: the United States, France, Great Britain, and the Soviet Union. On April 30, 1945, Hitler committed suicide in his Berlin bunker. Most of the major Nazi leaders who had not already committed suicide were in the hands of U.S. and British troops. Rather than shooting them on the spot as they were captured, or trying them immediately in summary proceedings, the United States pushed for a fair trial before an International Military Tribunal in which all accused would be given every opportunity to present their cases.

The tribunal would be committed to strict rules of evidence that had grown out of centuries of legal systems, the development of international criminal justice systems, and law and order among nations. The delegates from the Big Four powers had seriously heated debates that went on for many months. Finally, at the London Conference on August 8, 1945, they forged a charter agreement that established the International Military Tribunal.

Germany had been divided into four sectors by the victorious countries. The Russians had wanted the International Military Tribunal trial of the major Nazi leaders held in their sector of Berlin. However, Associate Supreme Court Justice Robert H. Jackson, U.S.

Chief of Counsel for War Crimes on the major Nazi leaders' trial, persuaded the other three countries to accept Nuremberg as the site of the trials.

The reasons for choosing Nuremburg were many. Zeppelin Field, located at the edge of Nuremberg, had been the site of huge Nazi Party rallies with Adolf Hitler. This massive stadium held 250,000 marching troops and citizens. It was from the grandstand in Zeppelin Field that Hitler had proclaimed: "The German form of life is definitely determined for the next one thousand years!"

Another consideration was that Adolf Hitler passed the infamous Nuremberg Laws here in 1935, depriving German Jews of citizenship and jobs, and prohibiting marriage between Jews and Aryans.

Ninety percent of this city, which before the war had 450,000 people and 130,000 buildings, had been destroyed by repeated bombings by the British Royal Air Force and the U.S. Air Force. Artillery barrages by the American Third and Forty-fifth Infantry Divisions had finished the devastation, leaving approximately 160,000 survivors and 17,000 buildings still standing. Nuremberg had over 30,000 bodies trapped beneath the rubble.

Nuremberg had been a beautiful, ancient historic city, a commercial center of the Middle Ages. Famous craftsmen and artists, including Albrecht Durer, were from Nuremberg. The city was the setting for the opera *Die Meistersinger von Nürnberg* by Richard Wagner, Hitler's favorite composer.

History's First International Criminal Trials

The Nuremberg War Crimes Trials held between November 1945 and April 1949 were the first international criminal trials in all of history. Four countries—the United States, Great Britain, France, and the Soviet Union—put the leaders of one country, Germany, on trial for crimes against humanity and calculated genocide. These acts were perpetrated over a period of twelve years from 1933, when Adolf Hitler came to power, until 1945, when World War II ended.

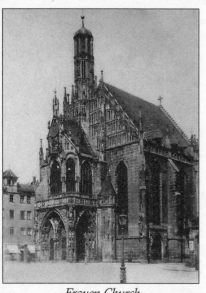

Frauen Church

Holy Ghost Hospital

Kaiser Castle

Isle of Schutt with synagogue

NUREMBERG BEFORE THE WAR

The International Military Tribunal for the trial of the major Nazi leaders was composed of one voting judge and one alternate judge from each of the Big Four victorious powers. The United States, Great Britain, and France had high ranking civilian judges, while the Soviet Union selected high ranking Russian military officers as judges.

At the end of the major Nazi leaders' trial, the twelve Subsequent Proceedings were held before several military tribunals, at times proceeding simultaneously, before American civilian judges. These were prosecuted by the United States only.

All of these trials were concerned with three major points: basic human rights and the dignity of life, the difference between good and evil, and indifference to evil.

In a crime there is always a perpetrator and a victim. If you look the other way, do not get involved, stay neutral, or remain silent, you will always help the perpetrator and never the victim. In Germany the Nazis were the perpetrators and the Jews and other targeted groups were the victims. The ordinary German population in general looked the other way when their Jewish neighbors were being rounded up and taken away. They did not get involved, did not ask why, did not protest. These silent bystanders helped the Nazi perpetrators by their silence, because of fears for their own safety, their own anti-Semitism, or just plain indifference. Far too few pastors and community leaders spoke up.

The Major Nazi Leaders' Trial

The horror story of Nazism began unfolding before the eyes and ears of the world in Nuremberg on November 20, 1945. The case for the trial of twenty-two major Nazi leaders was titled *In the Matter of the United States of America, the French Republic, the United Kingdom of Great Britain and Northern Ireland, and the Union of Soviet Socialist Republics against Hermann Wilhelm Goering, et al.*

The sixty-six page indictment detailed the four counts charged, which involved a common conspiracy to:

• seize power

- establish a totalitarian regime

- plan, prepare, initiate, and wage wars of aggression

- violate the laws of war

- commit crimes against peace, crimes against humanity, and crimes of persecution and extermination

- establish membership in a criminal organization declared so by the International Military Tribunal, commonly known as the SS.

There was no historical precedent in international law for these trials. Therefore, judicial precedent was established by the four victorious powers at the London Conference with the adoption of unambiguous rules of law governing the trials, set forth in the charter agreed to at this conference. Nineteen nations adhered to this agreement, which became basic international law that has been followed since that time. Justice Robert H. Jackson, Chief U.S. Prosecutor, detailed the points of the London Conference agreement in his October 7, 1946, report to President Truman.[1]

The Pretrial Gathering of Evidence

In the early stages of the war, the United States, Great Britain, France, and the Soviet Union had vowed to bring the leading Nazis to trial. Beginning in 1941—four years before the end of the war—it was learned that the Nazis were executing innocent hostages in retaliation for attacks on German forces who were occupying overrun countries. On October 25, 1941, President Roosevelt denounced such illegal executions and warned that those responsible would face severe consequences.

On October 7, 1942, the United States and the United Kingdom announced that a United Nations War Crimes Commission would be established to list the names of those responsible and to collect and evaluate evidence.

A reasonable person might have thought that the Germans would keep the fewest possible records detailing their most heinous atrocities. But did they? No. The famous German efficiency required meticulous detail. Twelve years of war records were found stashed away, including orders by Hitler and others highest in command in the Nazi hierarchy, regarding every facet of power seizure and waging wars of aggression against all of the countries they invaded, orders to round up all the Jews in those countries and transport them to concentration camps, and orders to perform horrific medical experiments.

Of course, as the Nazis conducted their aggressive expansion by force of arms, it never entered their heads that their Thousand-Year Reich might be defeated and their poisonous detailed records would in the greatest measure serve to convict them of their crimes against humanity at the bar of justice. And, as they were determined to build a super Aryan race of pure blood, they did not view as criminal their annihilation of "inferior, polluting" races and "subcultures" such as Jews, Gypsies, and Slavs.

Undoubtedly, Allied bombs had destroyed many records. However, thousands of records were recovered by the advancing Allied Forces in party or government offices. Then, when the Germans realized that their Third Reich just might go down in devastating defeat, they stashed all records they could in selected hiding places. The Allies found records behind a false wall in an abandoned castle. In another castle, nearly complete records of the German Foreign Office, weighing almost five hundred tons, were discovered. Poland had been invaded by Germany in September 1939; upon his arrest by Allied forces, the Nazi Governor General of Poland surrendered his voluminous diaries.

Particularly valuable were captured personal files of the Reich SS Leader and Chief of the German police, Heinrich Himmler. These documents were extremely important in establishing responsibility for crimes against humanity committed by the doctor defendants in the medical case that I worked on. Adolf Hitler had charged Himmler with the implementation of the Final Solution—the extermination of the Jews. At the end of the war in May 1945, Himmler attempted to flee in disguise, but was captured by British forces. When a doctor was ordered to search him, he bit down on a cyanide capsule hidden in his mouth and was dead within a few minutes.

Most of the atrocities were carefully recorded by written documentation, film, or photography. Because tens of thousands of pieces of documentary evidence had been captured by the Allies from various hiding places, most facts presented at the trials could not be denied or defended.

Hundreds of witnesses testified in pretrial hearings, but with such solid documentary evidence, the Big Four powers called only thirty-three witnesses. The defendants called sixty-six witnesses and answered 143 interrogatories. The major Nazi leaders' trial consumed 116 trial days, and concluded on August 31, 1946.

Of twenty-two defendants, nineteen were held accountable for their crimes individually, not collectively. Twelve were sentenced to death by hanging, including Martin Bormann in absentia. Ten were hanged at the Nuremberg Prison on October 16, 1946. Four hours before Hermann Goering was to be hanged, he bit down on a cyanide capsule that he had been able to conceal in his mouth, joining Hitler and Himmler in choosing suicide over taking responsibility for his actions and suffering the consequences.

November 6, 1946

I arrived in Nuremberg on November 6, three weeks after the hangings. The atmosphere was electric with what had happened on that historic October date, especially the suicide of the number one defendant, Hermannn Goering. It was particularly shocking because Colonel Burton C. Andrus, a rigorous military disciplinarian, was the Nuremberg prison commandant. He was noted for his strict orders to American soldiers to stand guard twenty-four hours a day in shifts, staring through the small window of each cell. Every movement and every part of the cell could be observed except a corner of the bathroom.

When I arrived, the British, French, and Soviets were packing up and going home or returning to their respective zones in Germany to conduct other war crime trials. After finishing the major Nazi leaders' trial, many of the lawyers, prosecutors, interpreters, judges, court reporters, document examiners, analysts, and clerks did not stay for the twelve Subsequent Proceedings.

The International Military Tribunal had finished their mission and purpose for being: to prove, expose, and justify severe punishment for atrocities committed by Germans. Justice Robert H. Jackson, who had been appointed by President Truman to be the Chief of Counsel for prosecuting war criminals in this first international military trial, made the following memorable statement during the trial:

> We must never forget that the record on which we judge these defendants is the record on which history will judge us tomorrow. To pass these defendants a poisoned chalice is to put it to our own lips as well.

In the end, the defendants eagerly drank from their own chalice, poisoned by their own atrocities. The entire world had been watching. It had been shown that this was not a trial of the victors over the vanquished, but of justice over evil. The Light of Goodness shone over the Darkness of Evil.

I have written this book based upon the official court reporters' transcript of the medical case, which I helped record. It is this record on which history will judge us, as Justice Jackson stated.

· 3 ·

The Subsequent Proceedings

THE TWELVE SEPARATE trials in the Subsequent Proceedings started on October 25, 1946, and continued until judgment in the last case was rendered in April 1949. These trials were prosecuted by the United States only, with American civilian judges sitting on military tribunals. Each tribunal consisted of three or more lawyers, admitted to practice for at least five years in the highest state courts or the Supreme Court of the United States.

The defendants in these Subsequent Proceedings included leading professional physicians, diplomats and politicians, the State Secretary of the Foreign Office of Germany, Cabinet Ministers, military leaders, SS leaders, industrialists, the Acting Minister of Justice, and jurists.

The twelve cases were:

- Case No. I, The Medical Case, charged twenty doctors and three medical assistants. This book will describe this case in condensed detail.

- Case No. II, The Milch Case, charged Erhard Milch, Field Marshal and State Secretary for Air.

- Case No. III, The Justices Case, charged the State Secretary Franz Schlegelberger and others in the Reich Ministry of Justice.

- Case No. IV, The Pohl Case, charged Oswald Pohl, Chief of the Economic and Administrative Office, and others.

- Case No. V, The Flick Case, charged Friedrich Flick, Leader of the German Industrial Steel and Coal Combine, and others.

- Case No. VI, The Farben Case, charged Karl Krauch, prominent Director of the I. G. Farben Industry, and others.

- Case No. VII, The Hostage Case, charged Wilhelm List, Commander-in-Chief in the Southeast, and others.

- Case No. VIII, The Race and Resettlement Case, charged Ulrich Greifeld, Chief of the Race and Resettlement Main Office, and others.

- Case No. IX, The Einsatzgruppen Case, charged Otto Ohlendorf, Chief of Einsatzgruppen "D," and others.

- Case No. X, The Krupp Case, charged Alfred Krupp and others in the Krupp Munitions Industry.

- Case No. XI, The Ministries Case, charged Ernst von Weizsaecker, State Secretary in the Foreign Office, and others.

- Case No. XII, The High Command Case, charged Wilhelm von Leeb, Army Group Commander-in-Chief, and others.

My First Nuremberg Home

After going through the ritual of presenting my orders to the proper military authorities when I landed in Nuremberg on November 6, I was given a briefing. Then I was given a top security pass, a supply of chlorine pills for drinking water, more information sheets, booklets, and forms to fill out. I was assigned a place to live, my first of three. With my suitcase and handbag, I climbed into a military vehicle and was driven by a corporal to my first Nuremberg home.

Riding along rubble-lined streets with piles of dirt, broken stone, and shattered bricks, I stared in silence at the gaping, bombed holes in the few still-standing apartment and office buildings, now just skeletons. Under the gray sky, everything seemed like a surreal charcoal drawing against the snow-covered ground. There was no color any-

Center of the medieval Walled City

The view from the castle

*Ruins of the Lorenz Church
in the Walled City*

Area near the Lorenz Church

NUREMBERG AFTER THE WAR

where. Very few vehicles were on the streets except for U.S. Army cars, jeeps, and buses. Small charred trees and shrubs, tipped with snow, tenaciously survived. A few drab-looking Germans, both men and women, were clearing rubble from side streets using handcarts and wheelbarrows. Occasionally, I saw a German hunched over a bicycle, zigzagging his way around potholes.

We arrived at a small two-story, three-bedroom house on Beulowstrasse, where I met my housemates. Both were on the Allied payroll—a young prim and proper British woman who spoke with a fast, clipped accent, and a pretty young French woman who greeted both the corporal and me in her slip. Her attitude, shown by her eyes, told me she saw nothing improper about her apparel—my second introduction to another culture. Two foreign languages confronted me: British English and French English! This was my first contact on this journey with women, other than the Icelandic Prime Minister's wife in Reykjavik.

The corporal told me that I would be picked up with the other women at 7:00 a.m. by a U.S. Army bus that stopped at all the residences. We would go first to breakfast at a large mansion with an American-maintained mess hall.

My housemates confirmed several shocking bits of information I had heard first from the major at Westover. In this bitter cold there was no heat or hot water. We had to bathe in ice-cold water—when we did. I learned the French and British thought we Americans were slightly addled with our daily shower ritual. According to my housemates, there was no need to bathe more than once a week anyway! In a short period of time, I got the "scent" of this philosophy not only in this house but in the courthouse as well. I dropped a chlorine pill in every glass of water I drank in this house without fail—otherwise, the water wasn't safe.

That night, totally exhausted after a wrenching, weeklong trip, I climbed into my bed, grateful for the thick featherbed comforter in the bone-chilling cold.

Early the next morning we climbed aboard the Army bus as promised the night before. My breakfast consisted of cold-storage eggs, pancakes and syrup, cereal, reconstituted milk, canned fruit, and powdered coffee. Other military and civilian personnel joined us in the mess hall. Somehow, this breakfast tasted delicious. I would get used to it, as it was virtually the same every day for over the next year and a half, with only slight variations.

After breakfast we were driven to the iron gates of the Palace of Justice, where most of us would work.

Vivien Spitz eating at the mess hall, November 1946

The Palace of Justice

The heavily damaged, but still standing, complex of the Palace of Justice stood on the western edge of Nuremberg. It was a huge, gray stone structure consisting of four buildings that stretched three blocks, housing courtrooms, offices, and the prison. Furtherstrasse, the main street, ran in front to the nearby city of Furth-im-Bayern, where other American and Allied personnel were housed. The Pegnitz River ran through Nuremberg behind the Palace of Justice.

In recent times the German Regional Court of Appeals had used this courthouse as a judicial arm of the Bavarian Government, now in the U.S. sector. Ironically, a sculpted tablet of the Ten Commandments hung over the door.

When the Allied bombing came, this famous German courthouse suffered extensive damage. Shattered windows, demolished rooms,

The Palace of Justice

and floor sections required extensive structural repair before the trials could take place.

In September 1945, under the close supervision of Lieutenant Evan Dildine of the 204th Combat Engineers Battalion, former SS troops (then prisoners of war) were busy restoring, repairing, and enlarging the seating capacity of the main courtroom. They had been sent to Nuremberg from other Army installations in the U.S. Zone of Germany by General George Patton for this purpose. Lieutenant Dildine told me that while working on the balcony, the prisoners piled too much debris on a weak spot, causing a cave-in. Several fell four floors to the basement, which killed one and injured three others.

The front section on the third floor had been badly damaged by American bombings. All necessary repairs were made in time for the opening of the major Nazi leaders' trial on November 20. The German prisoners of war were required to repair the building in which their Nazi superiors would be sentenced to prison or death.

To enter the front of the building on the Army bus, we rode through large iron gates fastened to stone pillars that connected the iron fences surrounding the building. The bullet-nicked archway and entrances were guarded by thirteen-ton U.S. Army personnel carriers with one GI posted on top of the turret and another seated next to the long bore of the cannon facing toward the street.

I walked up the five steps to the front entrance and showed my security pass to the American soldiers guarding the door. They were very formal, military, and unsmiling. I was a new person with whom they were unfamiliar, and they eyed me suspiciously. They carefully checked my pass. They checked everyone's credentials, including Chief Prosecutor General Telford Taylor's and any other officer, no matter how high the rank. Walking down long, cold corridors, I found my way to the office of Women's Army Corps Captain Sara Kruskall for my indoctrination. There was nothing warm or welcoming about Captain Kruskall, the fourth woman I met on this trip.

My Raw Orientation

Captain Kruskall made it very clear to me that the American court reporting section, although not in the military, was under military supervision. Even though I was a War Department contract employee with a high rating, I was still subject to court-martial for any behavior prohibited by the Code of Military Justice. At the time I did not know what behavior was covered by this code.

Because there were no banking facilities, U.S. currency was not allowed in occupied Germany. U.S. money was exchanged for occupation currency called scrip. Black-marketing was discouraged. I later learned what black-marketing meant.

Black-marketing, forbidden by the U. S. Military, was the sale by Germans and purchase by Allied personnel of valuable items (which were no longer valued by the Germans) such as Meissen and Rosenthal figurines and dinnerware, diamonds, jewelry, and silver, in an underground ready market. The medium of exchange was usually cigarettes and coffee, which could be used to buy food. There was always a German employed on the Allied payroll who had the connections and could make arrangements. One just needed to ask, "Where can I get Hummel figures?" or other specified items. It was always secretive.

My only acquired treasure was a Meissen figurine from Dresden of the Harlequin and the Ballerina, standing eleven inches tall. One of our American Army colonels told me he bought a new Volkswagen for four cartons of cigarettes, valued at $100 a carton.

However, when we went to country towns such as Garmisch-Partenkirchen and Regensberg, we could shop openly in their little stores. With cigarettes I bought some watercolor etchings, still hanging on my walls today. I watched a German man who had lost his arms in the bombing of Nuremberg as he laid back in a chaise lounge-type of chair and, with his pencil placed between his toes, drew scenes of Nuremberg. They are beautiful pieces of artwork. It is hard for people to believe when I tell them I watched him draw these lovely scenes the way he did.

We would be paid once a month, to include an overseas differential increase. I was paid about five thousand dollars a year. I would be provided with quarters, transportation to and from work, and a German maid to clean my living quarters. However, I was to pay for my meals supplied by the Army and for any purchases at the post-exchange. There were no facilities other than those provided by the Army for American and Allied personnel. I was to pay for any trips within or out of Germany upon obtaining orders.

We were not allowed to eat in the few open German restaurants because the Germans could not produce enough food for themselves. Their milk was not pasteurized and their produce was fertilized with human excrement, collected and carried in "honey wagons" that looked like large, hollowed-out logs. These were pulled by huge oxen that slowly, rhythmically clopped down the middle of cobblestone streets to their dispersal locations. I learned about this fertilizer harvest when I first saw strawberries the size of small apples.

I was issued ration cards for the Army post-exchange store (PX) and commissary where I could purchase some limited food items, toiletries, and cigarettes. Civilians were allowed to buy three bottles of hard liquor per month, but we were prohibited by the military code from providing any to GIs who worked for us in court or in our offices. They were allowed to have only beer and wine. An infraction of this rule would send me to Captain Kruskall's office on a much later occasion, where I was threatened with a court-martial if I ever again gave a bottle of hard liquor to one of our office GIs. How did she learn about it?

The soldier I gave it to had shared it with other GIs at the Noncommissioned Officers Club. The soldiers drinking it got in a fight, resulting in broken furniture and an intervention by Military Police. When the offending GIs were asked where they got the liquor, they replied in truthful fashion with my name. Then, although I knew the rule, I really learned what "prohibited behavior" meant.

When we had leave time (short or long), we could make trips to cities in the U.S., British, or French Occupation Zones—cities such as Paris, Brussels, Prague, or Amsterdam—or to cities in Switzerland. All rail transportation in the U.S. Zone was under the control of the U.S. Military and was free. There was a mess charge for food. We had to obtain orders and visas for these trips, depending on their destinations.

The Russian Occupation Zone was closed to us, and in order to get visas to enter the city of Berlin, we had to have an invitation from someone whom we knew within the city. That was not easy to obtain.

My orientation would continue every week that I was in Germany. American, Allied, and military personnel advised me based on their experience. I would learn the military lingo. Like most working on the trial, military or civilian, I could not speak German, but would learn simple greetings and certain important questions or statements.

Restrictive curfews were imposed on us. We could walk about the rubble-strewn city but were warned not to walk alone. We were not to be on the street after 7:00 p.m. for security reasons. Armed German terrorists were still hiding in basement rubble and catacombs under the medieval Walled City, which had been heavily bombed and shattered. Bombs thrown by die-hard terrorists had damaged U.S. Army facilities in Stuttgart. We were always to be on guard. I would eventually experience a frightful bombing of the Grand Hotel when I lived there—twenty-eight months after the end of the war!

Army jeeps were equipped with angle irons welded to every front bumper. These rose above the head of the driver to cut wires that might be strung across roads at night to decapitate American soldiers driving jeeps. The terrorists built roadblocks across the roads at night. Unfortunately, a new friend of mine, Alfred Kornfeld, a U.S. wartime correspondent for *Life Magazine,* hit one such roadblock when driving from Berlin to Nuremberg and was killed.

We could go to the Noncommissioned Officers Club, to the Red Cross ice rink and swimming pool, and to the German opera house. The opera house held fully staged opera performances by Germans. Movies arranged by U.S. Special Services were also shown at the opera house. The cost was thirty cents for civilians and fifteen cents for military. We could also go to the garish Stein Castle, where the international press had their Press Club.

The Officers Club in the Grand Hotel was our main center for socializing. It was reserved for U.S. and Allied military officers or civilian personnel working on the trials or visiting from other jurisdictions. We gathered in the cocktail lounge, dining room, and Marble Room ballroom to drink, talk, and eat in the plushest of our permitted Nuremberg locations.

There was no heat anywhere other than from fireplaces or an electric heater. Electric heaters were hard to come by, unless one knew a post-exchange supplier. Everyone wanted to be friends with Jack Barash from Miami, a civilian working with the PX who had an electric heater. It was comical to watch people in the lounge trying to get chairs closest to him. He, his wife Emma, and teen-age daughter eventually became good friends of mine, welcoming me to join them and their electric heater!

Meeting My Co-workers

From Captain Kruskall's office I walked down another long, dreary, cold hallway to the court reporters' office—a large room with many cheaply constructed desks and chairs and a few large tables. I received a warm welcome from Chief Reporter Charles Foster of California and met a dozen or so other reporters. Among them were three from my Detroit office who had been old enough to precede me to Nuremberg: Wayne Perrin, Gertrude Feldt, and Fern Primeau. It was amazing to think that of the approximately twenty-six highly qualified court reporters nationwide sent to Nuremberg, four were from my Detroit office!

Also from Michigan came Judge Robert M. Toms, for whom I had occasionally worked in the Detroit circuit court. He was a judge with an excellent reputation. Another Michigander, whom I had not known before, attorney George Murphy—a tall, jovial Irishman—came from Ann Arbor. He had been on the legal staff of the University of Michigan and was now appointed as a judge on the High Command Case, Case No. XII of the Subsequent Proceedings of the War Crimes Trials. Our small contingent from Michigan—a state that did not allow capital punishment—included these two judges who would now have to consider sentencing defendants to death.

Daughter of the Chicago German Bund Leader

The biggest surprise of all was Leonore Huber! She and I had been classmates and good friends at Gregg Business College in Chicago only four years before. Her perfect English belied the fact that of her twenty-six years, eighteen had been spent growing up in Germany, her country of birth. Of course she would be back home.

I greeted her with some trepidation, recalling the strange weekend in May 1943 I had spent at the Chicago apartment she shared with her parents.

I had lived seventy miles northwest in Woodstock, Illinois, a small farming community of six thousand. I got on the Northwestern 400 at 7:00 every morning, eating train smoke for breakfast and taking the train back home every evening—one and one-half hours each way. It was with some delight that I accepted Leonore's invitation to spend the weekend in the city with her and her parents.

Leonore explained that her folks could not speak English well so I would not be able to converse with them, but she would interpret when necessary, since she spoke fluent German. The first evening she showed me many snapshots of herself and her friends in Germany.

The bottom half of the pictures had been cut off because they were all in German military uniform, and she explained to me she did not want to see the uniform.

I observed her parents only casually the next day and did not try to converse with them other than to greet them. They spoke only in German to each other and to Leonore. And they did not make an effort to carry on any conversation with me through Leonore.

The war was exploding in 1943 all over Europe and the Pacific and I was aware that Germany was our enemy.

The radio was on and the news was blaring something about the liquidation of the Warsaw Jewish Ghetto in Poland by the Nazis. It was May 16, 1943. Then the true horrible meaning of the war occurred to me. I saw an immediate change in the demeanor of Herr and Frau Huber. They heard the news in English, and their eyes lit up with joy and delight. The tone of their excited and happy expressions in German indicated to me that whatever this news meant, it was great news to them. For me, anything the Nazis did was not good news. Strange, strange, indeed!

I could tell Leonore was embarrassed, and I was disturbed. I never forgot it. I finished college in 1943 and lost contact with her until I arrived in Nuremberg in November 1946. And there she was! Now we would be coworkers, but we were never to be close friends again.

Only when I told this same story to a new friend there—British Broadcasting Corporation news reporter Allen Dreyfus—a couple of months later, did I learn from him that Leonore's father, Herr Huber, "who could not speak English well," was the leader of the Chicago branch of the German-American Bund in 1943. On February 22, 1939, this subversive organization had staged a rally of twenty-two thousand Nazis in New York City's Madison Square Garden!

The Court Reporting Process

Chief Reporter Charles Foster of California had the authority to make team reporting assignments for the twelve trials that were to start soon. At times, two or more trials would proceed simultaneously. Six reporters usually made up one team, each spending fifteen minutes writing in court, then working a rotation schedule that provided a daily copy transcript by the end of the day.

I had indicated my interest in the medical case to Chief Foster and advised him that I had specialized in medical terminology in my college reporting courses. I was delighted that he selected me to be one of the six members of this daily copy reporting team.

The procedure that had been worked out on the IBM system for reporting the major Nazi leaders' trial would be followed for the subsequent trials. By this time, most of the bugs had been worked out.

Because of the many differing languages spoken by the people involved, everyone in the courtroom—the judges, attorneys, defendants, court reporters, press reporters, interpreters, monitors, translators, staff, and audience—had to wear earphones that enabled them to understand what was being said.

The defendants and their counsel had their dials turned to German. In the reporters' case, we turned the dial on the desk to English. The result was, except when an American judge or an English-speaking witness or attorney spoke, we were reporting the words of the interpreters. These areas could be clarified later by the interpreters and translators who went over the transcripts late in the day before they were printed overnight and delivered each morning to the judges, attorneys, other trial personnel, and the international press.

On the desks in front of the witnesses, judges, and attorneys were two lights that could be flashed on by the interpreters—yellow for SLOW DOWN, and red for STOP. In order to translate from German to English, the interpreters had to wait for the entire sentence to be spoken to get the vital verb at the end. Then the interpreter was forced to "telescope" the entire sentence as fast as possible.

When the temper of the German counsel or witness rose in heated argument, the rate of speech went up, putting the interpreter under great stress, often resulting in an incorrect interpretation or a struggle to find the correct words. It was then that the interpreter would flash the yellow or red distress light until he or she could catch up.

At times the interpreter was so hard pressed that, for example, *vacuum cleaner* became *dust sucker. Artificial insemination* became *artful fertilization.* Soon, the reporters and interpreters bonded, as we depended so much on each other. The reporters could never speak or interrupt the proceedings to have any of the hundreds of complex German words or names of cities, concentration camps, or organizations repeated. When they were spoken, we wrote sounds.

For this reason, an English-speaking German monitor—a German national who had been cleared of having been a member of the Nazi Party—sat next to us, writing in longhand words such as *Theresienstadt, soldatenkonzentrationslager, Haupt-sturmfuehrer,* and *Reichsluftfahrtministerium,* to mention a few.

After his or her fifteen-minute turn in court, each reporter would leave the courtroom when the next reporter entered and started recording. When leaving, we walked within touching distance of the defendants, then proceeded to the office where we typed what we had recorded on manual typewriters at our assigned desks.

Every word spoken in the courtroom was electronically recorded. These recordings could be used to compare to the reporter's transcript at the end of the day by a translator who corrected any misinterpretations made by the courtroom interpreters.

Each page of transcript, identified by the reporter's name and turn number, was then sent to the stenciling department for retyping on stencils. From there, the transcript was sent to the mimeographing department for printing and delivery to court participants, usually by the next morning. The making of this daily copy is a common procedure in U.S. courts and in the U.S. Senate and House of Representatives.

The American court reporters' transcripts were translated and printed in German as well. This was a daily laborious process that produced over 330,000 pages of transcript covering the twelve Subsequent Proceedings, including over 11,530 pages of the medical case.

· 4 ·

Case No. 1, The Medical Case

ON OCTOBER 25, 1946, the United States indicted twenty German doctors and three medical assistants on four counts in *The United States of America versus Karl Brandt, et al.* Thus commenced the first and most horrifying of the twelve subsequent trials.

Count I charged the Common Design or Conspiracy.

Count II charged War Crimes.

Count III charged crimes against humanity constituting murders, brutalities, cruelties, tortures, atrocities, and inhumane acts.

Count IV charged membership in a criminal organization declared so by the International Military Tribunal, commonly known as the SS.

Tribunal Members

The members of Military Tribunal I were:

- Walter B. Beals, Presiding Judge - Chief Justice of the Supreme Court, State of Washington

- Harold L. Sebring - Associate Justice of the Supreme Court, Florida

- Johnson T. Crawford - formerly Judge of a District Court, Oklahoma

Judges Harold L. Sebring; Walter B. Beals, presiding; Johnson Tal Crawford; and Victor C. Swearingen, alternate, in the courtroom at the Palace of Justice during the Nazi doctors' trial

- Victor C. Swearingen, Alternate - formerly Special Assistant to the Attorney General of the United States.

The indictment was served in German on each of the twenty-three defendants on November 5, 1946. I arrived in Nuremberg one day later.

The Arraignments

The arraignments took place on November 21, 1946.[1] Presiding Judge Walter Beals banged the gavel with such determination that it resounded throughout the large courtroom. He began:

We will now proceed to arraign the defendants on the cause now pending before this tribunal. As the names of the defendants are called, each defendant will stand and will remain standing until told to be seated. Mr. Secretary General of the Tribunal will call the roll of the defendants.

As their names were called, the defendants rose individually. I looked at each one. They were shabby-looking, either in unpressed suits, jackets and pants, or military uniforms stripped of all insignia. Many wore jackboots. They appeared to be resentful and arrogant. Some had straight tight lips; mean, hard looks on their faces; and set jaws. To my mind, the most evil-looking were Dr. Karl Brandt, with his piercing eyes, and Wolfram Sievers, with his black beard and pointed mustache. I dubbed him "Blue Beard." Everyone in the courtroom was silent as each defendant rose.

"If the Honorable Tribunal pleases, all of the defendants are in the dock."

"The defendants will be seated," said the judge. "The counsel for the prosecution will now proceed with the arraignment of the defendants."

Brigadier General Telford Taylor read out loud the four charges mentioned above and went on to say:

Between September 1939 and April 1945 all of the defendants herein unlawfully, willfully, and knowingly committed war crimes, as defined by Article II of Control Council Law No. 10, in that they were principals in, accessories to, ordered, abetted, took a consenting part in, and were connected with plans and enterprises involving medical experiments without the subjects' consent, upon civilians and members of the armed forces of nations then at war with the German Reich and who were in the custody of the German Reich in exercise of belligerent control, in the course of which experiments the defendants committed murders, brutalities, cruelties, tortures, atrocities, and other inhuman acts. Such experiments included, but were not limited to, the following:

- High-Altitude Experiments. Carried out in a low-pressure chamber in which the atmospheric conditions and pressures prevailing at high altitude (up to sixty-eight thousand feet) could be duplicated, many victims died as a result of these experiments and others suffered grave injury, torture, and ill treatment.

- Freezing Experiments. Victims were placed in a tank of ice water for up to three hours, or kept naked outdoors for hours at below freezing temperatures, during which numerous victims died.

By this time I was having a great deal of trouble remaining dispassionate emotionally and trying to keep my composure. The general continued:

- Malaria Experiments. Over one thousand involuntary subjects were infected by mosquitoes or by injections of extracts of the mucous glands of mosquitoes, who then contracted malaria, many of whom died, while others suffered severe pain and permanent disability.

- Lost (Mustard) Gas Experiments. Wounds were deliberately inflicted on victims and then infected with poisonous gas, some of whom died and others suffered intense pain and injury.

- Sulfanilamide Experiments. Wounds deliberately inflicted on experimental subjects were infected with streptococcus, gas gangrene, and tetanus, and then wood shavings and ground glass were forced into the wounds, resulting in deaths, serious injury and intense agony.

- Bone, Muscle, and Nerve Regeneration and Bone Transplantation Experiments. Sections of bones, muscles, and nerves were removed from the victims, resulting in intense agony, mutilation, permanent disability, and death.

- Sea Water Experiments. Subjects were deprived of all food and given only chemically processed sea water, causing great pain, suffering, serious bodily injury and madness.

- Epidemic Jaundice Experiments. Subjects were deliberately infected with epidemic jaundice resulting in pain, suffering, and death.

- Sterilization Experiments. Thousands of victims were sterilized by x-ray, surgery, and drugs, causing great mental and physical anguish.

- Spotted Fever (Typhus) Experiments. Hundreds of deliberately infected persons experimented upon died—over 90 percent.

- Experiments with Poison. Poisons were secretly administered to experimental subjects in their food, all of whom died or were deliberately killed to permit autopsies. Poison bullets were shot into other victims, who suffered torture and death.

- Incendiary Bomb Experiments. Burns were inflicted on subjects with phosphorous taken from the bombs, causing severe pain, suffering, and serious bodily injury.

Civilians and members of the armed forces of nations then at war with Germany were murdered in the exercise of belligerent control. One hundred twelve Jews were selected, killed, and defleshed for completing a skeleton collection for the

Reich University of Strasbourg in France under Nazi occupation.

Tens of thousands of Polish nationals alleged to be infected with incurable tuberculosis were ruthlessly exterminated while others were isolated in death camps with inadequate medical facilities.

Through the exercise of the "euthanasia" program of the German Reich, hundreds of thousands of human beings, including nationals of German-occupied countries, were murdered. This involved the systematic and secret execution of the aged, insane, incurably ill, deformed children, and other persons by gas, lethal injections and diverse other means in nursing homes, hospitals, and asylums. These people were termed "useless eaters" and a burden to the German war machine. Relatives of these victims were informed that they died from natural causes, such as heart failure. German doctors involved in the "euthanasia" program were also sent to Eastern occupied countries to assist in the mass extermination of Jews.

"I shall now call upon the defendants to plead guilty or not guilty to the charges against them," said Judge Beals. "Each defendant, as his name is called, will stand and speak into the microphone. At this time there will be no arguments, speeches, or discussion of any kind. Each defendant will simply plead either guilty or not guilty to the offenses with which he is charged by the indictment."

He began with Karl Brandt.

"Karl Brandt, are you represented by counsel in this proceeding?"

"Yes."

"How do you plead to the charges and specifications and each thereof set forth in the indictment against you, guilty or not guilty?"

"Not guilty."

"Be seated." Siegfried Handloser, are you represented by counsel in this cause?"

"No, I have no counsel yet."

"Do you desire that the Tribunal appoint counsel for you?"

"I hope that today or tomorrow I may receive an affirmative answer from a defense counsel."

"Are you at this time ready to plead to the indictment, guilty or not guilty?"

"Yes."

"How do you plead to the charges and specifications and each thereof set forth in the indictment against you, guilty or not guilty?"

"Not guilty."

"Be seated."

At this point the remaining defendants were individually arraigned. Counsel represented all. All pleaded not guilty to the indictment.

As a court reporter, although with only three years of experience in criminal courts in Detroit before going to Nuremberg, I was not surprised at the not-guilty pleas. I would have been surprised if anyone had pleaded guilty.

The Defendants

In many cases the defendants were distinguished German scientists, chief doctors and surgeons at medical clinics, institutes, hospitals, and universities throughout Germany. They were doctors and assistants at the concentration camps who performed or participated in the grisly medical experiments at Auschwitz, Dachau, Buchenwald, Ravensbrueck, Sachsenhausen, Natzweiler, Bergen-Belsen, Treblinka, and others.

Following is a brief description of each defendant:

1. Karl Brandt, Major General in the SS; Adolf Hitler's personal physician and chief architect of the program that turned doctors into torturers and murderers despite their Hippocratic Oath to heal and cure.
2. Siegfried Handloser, Lieutenant General, Medical Services.
3. Paul Rostock, Chief Surgeon of the Berlin Surgical Clinic.
4. Oskar Schroeder, Chief of the Medical Services of the Luftwaffe (Air Force).

5. Karl Genzken, Chief of the Medical Department of the Waffen SS.

6. Karl Gebhardt, Major General in the Waffen SS and President of the German Red Cross.

7. Kurt Blome, Plenipotentiary for Cancer Research.

8. Rudolf Brandt, Personal Administrative Officer to Reichsfuehrer SS Heinrich Himmler.

9. Joachim Mrugowsky, Chief Hygienist of the Reich Physician SS.

10. Helmut Poppendick, Chief of the Personal Staff of the Reich Physician SS.

11. Wolfram Sievers, Reich Manager of the Ahnenerbe Society.

12. Gerhard Rose, Brigadier General of the Medical Service of the Air Force.

13. Siegfried Ruff, Director, Department for Aviation Medicine at the Experimental Institute.

14. Hans Wolfgang Romberg, Staff Doctor at German Experimental Institute for Aviation.

15. Viktor Brack, Chief Administrative Officer in the Führer's Chancellery.

16. Herman Becker-Freyseng, Chief of the Department for Aviation Medicine.

17. Georg August Weltz, Chief of the Institute for Aviation Medicine.

18. Konrad Schaefer, Staff Doctor, Institute for Aviation Medicine.

19. Waldemar Hoven, Chief Doctor, Buchenwald concentration camp.

20. Wilhelm Beiglboeck, Consulting Physician to the Air Force.

21. Adolf Pokorny, Physician Specialist in Skin and Venereal Diseases.

22. Herta Oberheuser, Physician, Ravensbrueck concentration camp.

23. Fritz Fischer, Assistant Physician to defendant Gebhardt.

Twenty of the defendants sitting in the dock were doctors, and three were not: Rudolf Brandt, Wolfram Sievers, and Viktor Brack.

The defendants' dock. Bottom row of dock: Karl Brandt, Hitler's physician, (death); Siegfried Handloser, (life); Paul Rostock, (not guilty); Oskar Schroeder, (life); Karl Genzken, (life); Karl Gebhardt, (death); Kurt Blome, (not guilty); Joachim Mrugowsky, (death); Rudolf Brandt, (death); Helmut Poppendick, (10 years); Wolfram Sievers, (death)

Second row dock: Gerhard Rose, (life); Siegfried Ruff, (not guilty); Viktor Brack, (death); Hans Wolfgang Romberg, (not guilty); Hermann Becker-Freyseng, (20 years); Georg August Weltz, (not guilty); Konrad Schaeffer, (not guilty); Waldemar Hoven, (death); Wilhelm Beiglboeck, (15 years); Adolf Pokorny, (not guilty); Herta Oberheuser, (20 years); Fritz Fischer, (life). Lower right corner, German defense counsel; upper right corner, interpreters.

Office Chief of Counsel for War Crimes, US Army

The defendants fell into three main groups. Eight were members of the medical service of the German Air Force. Seven were members of the medical service of the SS. Eight, including the three who were not doctors, held top positions in the medical hierarchy.

All of the doctors violated the commandments of the Hippocratic Oath, which they had solemnly sworn to uphold and abide by, including the fundamental principle never to do harm—*primum non nocere.*

One doctor who will be mentioned frequently, Luftwaffe (Air Force) physician Dr. Sigmund Rascher, was not a defendant sitting in this dock. He and his wife had been executed near the end of the war for perpetrating a fraud on his Nazi superiors. The fraud involved the theft of babies by Rascher's wife in an illegal adoption procedure whereby she claimed she had given birth to them.

Heinrich Himmler will also appear frequently in the tribunal's documents and testimony. He was the Reichsführer-SS (Reich SS Leader) and Chief of the German police. Under orders from Führer Adolf Hitler, he implemented the extermination of Jews and other categories of people considered "undesirables" in the Final Solution. At the end of the war in May 1945, Himmler attempted to flee in disguise, was captured, and then committed suicide.

In a decree of July 1942, Hitler established a medical and health official under his direct control and appointed Karl Brandt to that position. Brandt had been his personal physician since 1934 and was thirty-eight at the time of this appointment. He became the supreme medical authority in the Reich in August 1944 and was the only one of the defendants who was directly answerable to Hitler.

Brandt, at age forty-two, sat in the prisoners' dock at Nuremberg on November 21, 1946.

Of the approximately 350 doctors who are estimated to have committed medical crimes, only these 20 doctors and 3 assistants were brought to the bar of justice and sat in the defendants' dock in the medical case in Nuremberg.

Other doctors were tried, convicted, and sentenced to death by hanging in other American military trials at Dachau. Many doctors got away, including the most evil and infamous, Dr. Josef Mengele— the "Angel of Death"—who experimented on and killed children (often twins) at Auschwitz. He successfully hid in Bavaria until his escape to South America.

The trial was a public trial conducted in open court, as were all trials. Each defendant selected German counsel. After the pleas of not guilty were taken at the arraignments on November 21, the tribunal adjourned until December 9, 1946.

A Respite from Initial Shock

This respite gave me and other reporters new to Nuremberg an opportunity to settle and get to know our colleagues who came from all over the United States.

It gave me a chance to prepare for living and working in a bombed-out, eerie city of ghosts. There was little contact and no socializing with the German population, although the nonfraternization order had ended. We were living in a closed society of American military, civilian, and Allied coworkers, working in the Nuremberg-Furth Enclave.

During those two weeks of adjournment, I became acclimated to what was the coldest, snowiest winter in Nuremberg in many years. Although there was a kitchen in the Beulowstrasse house—my first home there—I don't ever remember using it for any purpose other than to fix a cup of hot tea.

Occasionally I chatted briefly with my British and French housemates, but we had nothing in common in our work. They were clerical people in the documents section. We did have interesting conversations about their lives in London and Paris before they came to Nuremberg. I had never been to their countries and they had never been to mine.

Fortunately for me, I quickly became friendly with court reporters Piilani Ahuna of Honolulu, Hawaii, and Dorothy Fitzgerald of Cleveland, Ohio, both of whom had worked on the major Nazi leaders' trial, commonly referred to as Goering's trial. They stayed on in Nuremberg to work on the subsequent trials. Another friend I made through them was Siegfried (Sigi) Ramler of London, who had worked on Goering's trial and spoke several languages fluently.

It was very difficult to find linguists sufficiently qualified to become interpreters from German to English and English to German, but Sigi qualified and became an interpreter in the medical case. He held the court reporters in high regard for the work we did and I learned quickly how interdependent the reporters and interpreters became.

The weekend after the court adjourned on November 21, Lani, Sigi, and Dorothy invited me to join them at the Grand Hotel for breakfast and lunch and to take short walks around the nearby sections of the city. I had my camera and took my first pictures of the shattered city—just rubble and still-standing sections of buildings. One wall had a bathtub hanging from the second floor.

We would meet later in the Grand Hotel cocktail lounge—where everyone seemed to gather—and have dinner in the dining room. Lani and Sigi had sufficient seniority to be housed in the Grand Hotel. Dorothy lived in a large, elegant, three-story home at No. 8 Hebelstrasse with Anne Daniels of Washington, D.C. Anne had been Chief Reporter on Goering's trial, having arrived there directly from reporting the Potsdam Conference—attended by President Harry Truman, Prime Minister Clement Atlee of England, and President Josef Stalin of the Soviet Union—earlier that year.

Grand Hotel

The only standing building in the center of Nuremberg, the Grand Hotel towered over the rubble in the immediate vicinity. It was formerly one of the great hotels of Europe and had been the headquarters for Hitler and his top leaders during their visits to Nuremberg for huge Nazi Party rallies. The dining rooms, lobbies, and grand ballroom were lavishly decorated and furnished with heavy German furniture.

During the bombing of Nuremberg, the hotel had been almost split into two buildings. To get from the front office to the rear rooms, one had to walk the two planks placed across the crevasse on the third floor. Warrant Officer and court reporter Jack Rund of Washington, D.C., was one of the first to arrive at Nuremberg after the war to

The Grand Hotel, taken during the war, but prior to the 90-minute Allied bombing that destroyed the beautiful Walled City to the left.

record testimony in pretrial interrogations of Hermann Goering and the other major Nazi leaders, before their trial started on November 20, 1945. Jack told me that Bob Hope, during one of his U.S.O. appearances in Nuremberg for the troops, placed a chair halfway across the planks, sat on it, and declared it "the best room in Germany because of its southern, eastern, western, and northern exposures!"

The U.S. Army spent over one million dollars in 1945 to rebuild and repair the hotel to a livable condition. Open to civilian employees and military personnel of the Occupying Powers, the hotel became the center of American social life.

Across the street from the hotel stood the crumbled remains of the bombed Walled City. Only a still-standing turret and parts of the wall remained. Below, the dry moats were filled with debris. The black and gray skeleton of the main train station also stood across the street— its shattered windows staring hauntingly over at the hotel.

Just inside the front doors of the hotel, behind a half-circle bench desk at the lobby entrance, sat the U S. military policeman who checked security passes of everyone entering. Other nearby guards were his support staff.

In the large dining room was one round table that seemed to be reserved for my new court reporter friends, interpreters, and press people. I felt honored to be included in this interesting group.

Our waiter was a German named Henry, a tall, affable man with a pleasant, sincere smile, who had been cleared for employment. Only Henry and one young son had survived the brutal Allied bombing in which his wife and five other children died. He was grateful to have this job. We became his friends. Each week at the post-exchange we bought sundries and small supplies such as soap, toothpaste, and toothbrushes for him and his son. I remember giving him the glass of milk I ordered with dinner as time went on. He took it to the kitchen and saved it for his son. We always tipped the German waiters. The going rate was two cigarettes, which they used for bartering purposes. I had no idea where they lived. Was it in the basement rubble of one of those building skeletons, with many other German survivors huddled there, sharing whatever they had? I did not ask.

On weekend nights we often had dinner in the dining area that was part of the elegant ballroom named the Marble Room; we could also listen to the orchestra or band there. The top brass of the U.S. Army, realizing the daily horror stories we were hearing, arranged wonderful weekend entertainment in the Marble Room. Often they brought in shows from the Danish circuit—trapeze artists and dancers. There was always an orchestra for dancing, which played not only wonderful Viennese waltzes and peppy polkas, but also top American hit tunes of that era. German singers, with their accents, were often comical in their renditions of American tunes. This was the closest we got to an environment similar to life back in the States, which, along with short trips throughout Bavaria and to nearby countries, made it bearable to go back into the courtroom to face the next barrage of horror.

Without these weekend socializing experiences, which helped me block out mentally what I had heard in the courtroom the prior week, I would have had much trouble not showing emotion. The longer I was in Nuremberg the better I felt, as I could discuss my shock and dismay with other court reporters and members of the press who had been there for over a year working on the international major Nazi leaders' trial. After all, I had a one-year contract and could not just quit. The angrier I became at what I was hearing, seeing, and recording in the courtroom, the more motivated I became to overcome the initial shock and tough it out. I was not alone in these feelings, but I was the youngest reporter there—some were as much as twenty years older than I was.

Thanksgiving Day 1946

Our small group of reporters, interpreters, and journalists met in the Grand Hotel cocktail lounge for drinks—hot buttered rum was a favorite—and then had an American Thanksgiving dinner, with turkey and cranberries and prayers of gratitude, in the dining room. It might have been cold outside and the ground frozen under heavy snow, but the camaraderie in the lounge and dining room was warming. All winter the snow fell like frozen tears from drab skies.

On Friday November 29, a group of court reporters and soldiers who worked in our office climbed into a U.S. Army bus and left for a few days at the famous Bavarian resort Garmisch-Partenkirchen. It was my first trip and it became a time of intrigue and discovery. Here was a small, quaint mountain town with a uniquely picturesque alpine valley landscape, as if it had never suffered through a war. Old and modern frescoes decorated the gables of rustic houses. The finest decorations belonged to a house on Zugspitzstrasse where figures and patches of frescoes dated back to 1690. It was refreshing to have this rest away from the destruction of Nuremberg.

We went to the top of Germany's tallest mountain, the Zugspitze, and looked down on picturesque Lake Eibsee, nestled at the base of the mountains. It was deep blue in the middle and emerald green near the shore. The German shopkeepers were happy to sell us souvenirs: wood carvings and beautiful scenic etchings. They knew we were part of the American occupation forces. Our dealings with them were polite, but stiff. However, a few were so eager to appear friendly they bordered on fawning.

December 9, 1946

It was extremely chilly in the Palace of Justice. I put my coat on in the reporters' office, picked up my Parker pen and specially lined reporter's notebook, and walked the long icy hall to the huge double doors of the courtroom on the second floor of the eastern wing. I then entered for the first time the imposing room where I would be spending a good portion of the next nineteen months of my life. I took my coat off and laid it on a bench outside the doors and presented my security pass to the American military policeman, who opened one door. I took a deep breath and with great trepidation walked in, past the Nazi doctors and medical assistants in the defendants' dock and German defense counsel on my left. On my right were the American prosecutors and staff. The reporters' station was a long desk against the high bench of the four American judges. I turned around and sat down. It was 10:00 a.m.

I looked around the completely filled and enormous courtroom. It had beautiful mahogany panels and marble pillars. To my left sat the audience in the mezzanine. The international press gallery sat on the main floor. The interpreters' box was glass-enclosed and slightly raised, to the right of the prisoners' dock. The witness stand was to my right. U.S. Marshal Colonel Charles W. Mays was seated next to it. U.S. military policemen in white helmet liners, wearing belts over khaki uniforms, stood guard behind the dock, at each side of the dock, and at the main courtroom door to the left of the dock. Each courtroom door was under a large German appellate court medallion, which represented a different region of Germany.

I looked at the prosecutors to my left. They wore uniforms if military, suits if civilians. I looked at the defense counsel in black robes. Many would stuff crumpled newspapers under their robes to provide insulation against the freezing temperatures in the courtroom. We could hear the rustling every time they moved. (I was always dressed in layers—blouse, wool sweater, jacket and skirt—to withstand the cold.)

I looked at the defendants; the twenty-three doctors and medical assistants wore German army uniforms stripped of insignia, or civil-

The Nazi doctors' trial in session. In the upper left corner of the room are two newsreel cameramen. Two US court reporters sit at the far left of the desk in front of the judges. Vivien Spitz is the reporter on the end with her hand on her forehead. Next to the reporters sit two German monitors. General Telford Taylor (standing) is prosecuting. In the foreground are the German defense counsel, seated in front of the defendants' dock.

Office Chief of Counsel for War Crimes, US Army

ian suits. My eyes scanned all of them, coming to rest on the number one defendant in the first seat on the left in the dock, Dr. Karl Brandt, Hitler's personal physician and the architect of the experimental medical programs that had brought the defendants to this trial.

As I looked at Karl Brandt, his eyes locked onto mine—boring into me with such deep, evil intensity that I shuddered with a chill that went down my spine and froze me to my seat. I broke his gaze by lowering my eyes to the desk and prepared to start writing.

Defendant Karl Brandt,
Major General in the SS and
Adolf Hitler's personal physician

General Taylor's Opening Statement

Brigadier General Telford Taylor, Chief of Counsel for War Crimes, handsome with his military bearing, stood at the lectern and began the opening statement of the prosecution:

The defendants in this case are charged with murders, tortures, and other atrocities committed in the name of medical science. The victims of these crimes are numbered in the hundreds of thousands.

These nameless doomed were ordered in wholesale lots, like cattle, of two hundred Jews in good physical condition, fifty Gypsies, five hundred tubercular Poles, or one thousand Russians.

The mere punishment of the defendants . . . can never redress the terrible injuries which the Nazis visited on these unfortunate peoples. For them it is far more important that these incredible events be established by clear and public proof, so that no one can ever doubt that they were fact and not fable; and that this court . . . as the voice of humanity, stamp these acts, and the ideas which engendered them, as barbarous and criminal.[2]

General Taylor pointed out that the walls, towers, and churches of Nuremberg had been reduced to rubble by Allied bombs, but Germany had been destroyed decades earlier by the seeds sown in German medicine that permitted euthanasia and experimentation on people—a moral disintegration in the practice of medicine.

Then he outlined historical evidence of what he called the prostitution of German medicine under the Nazis. The attack on Jewish physicians started in Berlin in April 1933. They were put on a separate list from others, headed, "Enemies of the State or Jews." Insurance companies were no longer allowed to pay fees to Jewish physicians, and scientific and professional societies excluded them. Certification and licensing were withdrawn and Jewish doctors were forced to wear a blue shield emblazoned with the Star of David. Pharmacies put signs in their windows: "Jews Not Wanted." Finally, Jews were forbidden to practice medicine.

All principles of medicine became subordinate to the Nazi National Socialist population policy and racial concepts. In 1935, the Nazi Director of Public Health in the Ministry of the Interior, Dr. Arthur Guett, announced in a book entitled *The Structure of Public Health in the Third Reich*:

The ill-conceived "love of thy neighbor" has to disappear, especially in relation to inferior or asocial creatures. It is the supreme duty of a national state to grant life and livelihood only to the healthy and hereditarily sound portion of the people in order to secure the maintenance of a hereditarily sound and racially pure folk for all eternity. The life of an individual has meaning only in the light of that ultimate aim, that is, in the light of his meaning to his family and to his national state.[3]

Crimes of Mass Extermination

The degradation of medical science and research began with the Aryan racial theories. The weak and the mentally and physically handicapped were termed "life unworthy of life." The German Governor of northwest Poland, which was absorbed into the German Reich early in 1942, was exterminating Jews by the tens of thousands. He secured permission from Heinrich Himmler, Reich Leader SS, through Adolf Hitler, to exterminate over 230,000 Poles suffering from tuberculosis. Himmler cautioned him to carry out these exterminations inconspicuously. Defendants Rudolf Brandt and Blome were involved in what was termed "special treatment," carried out by ruthless extermination or sending the victims to isolated camps where thousands died.[4]

Illegal Euthanasia

On September 1, 1939, Hitler charged defendant Karl Brandt in writing with the responsibility of carrying out a widespread euthanasia program to provide a "mercy death" to those he considered incurable. An estimated five thousand mentally deficient, physically deformed, and diseased children were killed as a result of this directive.

Defendants Karl Brandt, Hoven, Brack, and Blome sent three hundred to four hundred Jews, mostly non-German, to their death in the killing station at Bernburg. The Ministry of the Interior then sent lists of doomed patients to insane asylums for transport to particular

USHMM

Defendant Kurt Blome,
Plenipotentiary for Cancer Research

killing stations. Relatives received falsified death certificates claiming death from natural causes.

By the summer of 1940 this secret became common knowledge in Germany. Church authorities and various legal officials protested in vain to the Minister of Justice and the Minister of the Interior that people were being murdered. Family members who received the falsified death certificates often did not believe them and sometimes challenged them.

In December 1940 Himmler told defendant Brack that the institution Grafeneck should be discontinued because "the population knows what's going on" at the constantly smoking crematory.

The idea of a "mercy death" began to take on a life of its own. The aged, the insane, and incurable people in nursing homes, asylums, and hospitals were some of those who were killed needlessly. The Czechoslovak War Crimes Commission estimated that at least 275,000 of these types of people, and those unfriendly to the Nazi regime, were killed.[5]

Protection of Animals

During General Taylor's summary of the charges against the doctors and assistants involving freezing, drowning, burning, and poisoning, in sheer irony he cited the law passed by the Nazis on November 24, 1933, to protect animals. This law was designed explicitly to:

... prevent cruelty and indifference of man towards animals and to awaken and develop sympathy and understanding for animals as one of the highest moral values of a people. The soul of the German people should abhor the principle of mere utility without consideration of the moral aspects.

The law sites further that all operations or treatments which are associated with pain or injury, especially experiments involving the use of cold, heat, or infection, are prohibited. . . .

Medico-legal tests, vaccinations, withdrawal of blood for diagnostic purposes, and trial of vaccines prepared according to well-established scientific principles are permitted, but the animals have to be killed immediately and painlessly after such experiments.[6]

Physicians were not permitted to use dogs to increase their surgical skill, but using human beings for such purposes was allowed.

The Tribunal then adjourned to December 10, 1946.

December 10, 1946

This day of the proceedings began as Mr. James McHaney of the U.S. prosecution staff made an introductory statement explaining when and how documentary evidence, records, and archives were captured and preserved by special units of the U.S. Army.

When the U.S. Army entered Germany, special military search teams captured and preserved enemy documents, records, and archives and assembled them in document centers. Then field teams were sent to these centers to sort, screen, and translate thousands of these documents to be sent to Nuremberg.

Mr. McHaney described how the German Medical Services were organized by listing captured German documents pertaining to the twenty-three defendants, their positions and responsibilities. Among these were empowerment decrees signed by Hitler, Subordination and Powers Duties, Special Powers, Tables of Organization, and documents marked "Secret," signed by Karl Brandt.[7] These were white paper documents that had been handled many times before and after the trial started. They were stacked in piles on the prosecutors' desk.

· 5 ·

High-Altitude Experiments

Ten prisoners were selected and were taken to the station as permanent experimental subjects; and they were told that nothing would happen to them.

—Walter Neff, concentration camp inmate

THE HIGH-ALTITUDE EXPERIMENTS were designed to test the limits of human endurance and existence at extremely high altitudes with and without oxygen. They were conducted at Dachau concentration camp from approximately March 1942 to about August 1942 for the German Air Force. The purpose was to duplicate atmospheric conditions that a German pilot might encounter in combat when falling great distances through space without a parachute and without a source of oxygen. These experiments were carried out by locking the victim in an airtight, low-pressure chamber provided by the German Air Force, then simulating high-altitude atmospheric conditions and pressures up to sixty-eight thousand feet.

The criminal proposal to conduct the high-altitude experiments was first made on May 15, 1941, by Luftwaffe (Air Force) physician Dr. Sigmund Rascher to the Reich Leader SS, Heinrich Himmler. Himmler authorized the experiments willingly. German aeronautical and naval combat and rescue experiments focused most intensely on these simulated high-altitude tests (above thirty-six thousand feet), tests on exposure to cold temperatures, and the ability of the human body to handle processed sea water (to be described later).

Defendant Romberg stated that four experiments were conducted: slow descent without oxygen, slow descent with oxygen, falling without oxygen, and falling with oxygen.[1] The first two were to simulate descent with the parachute open; the latter two, a free fall before the chute opened.

The human experimental subjects in the reports were referred to as VPs (*Versuchsperson,* meaning *experimental person*). The approximately two hundred subjects were selected at random. Russians, Russian prisoners of war, Poles, Jews of various nations, and German political prisoners were some of those selected. Of these two hundred, no more than forty had been condemned to death. (The fact that subjects of experiments had received death sentences was an argument forwarded by the defendants as justification for killing them.) Seventy-eight were killed by these experiments. Dr. Rascher promised some inmates that if they volunteered, they would be released, and because of this, a few volunteered. That promise was never kept.

A report written in May 1942 describes how some of these tests were conducted on Jewish professional criminals who had been condemned for *Rassenschande,* literally meaning *racial shame.* Racial shame, as defined by the Germans, was marriage or intercourse between Aryans and non-Aryans. ("Aryans" described pure blooded Germans.)

Defendant Weltz had jurisdiction over Dr. Rascher's activities. It is interesting to note that Weltz had approached two prominent experts in the field of aviation medicine, Dr. Lutz and Dr. Wendt, to take part in this experiment. Both refused on moral grounds, stating that the differences in the reactions of human subjects and animals were not sufficient to warrant carrying out hazardous experiments on human beings.

Because Weltz could not find specialists who would collaborate with Dr. Rascher, a novice in this field, the experiments did not begin until February 22, 1942. They were conducted at Dachau concentration camp, a short distance from Munich.

Defendant Georg August Weltz,
Chief of the Institute for
Aviation Medicine

Defendants Weltz, Ruff, Romberg, Rudolf Brandt, and Sievers were involved in the simulated parachute descent experiments. The mobile low-pressure chamber into which the experimental subjects were forced was shipped from defendant Ruff's institute in Berlin to

Defendant Siegfried Ruff, Director,
Department for Aviation Medicine
at the Experimental Institute

Dachau. The victims were individually locked in the airtight, ball-shaped compartment. Then the pressure was altered to simulate high-altitude atmospheric conditions up to 68,900 feet. Subjects might have additional oxygen supplied to them or they might not.[2]

All defendants knew that the proposed experiments on involuntary inmates were likely to result in death. The defendants claimed the experiments were to be performed on habitual and condemned criminals, referred to as "volunteers." Himmler ordered Dr. Rascher to pardon these victims only if they could be "recalled to life" after they had stopped breathing and their chests had been cut open. The "pardon" however, had conditions. As Himmler stated ". . . the person condemned to death shall be pardoned to concentration camp for life."[3]

In one report submitted by Dr. Rascher to Himmler, dated April 4, 1942, regarding his experiments he stated:

Only continuous experiments at altitudes higher than 10.5 kilometers (about 34,600 feet) resulted in death. These experiments showed that breathing stopped after about thirty minutes, while in two cases the electrocardiographically charted action of the heart continued for another twenty minutes.

The third experiment of this type took such an extraordinary course that I called an SS physician of the camp as witness, since I had worked on these experiments all by myself. It was a continuous experiment without oxygen at a height of 12 kilometers,[4] conducted on a thirty-seven-year-old Jew in good general condition. Breathing continued up to thirty minutes. After four minutes the VP began to perspire and to wiggle his head; after five minutes cramps occurred; between six and ten minutes breathing increased in speed and the VP became unconscious; from eleven to thirty minutes breathing slowed down to three breaths per minute, finally stopping altogether.

Severest cyanosis [bluish discoloration] developed in between and foam appeared at the mouth. ... About one-half hour after breathing had stopped, dissection was started.

Autopsy Report

The following is excerpted from Dr. Rascher's autopsy report on the "thirty-seven-year-old Jew in good general condition":

When the cavity of the chest was opened the pericardium [the sac surrounding the heart] was filled tightly [heart tamponade—compression of the heart by pericardial fluid]. Upon opening of the pericardium eighty cc. of clear yellowish liquid gushed forth. The moment the tamponade had stopped, the right auricle [atrium] began to beat heavily, at first at the rate of sixty actions per minute, then progressively slower. Twenty minutes after the pericardium had been opened, the right auricle was opened by puncturing it. For about fifteen minutes a thick stream of blood spurted forth. Thereafter clogging of the puncture wound in the auricle by coagulation [clot formation] of the blood and renewed acceleration of the action of the right auricle occurred.

One hour after breathing had stopped, the spinal marrow [soft organic material] was completely severed and the brain removed. Thereupon the action of the auricle stopped for forty seconds. It then renewed its action, coming to a complete standstill eight minutes later. A heavy subarachnoid oedema was found in the brain [swelling within the membrane that forms the blood/brain barrier]. In the veins and arteries of the brain a considerable quantity of air was discovered.

Photos of the brain were received in evidence.

Prosecution Exhibit 61, dated May 11, 1942, quoted an excerpt from a *Secret Report* from Dr. Rascher to Himmler:

... As a practical result of the more than two hundred experiments conducted at Dachau, the following can be assumed:

... Jewish professional criminals who had committed race pollution were used. The question of the formation of embolism [sudden blocking] was investigated in ten cases. Some of the VPs died during a continued high-altitude experiment. ... After the skull had been opened under water an ample amount of air embolism was found in the brain vessels and, in part, free air in the brain ventricles [cavities].

... After relative recuperation from such a parachute descending test had taken place, however, before regaining consciousness, some VPs were kept under water until they died. When the skull and the cavities of the breast and of the abdomen had been opened under water, an enormous amount of air embolism was found in the vessels of the brain, the coronary vessels, and the vessels of the liver and the intestines, etc.[5]

The research subject was intentionally killed to obtain these findings.

Dr. Rascher's experimental subjects in his above report to Himmler, dated May 11, 1942, involved "Jewish professional criminals" who had committed Rassenschande because they had had consensual sexual intercourse with German women.

An interim report submitted by Dr. Rascher stated: "The extreme fatal experiments will be carried out on specially selected VPs otherwise it would not be possible to exercise the rigid control so extraordinarily important for practical purposes."[6]

The defendants' argument that while the experiments may have killed the experimental subjects, they did not involve torture and pain, was not supported by photographic exhibits received in evidence. Some captured German film showing spasmodic convulsions and tortured and pained expressions totally rebut this argument.[7]

Prosecution Exhibit 66, NO-402[8] states: "After an ascent made as rapidly as possible, using oxygen apparatus with free flow, the mask was removed immediately upon attaining 49,200 feet altitude and the descent was begun."

At 49,200 feet, the experimental subject let the mask fall; he suffered severe altitude sickness and clonic convulsions [alternate muscular contraction and relaxation in rapid succession].

At 46,900 feet his arms were stretched stiffly forward; he sat up like a dog; his legs were spread stiffly apart. At 23,620 feet he had uncoordinated movements with his extremities. At 19,690 feet he had clonic convulsions and was groaning. At 18,040 feet he yelled loudly. At 9,520 feet he was yelling and convulsing his arms and legs; his head sank forward. At 6,560 feet he yelled spasmodically, grimaced, and bit his tongue. At zero feet he did not respond to speech and gave the impression of someone completely out of his mind.

Then after reaching ground level, it took twenty-four hours for the victim to regain normal cohesion. None of the victims had any recollection of the experiments.

Another argument used by the defendants was "necessity of the State." It was a common defense for incarcerating hundreds of thousands in concentration camps and subjecting them to slave labor, and murdering millions of Jews. The prosecution argued that "necessity of the State" was unfounded; that this is no defense. The experiments were "neither necessary nor a scientific success."[9]

Testimony of Walter Neff

Following is an extract from the testimony on December 17, 1947, of Tribunal witness Walter Neff, a concentration camp prisoner inmate. Prosecutor James M. McHaney was interrogating Neff.[10]

Prosecutor McHaney: When did the high-altitude experiments begin in Dachau?

Witness Neff: The first high-altitude experiments were on February 22, 1942. The so-called low-pressure chambers had been brought in earlier and dismounted. The exact time when the chambers came is not known to me. ...

Prosecutor: Will you tell the Tribunal who worked on these experiments?

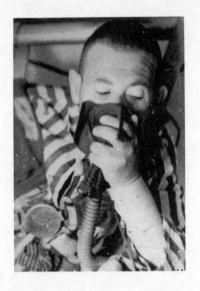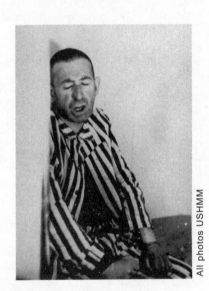

All photos USHMM

Inmate of Dachau concentration camp in low-pressure chamber, in different stages of simulated high altitude. Document NO-610. Prosecution exhibit 41.

Witness: The experiments were conducted by Dr. Rascher and Dr. Romberg. Ten prisoners were selected and were taken to the station as permanent experimental subjects; and they were told that nothing would happen to them. In the beginning, the first three weeks, the experiments went off without incident. One day, however, Rascher told me the next day he was going to make a serious experiment and that he would need sixteen Russians who had been condemned to death, and he received these Russians. Then I told Rascher that I would not help, and I actually got Rascher to send me away to the tubercular ward. On that day I know for certain that Rascher's SS man Endres or other SS men conducted these experiments. Dr. Romberg was not there that day. The SS man Endres took the Russian prisoners of war to Rascher and in the evening the parties were taken out.

On the next day when I returned to the station, Endres was already there and he said that two more, two Jews, would be killed. I am quoting what he said. I left the station again, but I watched to see who would be taken for the experiments. I saw the first one getting into the car. I could only see his profile. It seemed familiar to me. I knew that man worked in the hospital as a tailor. I tried to find out if it was really that man. I went to the place where he worked, and I was told that Endres had just taken the man away.

The first person that I informed was Dr. Romberg whom I met in the corridor. I told Romberg that this was not a person who had been condemned to death, that this was a clear case of murder on the responsibility of Endres. Romberg went with me to see Rascher to clear the matter up, but it was discovered that Endres had put this man in the experimental car because he had refused to make a civilian suit for him. Rascher sent the man back; Endres went with him and remarked: "Well, then you will get an injection today." I must say that Rascher interfered once more and put the man in safety into the bunker.

In the meantime, Endres had brought a second man up, a Czech whom I knew very well. Again it was Romberg together with me who talked to Rascher to stop this experiment or to inquire why a man like Endres was simply taking people who had never been condemned to death. Rascher went to the camp commandant, Piorkowski, who personally came to the station and Endres was transferred to Lublin immediately.

Prosecutor: About how many concentration camp inmates were subjected to these high-altitude experiments?

Witness: There were one hundred eighty to two hundred inmates who were subjected to the high-altitude experiments. ...

Prosecutor: I am asking you, witness, when the high-altitude experiments ended, that is, when they were completed.

Witness: During the course of June—maybe the beginning of July—the low-pressure chambers were taken away. I don't recollect the exact date, however.

Prosecutor: And you state that between February 22, 1942, and the end of June, or the beginning of July 1942, approximately one hundred eighty to two hundred concentration camp inmates were experimented on?

Witness: Yes.

Prosecutor: What nationalities were the experimental subjects?

Witness: I cannot say that with certainty but I think that approximately all nations were represented there; that is, all nations that were in the camp, mostly Russians, Poles, Germans, and Jews belonging to any nation. I do not remember any other nationalities being represented there.

Prosecutor: Were any of these experimental subjects prisoners of war?

Witness: Yes.

Prosecutor: What nationalities were they? Do you recall?

Witness: They were Russians.

Prosecutor: Now, will you tell the Tribunal how these experimental subjects were selected?

Witness: The experimental subjects who had to be subjected to severe experiments, experiments that would end in death, were requested by Rascher from the camp administration and then furnished by the SS; however, this procedure differed with the so-called series of experiments and a number of other experiments. For those experiments the people were brought into the experimental station straight from the camp, that is, from the blocks.

Prosecutor: Now, did they, to your knowledge, make any effort in the camp to secure volunteers for these experiments?

Witness: There were certain volunteers for these experiments. That was because Rascher promised certain persons that they would be released from the camp if they underwent these experiments. He sometimes promised them that they would be detailed to more favorable work.

Prosecutor: Now, about how many of such volunteers would you say there were for the high-altitude experiments?

Witness: I do not know the exact number. It was not very high; approximately ten inmates volunteered for that purpose. ...

Prosecutor: Now, other than these approximately ten persons who you state presented themselves as volunteers, were all the rest of the experimental subjects simply picked out and brought in and experimented on?

Witness: Yes.

Prosecutor: Were any of these prisoners experimented upon released from the concentration camp because they underwent the experiments?

Witness: There is only one man who was released after the high-altitude experiments.

Prosecutor: And who was that?

Witness: An inmate with the name of Sobota.

Prosecutor: And did Sobota assist Rascher in his experimental work other than simply undergoing the experiment? Was he something in the nature of an assistant to Rascher?

Witness: No. Sobota was one of those persons who had to undergo most of the experiments and he was also used on one experiment, which was conducted in the presence of the Reich Leader SS [Himmler]. ...

Prosecutor: Other than the prisoner Sobota, were there any other concentration camp inmates released as a result of undergoing the high-altitude experiments?

Witness: I know of no case except Sobota.

Prosecutor: Do you know of any cases where a prisoner condemned to death had his sentence commuted to life imprisonment because he underwent the high-altitude experiments?

Witness: No.

Prosecutor: Witness, were any political prisoners used in these high-altitude experiments?

Witness: Yes, there were political prisoners who were used in these experiments. All foreigners were considered political prisoners.

Prosecutor: Witness, tell the Tribunal how one could tell the difference between a political and a criminal prisoner in a concentration camp?

Witness: All inmates had certain squares with letters; the political inmates had red squares; the German political inmates had a plain red square; the Poles had a red square with a "P" marked on it; the Russians with an "R"; all nationalities could be identified by the first letter of their country. The red square with a yellow star was the Jew. The green square, on the other hand, was the sign of the so-called professional criminal. ...

Prosecutor: Now, was this square really a square or a triangle?

Witness: It was really a triangle with the head of the triangle pointed down to the earth. If it pointed upward, it indicated a member of the Wehrmacht [Army] who was sent to the camp for punishment.

Prosecutor: Witness, were any Jews experimented on in these high-altitude experiments?

Witness: Yes.

Prosecutor: Now, tell the Tribunal approximately how many prisoners were killed during the course of the high-altitude experiments?

Witness: During the high-altitude experiments seventy to eighty persons were killed.

Prosecutor: Did they experiment on prisoners other than those condemned to death?

Witness: Yes.

Prosecutor: Do you have any idea how many may have been killed?

Witness: There could have been approximately forty persons.

Prosecutor: That is, forty persons were killed who had not been condemned to death out of a total of seventy, did you say?

Witness: Yes. ...

Prosecutor: Can you remember approximately how many deaths Romberg witnessed during these high-altitude experiments, if any?

Witness: I can remember five cases where Romberg was present during cases of death; whether he was present on other occasions, I do not know. It is possible, but I am not sure of it.

Testimony of Defendant Rudolf Brandt

Following is a brief extract from the testimony of Defendant Rudolf Brandt with direct examination by his German lawyer, Dr. Kauffmann, from March 24-26, 1947.[11] Dr. Kauffmann began:

Defense counsel Kauffmann: Now I should like to speak to you about Document Book No. 2 concerning the high-altitude experiments of Dr. Rascher. You said this morning that you knew Rascher?

Witness Brandt: Yes.

Defense counsel: Did you see him frequently?

Witness: Very few times in the course of four to five years. ...

Defense counsel: But you do not want to deny that you knew that Rascher was carrying out experiments on human beings in Dachau?

Witness: Yes that I knew.

Defense counsel: Did you ever visit Dachau yourself?

Witness: No. I was never in Dachau or in any other concentration camp. ...

Defense counsel: Now, please turn to page fifty-three. This is a letter from Rascher to Himmler in which he makes suggestions to Himmler for the first time that human being experiments should be carried out in Dachau. In this letter he says that in these experiments he would certainly have to count on fatal consequences for some of the subjects. Do you remember receiving this letter? ...

Witness: I do not remember the letter. ...

Defense counsel: Now please look at page fifty-seven of the German document book. This is 1582-PS, Prosecution Exhibit 45, a letter from you to Rascher in which you tell him that, of course, prisoners will gladly be made available for high-altitude experimentation. Was this letter written on your own initiative or is it a case similar to all the others that you have brought up here, namely, a letter written on orders from Himmler?

Witness: This letter does not originate with me. It can be traced back to clear orders from Himmler. ...

Defendant Rudolf Brandt,
Personal Administrative Officer
to Reichsfuehrer SS Heinrich Himmler

Defense counsel: Now, please look at 1971-D-PS, Prosecution Exhibit 52, apparently a teletype message from Rascher to you. Here Rascher asks whether Poles and Russians are also to be pardoned if they have survived several severe experiments. In 1971-E-PS, Prosecution Exhibit 53, your answer is to be found ... In this letter you say that experimental subjects are not to be pardoned if they are Poles or Russians. This document was given particular stress by the prosecution, and its cruel and atrocious nature was emphasized. Do you remember this document or can you give us any explanation of how it came about that you signed this teletype message?

Witness: I cannot remember this communication.

Rudolf Brandt did not deny that he signed this message; he just said, "I cannot remember . . . ." This was a frequent response by a defendant when confronted with a document with his signature on it after having just testified that he knew nothing about it.

This is in contrast to the memory of the prior witness, Walter Neff, a prison inmate who under orders worked in the experimental station. At the time of the trial, he had been liberated and was eager to tell the world of the atrocities about which he appeared to have vivid memories.

Testimony of Defendant Dr. Romberg

Finally, the following are extracts from the testimony of Defendant Romberg under direct examination by his German lawyer, Dr. Vorwerk, from May 1-6, 1947.[12]

Defense counsel Vorwerk: Now, in your opinion, what is the distinction between your presence at the experiments on rescue from high altitudes and your occasional presence during Rascher's experiments?

Witness Romberg: In the experiments on rescue from high altitudes I was not merely present. I performed the experiments myself. ...

Defense counsel: When was the second death at which you were present?

Witness: That was a few days after my return to Dachau.

Defense counsel: Did the death of the experimental subject occur in a manner similar to the first case?

Witness: In general, yes. I don't know exactly what happened. As far as I recall, it was an experiment at a rather high altitude, and death occurred quicker, more suddenly.

Defense counsel: And when was the third death at which you were present?

Witness: That was right after that, on the next day, or the second day.

Reference was then made by the defendant's attorney to a letter 1971-B-PS, Prosecution Exhibit 51, and he asked Dr. Romberg, "And what does this letter indicate?"

Witness: Well, it showed that Himmler had actually ordered these experiments and that he, therefore, had complete official coverage, that the subjects were to be pardoned. It says in the letter: "Of course the person condemned to death shall be pardoned to concentration camp for life."...

Defense counsel: At that time, was there any possibility in Germany to resist, and in what did you see such possibility?

Witness: There were only three types of resistance possible. First of all, emigration for a person who was able; second, open resistance which meant a concentration camp or the death penalty, and to my knowledge, never met with any success;

third, passive resistance by apparent yielding, misplacing and delaying orders, criticism among one's friends, in short, what writers today call "internal emigration."

How scientific were the high-altitude experiments? Prosecution Exhibit 66 regarding "Experiments on Rescue from High Altitude," the report signed by Dr. Rascher and defendant Dr. Romberg, stated:

Since the urgency of the solution of the problem was evident, it was necessary, especially under the given conditions of the experiment to forego for the time being the thorough clearing up of purely scientific questions.[13]

This statement demonstrates that the defendants knew these experiments were not scientific and did not follow established medical protocols regarding voluntary subjects. In summary, 180 to 200 victims were subjected to this experiment, resulting in grave injury and 70 to 80 deaths.

Although defendants Schroeder, Gebhardt, Rudolf Brandt, Sievers, Ruff, Romberg, Becker-Freyseng, and Weltz were charged with special responsibility for and participation in criminal conduct involving high-altitude experiments, only Rudolf Brandt and Wolfram Sievers were convicted.

· 6 ·

Freezing Experiments

It hurts my racial feelings to expose to racially inferior concentration camp elements a girl as a prostitute who has the appearance of a pure Nordic and who could perhaps by assignment of proper work be put on the right road.

—Dr. Sigmund Rascher

FREEZING EXPERIMENTS WERE conducted from August 1942 to approximately May 1943 at Dachau, primarily for the benefit of the German Air Force. These investigated how to treat people who had been severely chilled or frozen. Ice water and dry land experiments simulated freezing conditions experienced by German fliers whose planes had crashed into the sea, or German Army troops fighting on the battlefield in subfreezing temperatures and deep snow. The purpose was to test different ways to rewarm surviving German fliers and troopers.

The defendants Karl Brandt, Handloser, Schroeder, Gebhardt, Rudolf Brandt, Mrugowsky, Poppendick, Sievers, Becker-Freyseng, and Weltz were charged with criminal conduct for conducting these freezing experiments.

The Department for Aviation Medicine, when defendant Becker-Freyseng was deputy, issued the research assignment.[1] Defendant Weltz and his subordinate Dr. Sigmund Rascher were ordered to per-

Defendant Helmut Poppendick,
Chief of the Personal Staff of
the Reich Physician SS

form the experiments. The experimental team was expanded to include Professor Dr. Holzloehner and Dr. Finke of Kiel University and all officers in the Medical Service of the Air Force.

Two types of freezing experiments were conducted: cold water freezing and dry freezing. Approximately 280 to 300 political prisoners, non-German nationals, and prisoners of war were used for 360 to 400 conducted experiments in freezing water. Eighty to 90 subjects died. Rascher conducted additional experiments, using 50 to 60 subjects. Of these, 15 to 18 individuals died.

The best way to describe these experiments is to go to the testimony of the Tribunal witness Walter Neff, a concentration camp inmate assistant. On December 17-18, 1946, Neff was questioned by Prosecutor James McHaney:

Prosecutor McHaney: When did the freezing experiments start?

Witness Neff: The first freezing experiments started during
  August or at the end of July ...

Prosecutor: All right. Suppose you describe the experimental basin.

Witness: The experimental basin was built of wood. It was two meters long and two meters wide. It was raised about fifty centimeters above the floor and it was in Block No. 5. In the experimental chamber and basin there were many lighting instruments and other apparatus that were used in order to carry out measurements. ...

Prosecutor: Now, will you tell the Tribunal approximately how many persons were used over the whole period? That is, including both groups that you have mentioned.

Witness: Two hundred and eighty to three hundred experimental subjects were used for these freezing experiments. There were really three hundred sixty to four hundred experiments that were conducted, since many experimental subjects were used for more than one such experiment—sometimes even for three.

Prosecutor: Now, out of the total of two hundred eighty or three hundred prisoners used, approximately how many died?

Witness: Approximately eighty to ninety subjects died as a result of these freezing experiments.

Prosecutor: Now, how many experimental subjects do you remember that they used in the Holzloehner-Finke-Rascher experiments?

Witness: During that period of time approximately fifty to sixty subjects were used for experimental purposes.

Prosecutor: Did any of these experimental subjects die?

Witness: Yes. During that period of time there were about fifteen, maybe even eighteen cases of death.

Prosecutor: When was that experimental series concluded?

Witness: It was concluded in the month of October. I think it was at the end of October ...

Prosecutor: And then Rascher continued experiments on his own?

Witness: Yes...

Prosecutor: How long did Rascher continue to experiment with freezing by cold water?

Witness: Until May 1943. ...

Prosecutor: Do I understand, then, that the experimental subjects used in the freezing experiments were political prisoners?

Witness: There were a number of political prisoners and also a number of foreigners, but there were also prisoners of war and inmates who had been condemned to death.

Prosecutor: These persons were not volunteers, were they?

Witness: No.

Prosecutor: Suppose you describe to the Tribunal exactly how these freezing experiments were carried out, that is, what tests they made, how they measured the temperature and how the temperature of the water was lowered in the basin, and so forth?

Witness: These basins were filled with water, and ice was added until the water measured three degrees [C.], and the experimental subjects were either dressed in a flying suit or were placed into the ice water naked. ...Now, whenever the experimental subjects were conscious, it took some time until so-called freezing narcosis set in. The temperature was measured rectally and through the stomach through the Galvanometer apparatus.

The lowering of the temperature to thirty-two degrees was terrible for the experimental subject. At thirty-two degrees the experimental subject lost consciousness. These persons were frozen down to twenty-five degrees body temperature, and now in order to enable you to understand this problem, I should like to tell you something about the Holzloehner and Finke period. During the period when Holzloehner and Finke were active, no experimental subject was actually killed in the water. Deaths occurred all the more readily because during revival the temperature dropped even further and so heart failure resulted. This was also caused by wrongly applied therapy, so that in contrast to the low-pressure experiments, deaths were not deliberately caused. In the air-pressure chamber, on the other hand, each death cannot be described as an accident but as willful murder.

However, it was different when Rascher personally took over these experiments. At that time a large number of the persons involved were kept in the water until they were dead....

Prosecutor: Do you recall the occasion when two Russian officers were experimented upon in the freezing experiments?

Witness: Yes.

Prosecutor: Will you relate that incident to the Tribunal?

Witness: Yes. It was the worst experiment, which was ever carried out. Two Russian officers were carried out from the bunker. We were forbidden to speak to them. They arrived at approximately 4:00 in the afternoon. Rascher had them undressed and they had to go into the basin naked. Hour after hour passed, and while usually after a short time, sixty minutes, freezing had set in, these two Russians were still conscious after two hours. All our appeals to Rascher asking him to give them an injection were of no avail. Approximately during the third hour one Russian said to the other, "Comrade, tell that officer to shoot us." The other replied, "Don't expect any mercy from this Fascist dog." Then they shook hands and said "Goodbye, Comrade." If you can imagine that we inmates had to witness such a death, and could do nothing about it, then you can judge how terrible it is to be condemned to work in such an experimental station.

After these words were translated for Rascher in a somewhat different form by a young Pole, Rascher went back into his office. The young Pole tried at once to give them an anesthetic with chloroform, but Rascher returned immediately and threatened to shoot us with his pistol if we dared approach these victims again. The experiment lasted at least five hours until death occurred. Both corpses were sent to Munich for autopsy in the Schwabing Hospital.

Prosecutor: Witness, how long did it normally take to kill a person in these freezing experiments?

Witness: The length of the experiment varied, according to the individual case. Whether the subject was clothed or unclothed also made a difference. If he was slight in build and if in addition to that he was naked, death often occurred after only eighty minutes. But there were a number of cases where the experimental subject lived up to three hours, and remained in the water until finally death occurred."

Reich Leader SS Heinrich Himmler wrote to Dr. Sigmund Rascher on October 24, 1942, about doctors or assistants who openly refused on moral grounds to participate in human experimentation without the victims' consent.[2] He said, "I regard these people as guilty of treason and high treason, who, still today, reject these experiments on humans and would instead let sturdy German soldiers die as a result of these cooling methods."

Concentration camp Dachau was where the majority of the religious community of prisoners was interned. They numbered over 2,070 clergymen, of whom more than 1,000 died in the camp. Although the majority of those interned were Polish Catholic priests, the community included Protestant, Orthodox, and Moslem clergymen. Over 300 Polish priests died in medical experiments or by torture.

One of the lucky survivors, Father Leo Miechalowski, came to Nuremberg and testified for the prosecution.[3] This is what he said:

Prosecutor McHaney: Now, Father, will you tell the Tribunal what happened to you after your arrest?

Witness Miechalowski: When I was arrested I was first kept in prison for two months, and from there we were sent into a cloister, and from there still other priests were assembled until about ninety priests had been assembled altogether, and from there were sent to Struthof near Danzig into the concentration camp which was located there. And, from there on the fifth or ninth of February we were transferred to Sachsenhausen-Oranienburg, which is located, near Berlin. On the thirteenth of December 1940, we were transferred again to Dachau. I was confined in Dachau until the arrival of the Americans—until we were liberated—that was on the twenty-ninth of April 1945.

Prosecutor: Now, Father, were you a political prisoner in Dachau?

Witness: Yes. I wore a red insignia which all those who had been arrested for political reasons had to wear this insignia.

Prosecutor: Now, Father, did there come a time when you were experimented on in the concentration camp at Dachau?

Witness: Yes. Malaria experiments and also on one occasion we were engaged in high-altitude experiments.

Prosecutor: Did you say high-altitude experiments, Father?

Witness: No, I said aviation experiments.

Prosecutor: And what do you mean by aviation experiments?

Witness: Well, I have said it because we were dressed in aviator's uniforms and then we were put into containers full of water and ice.

The witness was then questioned about the malaria experiments to which he had been subjected (described in chapter 7), after which the questioning continued as follows.

Prosecutor: Well, will you tell the tribunal about this other experiment?

Witness: During those malaria attacks on one occasion I was called by Dr. Prachtol and I was examined by a Polish physician, and Dr. Prachtol told me, "If I have any use for you, I will call you." However, I did not know what was going to be done with me. Several days later, that was on the seventh of October, 1942, a prisoner came and told me that I was to report to the hospital immediately. I thought I was going to be examined once more, and I was taken through the malaria station to block 5 in Dachau, to the fourth floor of block 5.

There—the so-called aviation room, the aviation experimental station was located there, and there was a fence, a wooden fence so that nobody could see what was inside, and I was led there, and there was a basin with water and ice, which floated on the water. There were two tables, and there were two apparatus on there. Next to them there was a heap of clothing that consisted of uniforms, and Dr. Prachtol was there, two officers in Air Force uniforms. However, I do not know their names.[4]

Now I was told to undress. I undressed and I was examined. The physician then remarked that everything was in order. Now wires had been taped to my back, also in the lower rectum. Afterwards I had to wear my shirt, my drawers, but then afterwards I had to wear one of the uniforms, which were lying there. Then I had also to wear a long pair of boots with cat's fur and one aviator's combination. And afterwards a tube was put around my neck and was filled with air. And afterwards the wires, which had been connected with me—they were connected to the apparatus, and then I was thrown into the water.

All of a sudden I became very cold, and I began to tremble. I immediately turned to those two men and asked them to pull me out of the water because I would be unable to stand it much longer. However, they told me laughingly, "Well, this will only last a very short time." I sat in this water, and I had— and I was conscious for one hour and a half. I do not know exactly because I did not have a watch, but that is the approximate time I spent there.

During this time the temperature was lowered very slowly in the beginning and afterwards more rapidly. When I was thrown into the water my temperature was lowered very slowly in the beginning and afterwards more rapidly. When I was thrown into the water my temperature was 37.6. Then the temperature became lower. Then I only had 33 and then as low as 30, but then I already became somewhat unconscious, and every fifteen minutes some blood was taken from my ear.

After having sat in the water for about half an hour, I was offered a cigarette. Later on I was given a little glass with Schnapps, and then I was asked how I was feeling. Somewhat later still I was given one cup of Grog. This Grog was not very hot. It was rather lukewarm. I was freezing very much in this water. Now my feet were becoming as rigid as iron, and the same thing applied to my hands, and later on my breathing became very short. I once again began to tremble, and afterwards cold sweat appeared on my forehead. I felt as if I was just about to die, and then I was still asking them to pull me out because I could not stand this much longer.

Then Dr. Prachtol came and he had a little bottle, and he gave me a few drops of some liquid out of this bottle, and I did not know anything about this liquid. It had a somewhat sweetish taste. Then I lost my consciousness. I do not know how much longer I remained in the water because I was unconscious. When I again regained consciousness, it was approximately between 8:00 and 8:30 in the evening. I was lying on a stretcher covered with blankets, and above me there was some kind of an appliance with lamps, which were warming me.

In the room there was only Dr. Prachtol and two prisoners. Then Dr. Prachtol asked me how I was feeling. Then I replied, "First of all, I feel very exhausted, and furthermore I am also very hungry." Dr. Prachtol had immediately ordered that I was to be given better food and that I was also to lie in bed. One prisoner raised me on the stretcher and he took me under his arm and he led me through the corridor to his room. During this time he spoke to me, and he told me, "Well, you do not know what you have even suffered." And in the room the prisoner gave me half a bottle of milk, one piece of bread and some potatoes, but that came from his own rations. Later on he took me to the malaria station,[5] block 3, and there I was put to bed, and the very same evening a Polish prisoner—it was a physician; his first name was Dr. Adam, but I do not remember his other name. He came on official orders. He told me, "Everything that has happened to you is a military secret. You are not to discuss it with anybody. If you fail to do so, you know what the consequences will be for you. You are intelligent enough to know that." Of course, I fully realized that I had to keep quiet about that.

On one occasion I had discussed these experiments with one of my comrades. One of the nurses found out about this and he came to see me and asked me if I was already tired of living, because I was talking about such matters. But, in the way these experiments were conducted, I do not need to add anything further to it.

Prosecutor: How long was it before you recovered from the effects of those freezing experiments?

Witness: It took a long time. I also have had several (pause) I have had a rather weak heart, and I have also had severe headaches, and I also get cramps in my feet very often.

Prosecutor: Do you still suffer from the effects of this experiment?

Witness: I still have a weak heart. For example, I am unable to walk very quickly now, and I also have to sweat very much. Exactly, those are the results, but in many cases I have had those afflictions ever since.

Prosecutor: Were you in good physical condition before you were subjected to malaria and freezing experiments?

Witness: Since the time of this starvation I weighed fifty-seven kilograms in Dachau. When I came to the camp I weighed about one hundred kilo; I lost about one-half of my weight. In the beginning, I was weighed, and I was in bed for about a week. And then my weight went down to forty-seven kilo.

Prosecutor: How much do you weigh now, Father?

Witness: I can not tell you exactly but I have not weighed myself lately, but I think at this time I weigh fifty-five kilogram.

Prosecutor: Do you know how you were rewarmed in these freezing experiments?[6]

Witness: I was warmed with these lamps, but I heard later that people were rewarmed by women.

Prosecutor: Do you know approximately how many inmates were subjected to the freezing experiments?

Witness: I can not tell you anything about this, because it was kept so secret; and because I was in there quite individually, and I was quite single during this experiment.

Prosecutor: Do you know whether anyone died as a result of this experiment?

Witness: I can not give you any information about that either. I have not seen anybody. But it was said in camp that quite a number of people died there during this experiment.

Women Used For Rewarming

Women who were used for rewarming in the freezing experiments were referred to as concentration camp prostitutes. In a memorandum dated November 5, 1942,[7] Dr. Rascher wrote:

For the resuscitation experiments by animal warmth after freezing, as ordered by the Reich Leader SS, I had four women assigned to me from the women's concentration camp Ravensbrueck.

One of the assigned women shows unobjectionably Nordic racial characteristics: blond hair, blue eyes, corresponding head and body structure, twenty-one and 3/4 years of age. I asked the girl why she had volunteered for the brothel. I received the answer: "To get out of the concentration camp, for we were promised that all those who would volunteer for the brothel for half a year would then be released from the concentration camp." To my objection that it was a great shame to volunteer as a prostitute, I was told: "Rather half a year in the brothel than half a year in the concentration camp." Then followed an account of a number of most peculiar conditions at Camp Ravensbrueck. Most of the reported conditions were confirmed by the three other prostitutes and by the female warden who had accompanied them from Ravensbrueck.

It hurts my racial feelings to expose to racially inferior concentration camp elements a girl as a prostitute who has the appearance of a pure Nordic and who could perhaps by assignment of proper work be put on the right road.

Therefore, I refused to use this girl for my experimental purposes and gave the adequate reports to the camp commander and the adjutant of the Reich Leader SS.[8]

The following is a letter from Rascher to Himmler dated February 17, 1943. The letter summarizes the effectiveness of the human rewarming process.

Munich, 17 February 1943

To the Reich Leader SS and Chief of the German Police
Heinrich Himmler
Berlin SW 11, Prinz Albrecht Str. 8

Dear Reich Leader,

Enclosed I present to you in condensed form a summary of the results of the experiments made in warming up people who have been cooled off by using animal heat.

Right now I am attempting to prove through experiments on human beings that it is possible to warm up people cooled off by dry cold just as fast as people who were cooled off by remaining in cold water. The Reich Physician SS, SS Gruppenfuehrer Dr. Grawitz, doubted very much that that would be possible and said that I would have to prove it first by one hundred experiments. Up to now I have cooled off about thirty people stripped in the open air during nine to fourteen hours at twenty-seven degrees to twenty-nine degrees. After a time, corresponding to a transport of one hour, I put these subjects in a hot bath. Up to now every single patient was completely warmed up within one hour at most; though some of them had their hands and feet frozen white. In some cases a slight fatigue with slightly rising temperature was observed on the day following the experiments. I have not observed any fatal results from this extremely fast warming up. I have not so far been able to do any warming up by "Sauna" as ordered by you, my dear Reich Leader, as the weather in December and January was too warm for any experiments in the open air, and right now the camp is closed on account of typhoid and I am not allowed therefore to bring in subjects for "Sauna" experiments.

With most obedient greetings and sincere gratitude, and Heil Hitler!

Yours very devotedly
(enclosure) Rascher

The enclosed document, labeled "Secret," read as follows:

Experiments for rewarming of intensely chilled human beings by animal warmth

A. Purpose of the Experiments:

To ascertain whether the rewarming of intensely chilled human beings by animal warmth, i.e., the warmth of animals or human beings, is as good or better than rewarming by physical or medical means.

B. Method of the Experiments:

The experimental subjects were cooled in the usual way—clad or unclad—in cold water of temperatures varying between four degrees C. and nine degrees C. The rectal temperature of every experimental subject was recorded thermoelectrically. The reduction of temperature occurred within the usual span of time varying in accordance with the general condition of the body of the experimental subject and the temperature of the water. The experimental subjects were removed from the water when their rectal temperature reached thirty degrees C. At this time the experimental subjects had all lost consciousness. In eight cases, the experimental subjects were then placed between two naked women in a spacious bed. The women were supposed to nestle as closely as possible to the chilled person. Then all three persons were covered with blankets. A speeding up of rewarming by light cradles or by medicines was not attempted.

C. Results:

1. When the temperature of the experimental subjects was recorded it was striking that an after-drop of temperature up to three degrees C. occurred, which is a greater after-drop than seen with any other method of rewarming. It was observed, however, that consciousness returned at an earlier point, that is, at a lower body temperature than with other methods of rewarming. Once the subjects regained consciousness they did

not lose it again, but very quickly grasped the situation and snuggled up to the naked female bodies. The rise of body temperature then occurred at about the same speed as in experimental subjects who had been rewarmed by packing in blankets. Exceptions were four experimental subjects who, at body temperatures between thirty degrees C. and thirty-two degrees C., performed the act of sexual intercourse. In these experimental subjects the temperature rose very rapidly after sexual intercourse, which could be compared with the speedy rise in temperature in a hot bath.

2. Another set of experiments concerned the rewarming of intensely chilled persons by one woman. In all these cases rewarming was significantly quicker than could be accomplished by two women. The cause of this seems to me that in warming by one woman only, personal inhibitions are removed, and the woman nestles up to the chilled individual much more intimately. Also in these cases, the return of complete consciousness was strikingly rapid. Only one experimental subject did not return to consciousness and the warming effect was only slight. This person died with symptoms suggesting cerebral hemorrhage, as was confirmed by subsequent autopsy.

D. Summary:

Rewarming experiments of intensely chilled experimental subjects demonstrated that rewarming with animal warmth was very slow. Only such experimental subjects whose physical condition permitted sexual intercourse rewarmed themselves remarkably quickly and showed an equally strikingly rapid return to complete physical well-being. Since excessively long exposure of the body to low temperatures implies danger of internal damage, that method must be chosen for rewarming which guarantees the quickest relief from dangerously low temperatures. This method, according to our experience, is a massive and rapid supply of warmth by means of a hot bath.

Rewarming of intensely chilled human beings by human or animal warmth can therefore be recommended only in such cases in which other possibilities for re-warming are not available, or in cases of specially tender individuals who possibly may not be able to stand a massive and rapid supply of warmth. As, for example, I am thinking of intensely chilled small children, who are best rewarmed by the body of their mothers, with the aid of hot water bottles.

Dachau, 12 February 1943.

(Signature) Dr. S. Rascher

SS Hauptsturmfuehrer

Testimony on the freezing experiments went on through April 14, 1947.

In separate experiments conducted privately by Dr. Rascher, fifty to sixty subjects were used, fifteen to eighteen of whom died.

The defendants Handloser, Schroeder, Rudolf Brandt, and Sievers were convicted of criminal conduct involving freezing experiments.

Defendant Siegfried Handloser,
Lieutenant General, Medical Services

· 7 ·

Malaria Experiments

▼

All of a sudden my heart felt like it was going to be torn
out. I became insane. I completely lost my language—my
ability to speak.

—Father Leo Miechalowski

OVER 1,084 INMATES of many nationalities, including Catholic priests,
were subjects in the experiments about malaria (testing immuniza-
tions and various treatments). These experiments were held at
Dachau concentration camp from approximately February 1942 to
April 1945, ending just before Germany surrendered on May 8, 1945.

Inmates considered to be healthy were deliberately infected with
malaria by infected mosquitoes, or were injected with malaria-infected blood. To maintain a constant source of malaria-infected blood,
three to five inmates per month were artificially infected with malaria
so their drawn blood could be used to infect other inmates.

Malaria, epidemic jaundice, and typhus were the principal diseases that broke out in German-occupied countries.

Although defendants Karl Brandt, Handloser, Rostock, Gebhardt,
Blome, Rudolf Brandt, Mrugowsky, Poppendick, and Sievers were
charged with special responsibility for and participation in criminal
conduct involving these experiments, only Sievers was convicted in
this trial. Sievers denied taking any part in malaria experiments.

*Defendant Paul Rostock, Chief
Surgeon of the Berlin Surgical Clinic*

The details of the malaria experiments came out in a separate trial commencing on November 13, 1945, in the courthouse on the grounds of Dachau concentration camp after the war ended on May 8, 1945, but prior to the beginning of the major Nazi leaders' trial in Nuremberg on November 20, 1945.

At Dachau a U.S. General Military Court, appointed November 2, 1945, tried forty doctors and staff in the case of *The United States versus Martin Gottfried Weiss, Friedrich Wilhelm Ruppert, et al.,* including Dr. Claus Karl Schilling. These defendants in the Dachau trial were charged and "convicted of offenses of the violations of laws and usages of war in that they acted in pursuance of a common design, did encourage, aid, abet and participate in the subjection of Allied nationals and prisoners of war to cruelties and mistreatments at Dachau concentration camp and its subcamps."[1]

Each accused was sentenced to death by hanging, except seven who were given sentences of five years to life of hard labor. On review of the sentences by the U.S. Military Government Court, the findings and sentences were upheld on January 24, 1946, with the exception of four whose charges were reduced.

Affidavits and evidence in the Dachau trial were received in evidence for the medical case at Nuremberg. Evidence came out in the Dachau trial that Dr. Claus Karl Schilling, after an arranged meeting with Heinrich Himmler, asked for and was given permission to carry out malaria experiments at Dachau. Schilling was not a defendant in this medical case, since he had already been convicted and sentenced to death by hanging in the Dachau trial.

Schilling was the most reprehensible doctor in the Dachau experiments, as he was perfectly willing to utilize Nazi experimental methods on involuntary camp victims at a time when other German doctors and scientists either refused to take part or fled the country. Schilling believed it was his duty to humanity to find a cure for malaria no matter what life-threatening methods were used on involuntary camp inmates.

A pretrial affidavit of Dr. Schilling, in his own handwriting, was executed on October 30, 1945, before 2nd Lt. Werner Conn. This affidavit was admitted into evidence as Prosecution Exhibit 122. Schilling stated that he personally inoculated nine hundred to one thousand prisoners. Many Catholic priests were used in this experiment. He named Fathers Wicki and Stachowski, who died, Rupieper, Peter Bower, Gustav Spitzick, Amon Burckhardt, Fritz, Keller, and Kasinemar Gasimer Rikofsky.

Many inmates who had been infected with malaria died from tuberculosis, dysentery, and typhus. According to the affidavit, Schilling observed an autopsy on one victim and requested the brain, liver, kidney, spleen, and a piece of stomach.[2]

In the Dachau trial, an inmate Catholic priest, Father Koch, testified that he was first x-rayed and then sent to the malaria station. Put into a small room, he had to hold a box of mosquitoes for half an hour every day for one week. Every afternoon another box of mosquitoes was put in between his legs while he was in bed. A blood smear was taken from his ear each morning.

Father Koch left the hospital after about seventeen days. Eight months later he had a malaria attack, which recurred every three weeks for six months. He suffered high fever, chills, and joint pains. Russian and Polish prisoners were infected by injections of the mosquitoes themselves or by extracts of the mucous glands of the mosquitoes. Malaria directly caused thirty deaths, while complications as side effects of malaria caused three hundred to four hundred deaths, one-third of the original twelve hundred experimental victims.

Extracts from the Testimony of Father Leo Miechalowski

Father Leo Miechalowski, a survivor of both the malaria and freezing experiments, who testified for the prosecution earlier about undergoing freezing experiments in this trial, also testified as follows about the malaria experiments.

Prosecutor: Now, Father will you tell the Tribunal just what happened when you were experimented on with malaria? That is, when it happened and how you happened to be selected?

Witness Miechalowski: I was that weak that I fell down on the road because everybody was hungry in the camp. I wanted to be transferred to another assignment later on where we got some bread to eat between meals so my health could improve by the additional food. One man arrived and selected about thirty people for some easy labor. I also wanted to be selected for this assignment and those who had been selected for this work were led away. We went in the direction where the work was located and at the very last moment, instead of going to the place of work we were led to the camp hospital.[3] We did not know what was going to be done with us there. I thought to myself that perhaps this was going to be some detail for easier work in the hospital.

We were told that we should undress, and after we had undressed ourselves our numbers were taken down, and then we asked what was going on, and they told us, smilingly, "this is for air detail." But we were not told what was going to be done with us. Then the doctor came and told us all to remain and that we were to be x-rayed. Now that our numbers had already been taken down, we were supposed to go to our blocks. I sat for two days in the block, and afterwards I was again called to the hospital, and there I was given malaria in such a manner that there were little cages with infected mosquitoes, and I had to put my hand on one of the little cages and a mosquito stung me, and afterwards I was still in the hospital for five weeks. However, for the time being no symptoms of the disease showed themselves.

Somewhat later, I don't exactly recall, two or three weeks, I had my first malaria attack. Such attacks recurred frequently, and several medicines were given to us for—against malaria. I was given such medicine as neo-salvasan. I was given two injections of quinine. On one occasion I was given atabrine, and the worst was that one time when I had an attack I was given so-called Perifere. I was given nine injections of that kind, one every hour, and that every second day through the seventh injection.

All of a sudden my heart felt like it was going to be torn out. I became insane. I completely lost my language—my ability to speak. This lasted until evening. In the evening a nurse arrived and wanted to give me the eighth injection. I was then able to speak, and I told the nurse about all of the complications I had had and that I did not want to receive the injection. The nurse had already poured out the injection and said that he would report this to Dr. Schilling. After approximately ten minutes, another nurse arrived and said that he would have to give me the injection after all. Then I said the same thing again, that I was not going to have the injection. However, he told me that he had to carry out that order. Then I replied that no matter what order he had, I would not be willing to commit suicide.[4]

Then he went away and returned once again after ten minutes. He told me, "I know you know what can happen if you don't accept the injection." Then I said in spite of everything, "I refuse to receive another injection and that I would tell that to the professor." I requested that he himself know that I would not be willing to receive the injection. So that the nurse would not have any further difficulty after twenty minutes, Dr. Ploettner came with four inmate nurses and he talked to my comrades. "There is going to be a big row here."

Then I said, "If I have resisted for such a long time I will continue to do so." Dr. Ploettner, however, was very quiet. He only reached for my hand and he checked my pulse, then touched my head and asked me what complications I had had. I told him what I had had after that injection. And then he told the nurse to give me two tablets in order to remove the headache and the pains in my kidneys.

When I had been given that, Dr. Ploettner was about to leave and told the nurses that they were to give me the rest of the injections. Then I said, "Hauptsturmfuehrer, I refuse to be given that injection."

The physician turned around after I had said that and looked at me and said, "I am responsible for your life, not you." ... He told the nurse, the nurses complied with his order, and it was then they gave me this injection. It was the same one to whom I had previously told that I did not want to have another injection. It was only strange that after the eighth injection no results happened as they had done previously, so that in my opinion I think that the nurse gave me some other injection.

On the morning I was given the ninth injection. When I woke up in the morning, the results were then as usual. I became sick and I began to feel cold, and I had a high fever.

[All injections were experimental medications for the treatment of malaria.]

Prosecutor: Father, do I understand you to say that you were injected with malaria in the middle of 1942?

Witness: It was approximately in the middle of 1942 when I was infected with malaria.[5]

Prosecutor: And you were not asked your consent to the malaria experiment?

Witness: No. I was not asked for my consent.

Prosecutor: And you did not volunteer for this experiment?

Witness: No. I was taken in the manner which I have just described.

Prosecutor: Did you make any protest?

Witness: In 1942 it was very difficult in the camp to lodge any protest. When I protested with this eighth injection, which I was to be given, I clearly realized that it would have the most serious consequences for me. Later on such things could be risked, but in that year I still think that I would have been unable to do that, and I don't think it would have been to any avail.

Prosecutor: Now, how many people were experimented on with you, that is, malaria experiments?

Witness: In the hospital when I had my attacks, there were approximately fifty to sixty people; the numbers changed.

Prosecutor: And do you know the approximate total number of inmates experimented on with malaria in Dachau?

Witness: Towards the end I heard that approximately twelve hundred prisoners were subjected to these experiments.

Prosecutor: Do you know whether or not any of those inmates died as a result of the malaria experiments?

Witness: Several have died, but if this was the direct result of malaria, I do not know. I know of one case when the patient died after having been given Perifere injections. Then, I still know another priest who died, but afterwards—and prior to his death he was sent to another room.

Prosecutor: Was it customary to transfer patients out of the block in which they were conducting the malaria experiments if it appeared that they might die?

Witness: It looked to me as if this patient of whom I have just spoken had been moved for the reason so it could not be seen that it happened in the case of malaria, but I do not know if people died as a result of malaria because I am not an expert on the subject.[6]

Prosecutor: How many recurrences of malaria fever did you have, Father?

Witness: I cannot give you the exact number anymore. However, those attacks recurred frequently, I think about five times, and then I still had treatment in bed for some time, and then there were several more, and altogether I had ten attacks, one every day. Then I reached a temperature of 41.6.

Prosecutor: Do you still suffer any effects from the malaria?

Witness: I still have had some after-effects, but I do not know if this is only of malaria because I was also subjected to another experiment.

Father Miechalowski then testified to being subjected to freezing experiments already detailed in chapter 6.

Extracts from the Testimony of August H. Vieweg

The following is an extract from the testimony of August H. Vieweg, a victim used in a malaria experiment. Mr. Hardy questioned him:

Prosecutor Hardy: While you were an inmate at the concentration camp, did you ever undergo any medical experiments?

Witness Vieweg: I was used for malaria experiments by Professor Dachfinney at the Dachau concentration camp.

Prosecutor: How many times were you subjected to the malaria experiments by Dr. Schilling?

Witness: On five occasions I received injections of five cubic centimeters of highly infectious malaria blood.

Prosecutor: Would you kindly tell the Tribunal what effect these experiments had on you; that is, did you have high fever, serious illness, and so forth?

Witness: Quite often I ran a very high temperature. I got into a very exhausted condition, and after the injection, I received large doses of medical drugs, quinine, ephedrine, and many others. I was in bed for weeks, and after one treatment there were twenty to twenty-six occasions in the course of the years 1943, 1944, 1945, and 1946 when I had malaria attacks, so that for a long time I was unable to work.

Prosecutor: At the present time do you have recurrences of this malaria fever?

Witness: This last year I was in the hospital from August first to fifteenth, again with malaria attacks.

Prosecutor: How many recurrences of malaria have you endured since you were experimented on by Dr. Schilling?

Witness: After my treatments in the experimental station had been concluded I stayed with Dr. Schilling, and there were twenty occasions when I was treated for recurrences.

Prosecutor: Are you completely cured now, witness?

Witness: No.

Prosecutor: After you had undergone the various experiments at the hands of Dr. Schilling, did you then become a worker in Dr. Schilling's laboratory?

Witness: After my first so-called immunization treatment had been concluded, the chief medical officer of that department sent me over to Dr. Schilling's department for laboratory duties.

Prosecutor: Witness, we will go back to the malaria experiments for the moment. What was the nationality of the people used for the malaria experiments, what type of people were they?

Witness: The biggest proportion, approximately two hundred patients, used for the malaria experiments were Germans, a large proportion were Polish priests, and the rest were partly Russians, some Yugoslavs, and some Poles.

Prosecutor: Were any prisoners of war used in these experiments?

Witness: Of the Russians, many were prisoners of war.

Prosecutor: What was the total number of people used in these malaria experiments from your knowledge?

Witness: According to my knowledge, one thousand eighty-four experimental subjects were used for the malaria experiments.

Prosecutor: Will you kindly tell us, witness, how many of these subjects used in the malaria experiments died as a result of the experiments?

Witness: According to my knowledge seven or eight died at the malaria station, either directly or because of the treatment with drugs. I can describe the details if you like. The first case was an Austrian who afterwards became ill because of these malaria experiments. The assistant at that time, Dr. Brachtel, who was at the same time the deputy physician at the hospital, made a liver puncture and the patient bled to death.

Prosecutor: Witness, then you state from your knowledge that seven or eight died from the experiments. Of that number who died, did the deaths occur in the malaria station itself?

Witness: This was the number of dead who were not transferred by us to another department, but who died at our station or a few hours after they had been transferred to another station.

Prosecutor: Have you any knowledge as to what happened to some of the other patients who were transferred to some other station after they were experimented on? That is, did some others die after they were experimented on?

Witness: Of our patients, during the years after they came to us for observation, I can recollect that another sixty patients died. I cannot say for certain they died of malaria or other results of the experiments.

Dr. Schilling's defense during his trial at Dachau was that his work was part of his duty; that it was unfinished; and that the Dachau court should do what it could to help him finish his experiments for the benefit of science.[7]

I did not report the Dachau trial, which was not one of the thirteen Nuremberg Trials. However, it was obvious that Dr. Schilling considered experiments for the "benefit of science" to take precedence over the benefit of his patients. This thinking was prevalent among the Nazi doctors. The judges in their ruling on this medical case established the Nuremberg Code of ten points as a guideline to end this perverse thinking and to conform medical practice to the Hippocratic Oath.

· 8 ·

Bone, Muscle, and Nerve Regeneration and Bone Transplantation Experiments

What kind of recompense can the world offer to those who were operated on in such a manner? What kind of justice has the world for those who carried out such operations?

—Prisoner Dr. Zofia Maczka

SOME OF THE most savage, sadistic, and inhumane experiments were those involving regeneration of bones, muscles, and nerves, and transplantation of bones. Sections of bone were removed, legs were removed at the hips, arms were removed, including the shoulder blades, and muscles and nerves were removed from healthy concentration camp inmates, and then the attempt was made to transplant these body parts to other victims. These attempts usually resulted in death. But, for those who lived, mutilation and permanent disability resulted.

The same group of young Polish women inmates at the women's concentration camp of Ravensbrueck who underwent sulfanilamide experiments (to be described later) was forced to undergo the bone, muscle, and nerve regeneration and bone transplantation experiments. These two experiments occurred during the same period of time.

Dr. Fritz Fischer (Waffen SS), a defendant in the medical case who had been fellow defendant General Karl Gebhardt's assistant, stated in his affidavit that Evipan and ether were used as anesthetics. Incisions were made at the outer side of the upper leg, and muscle was removed. Then the wound was closed and a cast applied. After one week the wound was split open, and more muscle was removed.[1]

Defendant Dr. Herta Oberheuser stated in her affidavit that her assigned duties were to select young, healthy Polish inmates, to assist at all surgical procedures, and to give post-operative care. She stated that fifteen to twenty inmates were subjected to this experiment from the end of 1942 and into 1943.

Dr. Maczka stated that defendant Gebhardt supervised both the sulfanilamide and bone, muscle, and nerve experiments. She admitted that not one subject was pardoned after experimentation. From subsequent testimony, it became evident that Dr. Oberheuser utterly neglected basic nursing requirements and her treatment of subjects was cruel and abusive.

Although I had gained a clue from the prosecutors' opening statements to the judges what they expected the evidence to prove, I, as a court reporter, was never given advance information of the detailed charges against any of the defendants. I remained unaware of how horrifying the witnesses' testimony would become until I heard their words coming from their own mouths and recorded them verbatim.

Prosecution Exhibit 232, received in evidence, is an affidavit of prisoner Dr. Zofia Maczka taken on April 16, 1946 (after the war), concerning experiments conducted at Ravensbrueck women's concentration camp from the summer of 1942 and continuing on for a year. Doctors Fischer and Oberheuser, under the direction of Dr. Gebhardt, were indicted on this testimony.

Testifying for the prosecution, Dr. Maczka was a practicing physician and graduate of the University of Krakow medical school. As a prisoner, she was assigned to be the x-ray technician in the Ravensbrueck concentration camp. She testified that in the course of her duties she observed approximately thirteen cases of experiments performed on the bones of inmates. She testified that three kinds of bone operations were performed: fractures, bone transplantations, and bone splints. Some of the Polish girls were operated on several times.

Dr. Maczka took x-ray pictures of prisoner Krystyna Dabska, which showed that small pieces of the fibulae (the bones of the leg) had been removed, and in one leg the periosteum (connective tissue covering the bone) had been removed.

Zofia Baj, Janina Marezewska, and Leonarda Bien suffered bone fracture experiments. Dr. Maczka stated: "The tibia (shin bone) was broken in several places..." which impeded locomotion. Bone incisions were performed on Barbara Pietczyk, a sixteen-year-old Polish girl who was operated on six times.[2] Pieces of both tibia were cut out.

Dr. Maczka stated that multiple muscle experiments were carried out on the same subject. Certain muscles were removed from Maria Grabowska, who later developed osteomyelitis (inflammation of the bone). In subsequent operations additional pieces were cut out, always at the same place so that the legs got thinner and weaker all the time.[3]

Dr. Maczka testified that about ten feeble-minded inmates were selected in the transplantation experiment. Whole limbs were transplanted from one person to another. One case was a leg amputation. Then the experimental subject was killed.

In another case, an abnormal woman was operated on, and her whole arm and shoulder blade were removed, making it impossible for her to raise her remaining arm above the horizontal.[4]

Dr. Maczka stated that seventy-four Polish political prisoners were the victims—all healthy, aged sixteen to forty-eight.

She testified that all leg operations were done under anesthetic. The calf of the leg was opened, and wounds were deliberately infected with staphylococcus, gas gangrene, and tetanus. The first three died after a few days.

She stated:

On the operating table, the bones of the lower part of both legs were broken into several pieces with a hammer.... The muscle experiments consisted of many operations always on the same spot, the upper or lower part of the leg. At each further operation larger and larger pieces of muscles were cut out. Once a small piece of bone was planted into a muscle.... During nerve operations parts of nerves were removed.

When asked, "What problem did Professor Gebhardt and his school wish to solve by these experiments?" Dr. Maczka replied, "The problem of the regeneration of bones, muscles, and nerves. Was the thing carried out?" she asked rhetorically. "No. It was not checked at all, or only insufficiently."

Dr. Maczka stated that "special operations" were carried out at the same time on mentally ill prisoners:

> ... amputations of the whole leg (at the hip joint) were carried out, or on others, amputation of the whole arm (with the shoulder blade) were carried out. Afterwards the victims (if they still lived) were killed by means of Evipan injections and the leg or arm was taken to Hohenlychen. ... Ten such operations, approximately, were carried out.
>
> During the whole of the time these operations were carried out, I was employed as a worker in the ward and investigated this matter, risking my own life, with the idea that it was my duty, if I were saved, to tell the truth to the world. I conclude my statement with two questions: What kind of recompense can the world offer to those who were operated on in such a manner? What kind of justice has the world for those who carried out such operations?

The affidavit of Gustawa Winkowska corroborated Maczka's testimony concerning the transplantation of whole limbs and established that the experimental subjects were later killed.[5]

Prosecution Exhibit 230 was an affidavit of Dr. Zdenka Nedvedova-Nejedla, who stated that she arrived in a transport from

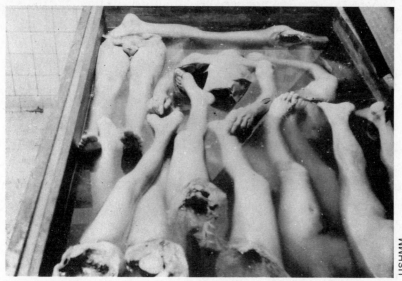

A bin of severed legs from a concentration camp

Auschwitz and worked as a doctor prisoner in Ravensbrueck. She stated:

> Operations were performed on one Yugoslav, one Czech, two Ukrainian, two German, and about eighteen Polish women, of whom six were operated on by force in the bunker with the help of SS men. Two of them were shot after their operation wounds had healed. After operations, no one except SS nurses was admitted to the persons operated on. Whole nights they lay without any assistance and it was not permitted to administer sedatives even against the most intensive post-operational pains. From the persons operated on, eleven died or were killed, and seventy-one remained invalids for life.

In the final defense plea for Defendant Gebhardt, his lawyer stated, referring to transplanting the shoulder blade in the above case:

> This experiment was justified in this particular case as it took place for the benefit of a patient in serious danger. The exper-

imental person from whom the shoulder blade was taken was also a member of the Resistance Movement, and she, too, thus escaped execution. Furthermore, the shoulder blade in question belonged to a hand restricted in its function.[6]

On December 20, 1946, just before Christmas, a thirty-seven-year-old Polish woman from Warsaw named Vladislava Karolewska, a lucky survivor, was able to come to Nuremberg and testify as a witness. She was called to the stand by the prosecutor for the United States, and testified during my turn in the courtroom. She was an experimental subject in both the sulfanilamide and bone, muscle, and nerve experiments, operated on a total of six times by Dr. Fischer, beginning August 14, 1942.

She identified defendants Gebhardt, Fischer, and Oberheuser as having cut into her body and experimented on her, forcibly anesthetizing her without preoperative care, her body still filthy from the camp.

Extracts from the Testimony of Vladislava Karolewska

The direct examination was conducted by Prosecutor McHaney as follows.[7]

Prosecutor McHaney: What is your name, please?

Witness Karolewska: Karolewska.

Prosecutor: Were you born on March 15, 1909 at Yeroman?

Witness: I was born on March 15, 1909 in Yeroman.

Prosecutor: You are a citizen of Poland?

Witness: Yes, I am a Polish citizen.

Prosecutor: And have you come here as a voluntary witness?

Witness: Yes, I came here as a voluntary witness.

Prosecutor: What is your home address?

Witness: Warsaw, Inzynierska Street, No. 9, Flat No. 25.

Prosecutor: Are you married?

Witness: No.

Prosecutor: Are your parents living?

Witness: No, my parents are dead.

Prosecutor: Will you tell the Tribunal what education you have received?

Witness: I finished elementary school and completed the training school for teachers in 1928.

Prosecutor: And what did you do between 1928 and the beginning of the war in 1939?

Witness: I worked as a teacher in a children's school in Grudenz.

Prosecutor: And when did you leave that post?

Witness: I finished my work in June 1939 and went on holiday.

Prosecutor: And did you go back to this position after your holiday?

Witness: No, I did not go back because the war broke out and I stayed in Lublin.

Prosecutor: And what did you do while you were in Lublin?

Witness: I lived with my sister and did not work at all.

Prosecutor: Were you a member of the Polish Resistance Movement?

Witness: Yes, I was.

Prosecutor: And what did you do in the Polish Resistance Movement?

Witness: I was a messenger.

Prosecutor: And were you ever arrested for your activity in the Resistance Movement?

Witness: I was arrested on the 13th of February 1941 by the Gestapo.

Prosecutor: Was your sister arrested with you?

Witness: Two sisters and two brothers-in-law were arrested with me on the same day.

Prosecutor: What happened to you after you were arrested?

Witness: I was taken to the Gestapo.

Prosecutor: And what did the Gestapo do with you?

Witness: The first day the Gestapo took down my personal data and sent me to the prison in Lublin.

Prosecutor: And then what happened? Just go on and tell the complete story about what the Gestapo did with you and where you went.

Witness: I stayed two weeks in the prison in Lublin, and then I was taken again to the Gestapo. There I was interrogated and they wanted to force me to confess what kind of work I used to do in the Resistance Movement. The Gestapo wanted me to give them the names of persons with whom I worked. I did not want to tell them the names and, therefore, I was beaten. I was beaten by one Gestapo man, with brief intervals, for a very long time. Then I was taken to a cell. Two days later, at night, I was taken again to the Gestapo for interrogation. There I was beaten again. I stayed in the Gestapo office one week and then I was taken back into the prison in Lublin. I stayed in the prison 'til September 21, 1941. Then I was transported with other prisoners to the concentration camp Ravensbrueck, where I arrived on the 23rd of September 1941. ...

Prosecutor: All right. Will you tell the Tribunal what happened to you at Ravensbrueck?

Witness: At Ravensbrueck our dresses were taken away from us and we received the regular prison dress. Then I was sent to the block and I stayed in quarantine for three weeks. After three weeks we were taken to work. The work was hard physical work. In the spring I was given other work and I was transferred to the workshop, which was called in German "Betrieb." The work I did there was also very hard, and one week I had to work in the daytime and the next week at night. In the spring the living conditions in the camp grew worse and worse, and hunger began to reign in the camp. The food portions were smaller. We were undernourished, very exhausted, and we had no strength to work.

In the spring of the same year, shoes and stockings were taken away from us and we had to walk barefoot. The gravel in the camp hurt our feet. The most tiring was the so-called "roll calls," which we had to stand several hours, sometimes even four hours. If a prisoner tried to put a piece of paper underneath her feet, she was beaten and ill-treated in an inhuman way. We had to stand at attention at the roll call place and we were not allowed to move our lips, because then we were supposed to be praying and we were not allowed to pray.

Prosecutor: Now, witness, were you operated on while you were in the Ravensbrueck concentration camp?

Witness: Yes, I was.

Prosecutor: When did that happen?

Witness: On July 22, 1942, seventy-five prisoners from our transport that came from Lublin were summoned to the chief of the camp. We stood outside the camp office, and present were Kogel, Mandel, and one person whom I later recognized as Dr. Fischer. We were afterwards sent back to the block and we were told to wait for further instructions.

On the 25th of July, all the women from the transport of Lublin were summoned by Mandel, who told us that we were not allowed to work outside the camp. Also, five women from the transport that came from Warsaw were summoned with us at the same time. We were not allowed to work outside the camp. The next day seventy-five women were summoned again and we had to stand in front of the hospital in the camp. Present were Schiedlausky, Oberheuser, Rosenthal, Kogel, and the man whom I afterwards recognized as Dr. Fischer.

Prosecutor: Now, witness, do you see Oberheuser in the defendants' dock here?

The interpreter interjects: "The witness asks for permission to go near to the dock to be able to see them."

Prosecutor: Please do.

I watched the witness leave the stand, walk over to the dock, face the only woman defendant, Dr. Oberheuser, in the second row and point at her.

Prosecutor: And Fischer?

While still standing in front of the defendants' dock, the witness pointed at Dr. Fischer.

Prosecutor: Witness, you have told the Tribunal that in July 1942 some seventy-five Polish girls, who were in the transport from Lublin, were called before the camp doctors in Ravensbrueck.

*Defendant Fritz Fischer, Assistant Physician
to defendant General Karl Gebhardt*

Witness: Yes.

Prosecutor: Now, were any of these girls selected for an operation?

Witness: On this day we did not know why we were called before the camp doctors, and on the same day ten out of twenty-five girls were taken to the hospital, but we did not know why. Four of them came back and six stayed in the hospital. On the same day six of them came back to the block after having received some injection, but we did not know what kind of injection.

On the 1st of August, those six girls were called to the hospital again; those girls who received injections were kept in the hospital, but we could not get in touch with them to hear from them why they were put in the hospital. A few days later one of my comrades succeeded in getting close to the hospital and learned from one of the prisoners that all were in bed and that their legs were in casts.

On the 14th of August, the same year, I was called to the hospital and my name was written on a piece of paper. I did not know why. Besides me, eight other girls were called to the hospital. We were called at a time when executions usually took place and I thought I was going to be executed because some girls had been shot down before.

In the hospital we were put to bed and the ward in which we stayed was locked. Then a German nurse arrived and gave me an injection in my leg. After this injection I vomited and I was weak. Then I was put on a hospital cot and they brought me to the operating room ... Then I lost consciousness and when I revived I noticed that I was in a proper hospital ward. I recovered consciousness for a while and I felt severe pain in my leg. Then I lost consciousness again. I regained consciousness in the morning, and then I noticed that my leg was in a cast from the ankle up to the knee and I felt very great pain in this leg and had a high temperature. I noticed also that my leg was swollen from the toes up to the groin. The pain was increasing and the temperature, too, and the next day I noticed that some liquid was flowing from my leg.

The third day I was put on a hospital trolley and taken to the dressing room. Then I saw Dr. Fischer again. He had on an operating gown and rubber gloves on his hands. A blanket was put over my eyes, and I did not know what was done with my leg but I felt great pain and I had the impression that something must have been cut out of my leg... Two weeks later we were all taken to the operating theater again, and put on the operating tables. The bandage was removed, and that was the first time I saw my leg. The incision went so deep that I could see the bone ...

On 8 September I went back to the block. I couldn't walk. The pus was draining from my leg; the leg was swollen up and I could not walk. In the block I stayed in bed for one week; then I was called to the hospital again. I could not walk and I was carried by my comrades.

In the hospital I met some of my comrades who were there after the operation. This time I was sure I was going to be executed because I saw an ambulance standing outside the office, which was used by the Germans to transport people intended for execution. Then we were taken to the dressing room where Doctor Oberheuser and Doctor Shiedlausky examined our legs. We were put to bed again, and on the same day, in the afternoon I was taken to the operating theater and the second operation was performed on my leg. I was put to sleep in the same way as before, having received an injection. This time I again saw Doctor Fischer. I woke up in the regular hospital ward, and I felt a much greater pain and had a higher temperature. The symptoms were the same. The leg was swollen and the pus flowed from my leg... After this operation I felt still worse, and I could not move. While I was in the hospital, Dr. Oberheuser treated me cruelly.

Prosecutor: Witness you have told the Tribunal that you were operated on the second time on the 16th of September 1942? Is that right?

Witness: Yes.

Prosecutor: When did you leave the hospital after this second operation?

Witness: After the second operation I left the hospital on October 6.

Prosecutor: Was your leg healed at that time?

Witness: My leg was swollen up, caused me great pain, and the pus drained from my leg.

Prosecutor: Were you able to work?

Witness: I was unable to work, and I had to stay in bed because I could not walk.

Prosecutor: Do you remember when you got up out of bed and were able to walk?

Witness: I stayed in bed several weeks, and then I got up and tried to walk.

Prosecutor: How long was it until your leg was healed?

Witness: The pus was flowing from my leg till June 1943; and at that time my wound was healed.

Prosecutor: Were you operated on again?

Witness: Yes, I was operated on again in the bunker.

Prosecutor: In the bunker? That is not in the hospital?

Witness: Not in the hospital but in the bunker... At the end of
February 1943, Dr. Oberheuser called us and said, "Those
girls are new guinea pigs;" and we were very well known
under this name in the camp. Then we understood that we
were persons intended for experiments, and we decided to
protest against the performance of these operations on
healthy people.

We drew up a protest in writing and we went to the camp
commandant. Not only those girls who had been operated on
before but other girls who were called to the hospital came to
the office. The girls who had been operated on used crutches
and they went without any help. We did not get any answer;
and we were not allowed to talk to the commandant.

On 15 August 1943, a policewoman came and read off the
names of ten new prisoners. She told us to follow her to the
hospital. We refused to go to the hospital because we thought
that we were intended for a new operation. ... All prisoners in
the camp were told to stay in the blocks. All of the women
who lived in the same block where I was were told to leave the
block and stand in line in front of Block 10 at a certain time.
Then the Overseer Binz appeared and called out ten names,
and my name was among them.

We went out of the line and stood before Block 9 in line.
Then Binz said: "Why do you stand in line as if you were to
be executed?" We told her that operations were worse for us
than executions and that we would prefer to be executed
rather than to be operated on again... In the meantime one
fellow prisoner who used to work in the canteen walked past.
She told us that Binz had asked for help from SS men to take
us to the hospital by force... Then Binz and the camp police
appeared. They drove us out from the lines by force. She told
us that she was putting us into the bunker as punishment for
not following her orders.

Five prisoners were put into each cell although one cell was only intended for one person. The cells were quite dark, without lights. We stayed in the bunker the whole night long and the next day... The woman guard of the bunker unlocked our cell and took me out. I thought that I was to be interrogated or beaten. She took me down the corridor. She opened one door and behind the door stood SS man Dr. Trommel. He told me follow him upstairs. Following Dr. Trommel, I noticed there were other cells, with beds and bedding. He put me in one of the cells. Then he asked me whether I would agree to a small operation. I told him that I did not agree to it because I had already undergone two operations. He told me that this was going to be a very small operation and that it would not harm me. I told him that I was a political prisoner and that operations could not be performed on political prisoners without their consent.

He told me to lie down on the bed; I refused to do so. He repeated it twice. Then he went out of the cell and I followed him. He went quickly downstairs and locked the door. Standing in front of the cell I noticed a cell on the opposite side of the staircase, and I also noticed some men in operating gowns. There was also one German nurse ready to give an injection. Near the staircase stood a stretcher. That made it clear to me that I was going to be operated on again in the bunker.

I decided to defend myself to the last. In a moment Trommel came back with two SS men. One of these SS men told me to enter the cell. I refused to do it, so he forced me into the cell and threw me on the bed.

Dr. Trommel took me by the left wrist and pulled my arm back. With his other hand he tried to gag me, putting a piece of rag into my mouth, because I shouted. The second SS man took my right hand and stretched it. Two other SS men held me by my feet. Immobilized, I felt somebody giving me an injection. I defended myself for a long time, but then I grew weaker. The injection had its effect; I felt sleepy. I heard Trommel saying, "That is all."

I regained consciousness again, but I don't know when. Then I noticed that a German nurse was taking off my dress; I then lost consciousness again; I regained it in the morning. Then I noticed that both my legs were in iron splints and were bandaged from the toes up to the groin. I felt a severe pain in my feet, and had a temperature.

On the afternoon of the same day, a German nurse came and gave me an injection. In spite of my protests; she gave me this injection in my thigh and told me that she had to do it.

Four days after this operation a doctor from Hohenlychen arrived; again I was given an injection to put me to sleep, and as I protested he told me that he would change the dressing. I felt a higher temperature and a greater pain in my legs.

Prosecutor: How many times did you see Gebhardt?

Witness: Twice.

Prosecutor: I will ask you to step down and walk over to the defendants' dock and see whether or not you find the man Gebhardt sitting in the dock?

Witness: The witness complied and pointed to the defendant Gebhardt.

Prosecutor: Thank you. Sit down.

"Do any of the defense counsel desire to cross-examine this witness?" interjected Judge Beal.

The counsel for the defendants Gebhardt, Oberheuser, and Fischer—Mr. Seidl—replied, "I do not intend to cross-examine this witness, but this does not mean that my clients admit the correctness of all statements made by this witness."

"Does any other of the defense counsel desire to examine the witness?"

None of the lawyers responded.

Defendant Karl Gebhardt,
Major General in the Waffen SS and
President of the German Red Cross

Extract from the Testimony of Expert Witness Dr. Leo Alexander

Prosecutor McHaney: Doctor, can you express any opinion as to the purpose of the type of operation to which she [Karolewska] was subjected, that is the bone removal?

Witness Alexander: I think it must have been one of the experiments which aimed at the question of regeneration of bone or possible transplantation of bone. Chances are that this tibial graft was either implanted in another person or that grafts had been exchanged. Of course today, three years after the experiment, no trace of transplantation is left in this individual. Or if the object was, as alleged in some statements I have seen, that tibial grafts were exchanged between the two legs, one must conclude that the experiment was negative because there is no evidence that a graft took.

All we see now are the consequences of removal of a graft, and the graft had included the entire compact part of the bone, otherwise the repair would have been better. If some part of the compact had remained, the periosteum [connective tissue covering the bone] would have probably regenerated and today, three years after the operation, no x-ray would have shown the defect. So I feel that rather deep grafts were taken which went down into the spongiosa. Whether anything was replaced that later was destroyed, I do not know, except the patient stated that there was a purulent discharge, indicating that the wound had become infected, and her statement of a subsequent operation, in fact, if I am not mistaken, two subsequent operations, indicates the probability that the grafts did not take and that they were removed after infection had become obvious.[8]

A doctor prisoner, Zdenka Nedvedova-Nejedla of Prague, Czechoslovakia, arrived at Ravensbrueck in a transport from Auschwitz on August 19, 1943, and worked until May 1945. In her affidavit concerning experimental operations conducted on fellow inmates, she stated, "All women on whom experimental operations had been performed were placed in one block, and they were generally known as 'rabbits.'"[9]

She learned from nursing personnel that cultures of streptococcus, staphylococcus, tetanus, and gas phlegmon were injected into the wounds to produce osteomyelitis (inflammation of the bone) experimentally.

Parts of leg bones as long as five centimeters were removed. Victims were immediately killed after the operation by an Evipan injection.

Arm and leg specimens were wrapped in sterile gauze and taken to the SS hospital nearby for attempted transplantation to wounded German soldiers.

Only SS nurses were admitted to the inmates operated upon. All night the inmates lay in intense pain because sedatives were not permitted to be administered. Eleven died or were killed and seventy-one remained invalids for life.[10]

Defendants Gebhardt, Oberheuser, and Fischer were convicted of criminal conduct for their responsibility in conducting these experiments.

· 9 ·

Mustard Gas Experiments

The general need for experiments on human beings ... has been recognized by all nations as a military necessity.

—Dr. Karl Brandt

WOUNDS CAUSED BY chemical warfare agents were of grave concern to military medical circles of Germany. Experiments with Lost, an asphyxiating poison gas commonly known as mustard gas, were conducted at Sachsenhausen, Natzweiler, and other concentration camps over the entire period of the war (September 1939 to April 1945) for the benefit of German armed forces. Hitler issued a decree in March 1944 ordering Defendant Karl Brandt to push medical research on gas warfare. The Germans needed an effective pharmaceutical treatment for burns caused by mustard gas.

Wounds were deliberately inflicted on camp inmates and mustard gas applied to the wounds. Other inmates were forced to inhale the gas, take it internally in liquid form, or be injected with gas. A 1939 report described instances where wounds were inflicted on both arms of the "human guinea pigs" and then infected. "The arms in most of these cases are badly swollen and pains are enormous."[1]

Inmates of the Natzweiler concentration camp were used in these experiments, beginning in November 1942. The experiments were conducted by Professor Dr. Hirt, from the University of Strasbourg in

Nazi-occupied France, and defendant Wolfram Sievers collaborated. Approximately 220 Russian, Polish, Czech and German inmates became involuntary subjects. About 50 died.

One group of experiments used a chemical warfare agent called phosgene—a suffocating and highly poisonous gas. Forty Russian prisoners of war, described as middle-aged, weak, and underfed, were treated with an experimental drug against phosgene poisoning after exposure. Four died. The rest suffered severe edema and had abnormally large amounts of fluid in their lungs.

A report dated March 31, 1945, by Ferdinand Holl described experiments with mustard gas at Neuengamme concentration camp.[2] Holl was a miner by profession, a political prisoner during the war, and a camp hospital inmate Kapo (trustee) who testified for the prosecution on January 3, 1947. He stated that despite the fact that Dr. Hirt had promised inmates that he would intervene with Himmler, requesting they be released if they volunteered—no one volunteered.

Holl's report stated:

> The first experiments were attended by Professor Hirt. After that it was a German aviation officer who carried out the experiments. The prisoners were stripped completely naked. They came into the laboratory one after the other. Then I had to hold their arms and a drop of this fluid was rubbed on their arm ten cm. above their forearm.
>
> Then the people who had been treated accordingly had to stand waiting with their arms spread out. After about ten hours, maybe it was a bit longer, burn injuries began to cover their whole body. Their bodies were burnt in all of those places where fumes from this gas reached. Some of the people also went blind. The pain was so tremendous that one could hardly stand being near the victims.
>
> Then they were photographed each day; all of the injured parts of their bodies: i.e. each of their burnt areas. About on the fifth or sixth day we had our first death. At that time the dead were sent to Strasbourg, because there was no crematorium in the camp.

The dead man was sent back and was "dissected" in the Ahnenerbe [SS research foundation]. His intestines, lungs and so forth were completely eaten away. Then, during the following several days seven more people died. This treatment lasted about two months until they were more or less transportable; then these people were sent to a different camp.

On the following day, that is, on the seventh day of the experiment, another seven of the experimental subjects died.

The remaining twenty-two were sent to another camp.[3] Holl's report went on to say:

Other experiments on concentration camp inmates of the Natzweiler concentration camp were carried out in the gas chamber... The experimental subjects had to enter this gas chamber two by two. They had to smash small ampules, which contained the liquid. The liquid evaporated and the experimental subject then had to inhale the resulting vapor. Usually the experimental subjects became unconscious.

Holl describes what happened after further observation:

The breathing organs of the experimental subjects were likewise destroyed. Their lungs had been eaten away by the gas. About one hundred fifty concentration camp inmates were experimented upon in this manner.[4] Approximately the same percentage as in the first series died as a result of this type of experimentation.

Other lost [mustard] gas experiments were carried out by means of injection... in a special room adjoining the crematorium. The victims...died without exception.

Another type of experiment was carried out on the experimental subjects, who had to take the liquid orally.

The witness Holl was transferred before Christmas 1943 to another camp, so he could not report on the continuing results of these experiments. He returned once a month to Natzweiler "and was therefore able to observe that the Lost [mustard] gas experiments continued until autumn 1944, when the Natzweiler concentration camp was liberated by the Allies."

From Holl's testimony it was proved that two hundred twenty inmates were forced to undergo these experiments and about fifty died.

Defendant Karl Brandt's defense was that "all nations" do it, *du tocque*—you did it, too.[5] He said, "The general need for experiments on human beings, and only those are relevant here, has been recognized by all nations as a military necessity."

In a memorandum from defendant Sievers to defendant Rudolf Brandt, dated November 3, 1942, Sievers was quoted as writing, "We are not conducting these experiments, as a matter of fact, for the sake of some fixed scientific idea, but to be of practical help to the armed forces and beyond that to the German people in a possible emergency."[6]

The court noted that Sievers was outraged that the Natzweiler camp officials asked that they be paid for providing inmates for the mustard gas experiments.

Defendants Karl Brandt, Rudolf Brandt, and Wolfram Sievers were convicted of special responsibility for and participation in these crimes. Defendants Handloser, Rostock, Gebhardt, and Blome, who had also been charged, were acquitted.

· 10 ·

Sulfanilamide Experiments

Death is victory. You must suffer for it, and you will never
get out of the camp.

—Ravensbrueck camp overseer Binz

AFTER HEAVY CASUALTIES from gas gangrene on the Russian Front in
the winter of 1941-42, following the German attack on Russia, sulfanilamide experiments were conducted to evaluate whether the drug
could be used on soldiers in the field to improve their survival during
lengthy transports to base hospitals. The Allies referred to sulfanilamide as the "miracle drug." Hearing this claim, German soldiers
questioned their medical officers—why weren't they using it? If
wounds could not be treated in the field, then it was necessary to have
front line hospitals to treat soldiers surgically.[1]

To test the effectiveness of sulfa on infections, experiments were
conducted at the women's concentration camp Ravensbrueck from
July 20, 1942, until August 1943.

Fifteen male inmates and sixty Polish women inmates were experimented on—the women in five groups of twelve each.

Defendant Gebhardt in a preliminary report dated August 29,
1942, stated,

By order of the Reich Leader SS, I started on July 20, 1942 at Ravensbrueck concentration camp for women on a series of clinical experiments with the aim of analyzing the sickness known as gas gangrene...and to test the efficacy of the known therapeutic medicaments.

In addition, the simple infections of injuries which occur as symptoms in war, surgery had also to be tested; and a new therapeutic treatment, apart from the known surgical measures, had to be tried out."[2]

Preliminary experiments in July 1942 were carried out on fifteen male concentration camp inmates to determine how to bring about gangrene infection artificially. An incision ten centimeters long was made into the muscle, and wood shavings were added to the infectious bacteria forced into the wounds. Efforts continued after each initial experiment to make the gangrene infection more serious.

Experiments were then continued on the female Polish inmates.

The affidavit of Defendant Fischer stated that "three series of operations were performed, each involving ten persons, one using the bacterial culture and fragments of wood, the second using bacterial culture and fragments of glass, and the third using culture plus glass and wood."[3]

Because no deaths had occurred, "In order to make the gangrene infections still more severe, a new series of experiments involving twenty-four Polish female inmates was carried out. In this series, the circulation of blood through the muscles was interrupted in the area of infection by tying off the muscles on either end. This series of experiments resulted in very serious infections and a number of deaths occurred."[4]

Evidence proved that five died as a direct result of the experiments, and six were executed by shooting at a later date.[5]

Four Polish women subjects testified before the Tribunal. Only healthy inmates were used, none volunteered. They protested against the experiments, both orally and in writing. They were convinced that they were going to die anyway and stated they would have preferred death to continuing in the experiments.[6]

The women testified that "seventy-four Polish women, one German, and one Ukrainian women were experimented upon." The additional sixteen women mentioned by the witnesses may well have been subjects in the bone, muscle, and nerve regeneration experiments.[7]

The witness Kusmierczuk was a Polish national woman who arrived at Ravensbrueck in the fall of 1941.[8] Operated on in the sulfanilamide experiments in October 1942, she developed a serious infection. Her wound did not finally heal until June 1944. She suffered permanent injuries.

The expert inmate witness, Maczka, who had been arrested for belonging to the Resistance Movement, worked as an x-ray technician. She testified to the deaths of five Polish subjects in the sulfanilamide experiments. One of the worst cases involved a healthy twenty-three-year-old Polish girl named Kurowska who was artificially infected with gangrene. Her leg became blacker and more swollen. After being given care for only the first few days, she was taken to Room 4 in the camp hospital. After lying in unbelievable pain for days, she finally died.

Maczka testified that immediate amputation would have saved her life. Had a German soldier's life been endangered by gangrene, an amputation would have been undertaken.

Kusmierczuk was the only survivor of that series of experiments. All of these subjects suffered severe pain. The Tribunal was able to view the mutilations to which the Polish witnesses who testified were subjected. Photos of their scars were received in evidence, forming a permanent part of the record.

Defendant Oberheuser ordered that many of the victims were not to be given medicine or morphine.[9] They were given bandages only from time to time, resulting in a terrible odor of pus in the rooms.

The witness Broll-Plater testified, "My leg pained me; I felt severe pain; and blood flowed from my leg. At night we were all alone without any care. I heard only the screaming of my fellow prisoners, and I heard also that they asked for water. There was nobody to give us any water or bed pans."[10]

The witness Karolewska, a subject in the bone, muscle, and nerve transplantation experiment, was also a subject in the sulfanilamide experiments. A fortunate survivor who was able to come to Nuremberg and testify, she stated:

> I was in my room and I made the remark to fellow prisoners that we had been operated on under very bad conditions and were left here in this room, and that we were not given even the possibility to recover. This remark must have been heard by a German nurse who was sitting in the corridor...
>
> The German nurse entered the room and told us to get up and dress. We answered that we could not follow her order because we had great pains in our legs and could not walk. Then the German nurse came into our room with Dr. Oberheuser.
>
> Dr. Oberheuser told us to dress and go to the dressing room. We put on our dresses; and being unable to walk, we had to hop on one leg going to the operating room. After one hop, we had to rest. Dr. Oberheuser did not allow anybody to help us.
>
> When we arrived at the operating room quite exhausted, Dr. Oberheuser appeared and told us to go back because a change of dressing would not take place that day. I could not walk, but somebody, a prisoner whose name I do not remember, helped me to get back to the room.[11]

Defendant Fritz Ernst Fischer, in his affidavit of November 19, 1946, concerning sulfanilamide experiments conducted in the concentration camp Ravensbrueck (Prosecution Exhibit 206), stated that the first of the series of experiments involved five persons. An incision was made five to eight centimeters in length and one to one and a half centimeters in depth on the outside of the lower leg.

He stated that the gangrenous bacterial cultures were put in dextrose and then spread into the wound, which was then closed and a cast applied. "No serious illnesses resulted from these initial operations."[12]

Defendant Herta Oberheuser, Physician,
Ravensbrueck concentration camp

Then a third and fourth series of operations were performed using new more virulent cultures each time. Since the infections conducted thus far "were not typical of gangrenous battlefield infections..." it was then decided to add wood shavings and ground glass to the cultures forced into the wounds.

When Dr. Grawitz asked him, "How many deaths have there been?" and he reported there had not been any, Dr. Grawitz ordered the next series of experiments to be undertaken by inflicting actual bullet wounds on the patients.

When a decision was made not to do this experiment, two additional sets of experiments were ordered. In the second set, streptococcus and staphylococcus cultures were forced into the wounds, resulting in severe infection, high temperatures, and swelling.

Incisions were made on the lower part of the leg in all experiments to make amputation possible. Because inflammation was so rapid and the resulting infections became acute in three weeks, no amputations were made.

Defendant Dr. Gebhardt in a report to a Wehrmacht (Army) conference declared, "I bear the full human, surgical, and political responsibility for these experiments." No criticism by the Wehrmacht physicians at the conference was raised.

In a supplemental affidavit, Defendant Fischer stated, "As a result of these experiments, three people died." [13]

Testimony of Jadwiga Dzido

On December 20, 1946, Jadwiga Dzido was called as a witness by the prosecution. A portion of her testimony follows.[14]

Prosecutor Hardy: Witness, what is your full name?

Witness Dzido: Jadwiga Dzido. ...

Prosecutor: Witness, you were born on January 26, 1918?

Witness: Yes.

Prosecutor: You are a citizen of Poland?

Witness: Yes.

Prosecutor: Have you come here to Nuernberg voluntarily to testify?

Witness: Yes.

Prosecutor: Would you kindly tell the Tribunal your present home address?

Witness: Warsaw, Garnoslonska 14.

Prosecutor: Witness, are you married?

Witness: No.

Prosecutor: Are your parents living?

Witness: No.

Prosecutor: What education have you received?

Witness: I finished elementary school and high school at Warsaw. In 1937 I started to study pharmacology at the University of Warsaw.

Prosecutor: Did you graduate from the University in Warsaw?

Witness: No.

Prosecutor: What did you do after you had finished school in the University of Warsaw?

Witness: I started studying pharmacology at the University, and then when I was studying the second year, the war broke out.

Prosecutor: What did you do after the war broke out?

Witness: In 1939 I was working in a pharmacy during the holidays.

Prosecutor: Were you a member of the Resistance Movement?

Witness: In the autumn of 1940 I entered the Resistance Underground.

Prosecutor: What did you do in the Resistance Movement?

Witness: I was a messenger.

Prosecutor: Then were you later captured by the Gestapo and placed under arrest?

Witness: I was arrested by the Gestapo on March 28, 1941.

Prosecutor: What happened to you after your arrest by the Gestapo?

Witness: I was interrogated by the Gestapo in Lublin, Lukow, and Radzin.

Prosecutor: And what happened after that?

Witness: In Lublin I was beaten while naked.

Prosecutor: Did you then receive any further treatment from the Gestapo, or were you released?

Witness: I stayed in Lublin six weeks in the cellar of the Gestapo building.

Prosecutor: Then were you sent to the Ravensbrueck concentration camp?

Witness: On September 23, 1941, I was transported to the Ravensbrueck concentration camp.

Prosecutor: Now will you tell the court, Miss Dzido, in your own words what happened to you after you arrived at Ravensbrueck?

Witness: When I arrived in the Ravensbrueck concentration camp, I thought that I would stay there till the end of the war. The living conditions in the prison were such that we would not live there any longer. In the camp we had to work, but in the camp it was not so dirty, and there were not so many lice as used to be in the prison.

Prosecutor: What work did you do in the camp, witness?

Witness: I did physical work inside or outside the camp.

Prosecutor: Were you ever operated on in the Ravensbrueck concentration camp?

Witness: I was operated on in November 1942.

Prosecutor: Will you kindly explain the circumstances of this operation to the Tribunal?

Witness: In 1942 great hunger and terror reigned in the camp. The Germans were at the zenith of their power. You could see haughtiness and pride on the face of every SS woman. We were told every day that we were nothing but numbers, that we had to forget that we were human beings, that we had nobody to think of us, that we would never return to our country, that we were slaves, and that we had only to work. We were not allowed to smile, to cry, or to pray. We were not allowed to defend ourselves when we were beaten. There was no hope of going back to my country.

Prosecutor: Now, witness, did you say that you were operated on in the Ravensbrueck concentration camp in November 1942?

Witness: Yes.

Prosecutor: Now, on 22 November 1942, the day of this operation, will you kindly tell the Tribunal all that happened during that time?

Witness: That day the policewoman, camp policewoman, came with a piece of paper where my name was written down. The policewoman told us to follow her. When I asked her where we were going, she told me that she didn't know. She took us to the hospital. I didn't know what was going to happen to me. It might have been an execution, transport for work, or operation.

Dr. Oberheuser appeared and told me to undress and examined me. Then I was x-rayed. I stayed in the hospital. My dress was taken away from me. I was operated on November 22, 1942 in the morning. A German nurse came, shaved my legs, and gave me something to drink. When I asked her what she was going to do with me she did not give me any answer. In the afternoon I was taken to the operating room on a small hospital trolley. I must have been very exhausted and tired and that is why I don't remember whether I got an injection or whether a mask was put on my face. I didn't see the operating room.

When I came back I remember that I had no wound on my leg, but a trace of a sting. From that time I don't remember anything till January. I learned from my comrades who lived in the same room that my leg had been operated on. I remember what was going on in January, and I know that the dressings had been changed several times...

Prosecutor: Witness, will you step down from the witness box and walk over to the defendants' dock and see if you can recognize anyone in that dock as being at Ravensbrueck concentration camp during the period and during the time that you were operated on?

Jadwiga points.

Prosecutor: And who is that, witness?

Witness: Dr. Oberheuser...

Prosecutor: Do you recognize anyone else in that dock, witness?

Witness: Yes.

Prosecutor: Point out who else you recognize, witness.

Jadwiga points again.

Prosecutor: Who is that man, witness?

Witness: Dr. Fischer.

Prosecutor: Witness, have you ever heard of a person named Binz in the Ravensbrueck concentration camp?

Witness: I know her very well.

Prosecutor: Do you remember what time your friends were called to be operated on in August of 1943?

Witness: Yes.

Prosecutor: Will you kindly tell the Tribunal some of the details there and the names of the persons who were to be operated on?

Witness: In the spring of 1943 the operations were stopped. We thought that we could live like that till the end of the war. On the 15th of August a policewoman came and called ten girls.... We didn't want to let our comrades out of the block. The policewoman came, and the assistants, the overseers, and with them Binz. We were driven out of the block into the street. We stood there in line, ten at a time, and Binz herself read off the names of ten girls. When they refused to go because they were afraid of a new operation and were not willing to undergo a new operation, she herself gave her word of honor that it was not going to be an operation, and she told them to follow her.

We remained standing before the block. Then several minutes later our comrades ran to us and told us that SS men have been called for in order to surround them. The camp police arrived and drove our comrades out of the line. We were locked in the block. The shutters were closed. We were three days without any food and without any fresh air. We were not given parcels that arrived in the camp at that time.

The first day the camp commandant and Binz came and made a speech. The camp commandant said that there had never been a revolt in the camp and that this revolt must be punished. She believed that we would reform and that we would never repeat it. If it were to happen again, she had SS people with weapons.

My comrade, who knew German, answered that we were not revolting, that we didn't want to be operated on because five of us died after the operation and because six had been shot down after having suffered so much. Then Binz replied: "Death is victory. You must suffer for it and you will never get out of the camp." Three days later we learned that our comrades had been operated on in the bunker.

Prosecutor: Now, witness how many women, approximately, were operated on at Ravensbrueck?

Witness: At Ravensbrueck, seventy-four women were operated on. Many of them underwent many operations.

Prosecutor: Now, you have told us that five died as a result of the operations, is that correct?

Witness: Yes.

Prosecutor: And another six were shot down after the operation, is that correct?

Witness: Yes...

Prosecutor: When you were operated on, did you object?

Witness: I could not.

Prosecutor: Why?

Witness: I was not allowed to talk and our questions were not answered.

Prosecutor: Do you still suffer any effects as a result of the operation, witness?

Witness: Yes.

Prosecutor: Were you ever asked to sign any papers with respect to the operation?

Witness: Never.

Prosecutor: When did you finally leave Ravensbrueck?

Witness: On 27 April, 1945.

Prosecutor: Have you ever received any treatment since you have left Ravensbrueck in the last year?

Witness: Yes.

Prosecutor: Tell us what treatment you have received.

Witness: Dr. Gruzan in Warsaw transplanted tendons on my leg.

Prosecutor: When did he do that?

Witness: On 25 September, 1945.

The war ended on May 8, 1945, with Germany's surrender, so the treatments the witness refers to were only a little more than four months later.

Prosecutor: Do you have to wear any special shoes now, witness?

Witness: Yes, I should wear them, but I can't afford to buy them.

Prosecutor: What are you doing now, witness? Are you working now, or what is your occupation?

Witness: I am now continuing my studies which I started before the war.

Prosecutor: I see. I will ask the witness to identify these pictures.... Were these photographs taken of you in Nuernberg in the last day or two, witness?

Witness: Yes.

Prosecutor: Witness, would you kindly take your stocking and shoe off your right leg, please, and will you step out to the side and show the Tribunal the results of the operations at Ravensbrueck?

After removing her right stocking and shoe, Jadwiga Dzido stepped out of the witness stand, raised her mid-calf length skirt, put her leg out to the side, and showed the long, deep scars in her leg.

*Witness Jadwiga Dzido, who underwent sulfanilamide
and bone experiments while an inmate of the Ravensbrueck
concentration camp. Document NO-1082 A. Prosecution exhibit 214 A.*

Prosecutor: That's all, witness, you may sit down. I have no further question on direct examination, your Honor.

Judge: Is there any defense counsel who desires to cross-examine this witness?

Dr. Seidl, Counsel for defendants Gebhardt, Oberheuser, and Fischer steps up. "I do not want to cross-examine the witness; however, I do not wish the conclusion to be drawn that my clients admit all the statements made by the witness."

Testimony of Dr. Leo Alexander

Dr. Leo Alexander, a prominent Boston doctor, was called and sworn in as an expert medical witness for the prosecution, and the following excerpt is taken from his testimony on December 20, 1946.

Prosecutor Hardy: Dr. Alexander, have you examined Miss Dzido before today?

Dr. Alexander pointing to the scars on witness Jadwiga Dzido's leg.

Witness Alexander: Yes, sir, I did, on several occasions during the last three days.

Prosecutor: During your examination, did you have x-rays made of the patient's legs?

Witness: I did, sir.

Prosecutor: At this time I will introduce Document NO-1091, which is the x-ray of the witness, Miss Dzido. Dr. Alexander, in the course of your diagnosis of these x-rays, will you kindly diagnose this x-ray in English and then repeat in German for the benefit of the defendants?

Witness: Yes, sir.

Prosecutor: Doctor, will you identify that x-ray which carries Document NO-1091?

Witness: Yes. This is the x-ray, which included the lower two-thirds of the thigh bone, the femur, and the knee joint. ...

Prosecutor: Doctor, this x-ray you are referring to now is Document NO-1092?

Witness: This is Document NO-1091. The arrow points to the osteoporotic atrophy of the tibia. Document NO-1092 is the x-ray of the leg. It shows the fibula, which is the smaller of the two larger bones of the leg, about in the middle between the areas just mentioned under the bracket called BP. ...In pictures 1093 and 1094, it shows arthritic changes of the cuneiform [wedge shaped] navicula [foot bone] joints with narrowing of the joint spaces and increased marginal sclerosis. ...

This arthritis is due to the immobilization of the right foot. Secondary to the muscles and especially the paralysis of the perineal nerve. It is evidently arthritis of an immobilization nature which one sees also by inspection of the patient's foot. ...

Prosecutor: Doctor, in your opinion, from your examination of this patient, can you determine what was the purpose of the experiment?

Witness: It appears that in this experiment a highly infectious agent was implanted, probably without the addition of a bacteria static agent such as sulfanilamide, and for that reason the infection got out of hand and became very extensive.

These experiments were not scientifically successful and "were entirely unnecessary since similar results could have been achieved by the treatment of wound infections of German soldiers normally contracted during the course of the war."[15]

Defendant Gebhardt's defense was "that these women were members of the resistance movement who had been condemned to death and who were in this way given an opportunity to obtain a pardon and so to escape execution."[16]

Subsequent testimony proved that the surviving witnesses were never accorded a trial and had no opportunity to defend themselves. They were arrested, interrogated by the Gestapo, and sent to a concentration camp.[17]

Article 30 of the Regulations Respecting the Laws and Customs of War on Land annexed to the Hague Convention expressly provide that even a spy "shall not be punished without previous trial."

Defendants Karl Brandt, Handloser, Gebhardt, Mrugowsky, Oberheuser, and Fischer were convicted of having special responsibility for and participation in criminal conduct involving sulfanilamide experiments.

· 11 ·

Sea Water Experiments

Jews and Gypsies cannot become citizens.

—Reich Citizenship Law
September 15, 1935[1]

Dachau was the location for the sea water experiments, conducted primarily for the German Air Force and the German Navy. The
purpose was to develop a method of making sea water drinkable
through desalinization. German Air Force pilots who had crashed or
ejected into the sea and German sailors who survived ships that were
bombed and sunk might have to survive for long periods in the ocean.

A series of experiments was conducted from July to September
1944 on forty-four experimental subjects ages sixteen to forty-nine,
mostly German, Czech, and Polish Gypsies. No food was given for
five to nine days. Inmates in other camps were asked to volunteer for
a "cleaning up work detail" in Dachau, where they heard conditions
were better, and so they agreed to go. Then, at Dachau, they were told
by defendant Dr. Beiglboeck, who supervised the experiments, that
they were to participate in sea water experiments. This was the "cleaning up work detail."[2]

Beiglboeck had promised them extra rations and an easy work
detail. These promises were never kept. These victims were deceived.

On May 19, 1944, defendant Dr. Becker-Freyseng reported they had not been able to conduct sea water experiments on volunteers who were not camp inmates under sufficiently realistic conditions of sea distress. He reported that the Chief of the Medical Services of the Luftwaffe (German Air Force) was "convinced that damage to health had to be expected not later than six days after taking Berkatit [sea water processed to conceal the taste but not alter the saline content], which damage will result in permanent injuries to health and will finally result in death after not later than twelve days."[3]

The experimental subjects were divided into four groups. The first received no water at all. The second drank ordinary sea water. The third drank sea water processed by the Berka method, called Berkatit. The fourth drank sea water treated to remove the salt.

*Defendant Hermann Becker-Freising, Chief of
the Department for Aviation Medicine*

During the experiment those assigned to the "thirst group" received no food whatsoever. The others received sea-emergency rations—the shipwreck diet of one ounce per day of biscuits, sweetened condensed milk, butter, fat, or margarine and chocolate.

In June 1944 defendant Dr. Schroeder wrote to Heinrich Himmler (Chief of the Gestapo) regarding the third group who drank sea water processed to conceal the taste but not to alter the saline content (NO-185):

> From the medical point of view this method must be viewed critically, as the administration of concentrated salt solutions can produce severe symptoms of poisoning.
>
> As the experiments on human beings could thus far only be carried out for a period of four days, and as practical demands require a remedy for those who are in distress at sea up to twelve days, appropriate experiments are necessary.[4]

Defendant Oskar Schroeder, Chief of the Medical Services of the Luftwaffe

The Austrian prosecution witness Joseph Vorlicek, a prisoner at Dachau, acted as an assistant nurse in the experimental station during the sea water experiments. On one occasion he spilled some fresh water on the floor and forgot the rag that he used to mop it up, leaving it there. The experimental subjects seized the dirty rag and sucked the water out of it. Dr. Beiglboeck threatened to put Vorlicek in the experiments if it ever happened again.[5]

High Drama in the Courtroom

One of the most dramatic scenes of the trial occurred during my turn in the courtroom. Karl Hoellenrainer, a dark-haired man of small stature, nervous and very excitable, assumed the witness stand. The main courtroom of the Palace of Justice loomed very large before him. It was June 27, 1947.

Prosecutor Hardy: Now, witness, for what reasons were you arrested by the Gestapo on May 29, 1944?

The question was asked in English and simultaneously interpreted into German. The answer, given in German, was interpreted through the English channel of my earphones.

Witness Hoellenrainer: Because I am a Gypsy of mixed blood.

The Law for the Protection of German Blood and German Honor, dated November 14, 1935—another of the infamous Nuremberg Laws—prohibited marriage between Gypsies and Germans. "A marriage shall furthermore not be contracted if the progeny to be expected from it would endanger the purity of German blood."[6] The Germans considered Gypsies to be asocial, whether or not they had committed any crimes.

Karl Hoellenrainer was first sent to Auschwitz, then Buchenwald, and then Dachau, where sea water experiments tortured his mind and body for weeks. In his examination of the witness, Prosecutor Hardy asked Hollenrainer to identify the doctor who administered the experiments.

Prosecutor: Do you think you would be able to recognize that doctor if you saw him today?

Witness: Yes, immediately. I would recognize him at once.

Prosecutor: Would you kindly stand up from your witness chair, take your earphones off, and proceed over to the defendants' dock, and see if you can recognize the professor that you met at Dachau?

Everyone in the courtroom waited tensely. I watched this little man as he stood up. He paused for just a moment with his eyes seemingly fixed on a doctor in the second row of the prisoners' dock.

Then in a flash he was gone from the witness stand! Seeming to leap over the ends of the German defense counsels' tables, he appeared to be almost flying through the air toward the prisoners' dock with his right hand stretched high, clutching a dagger, reaching for Dr. Beiglboeck, the consulting physician to the German Air Force.

Defendant Wilhelm Beiglboeck,
Consulting Physician to the Air Force

Amid the scramble of defense attorneys bending away from him, and the momentary shock and confusion in the courtroom, three American military policemen rushed from behind the prisoners' dock and grabbed Hoellenrainer, nearly in midair. They subdued him just

161

short of his target, preventing him from delivering his own brand of justice.

I did not see a weapon but was told later by an American military police officer that the witness had been able to conceal a small dagger on his person.

Minutes later, order was restored in the courtroom. The witness stood before Presiding Judge Walter Beals of Seattle.

Judge Beals: Will the marshal bring the witness before the bar of this court? Will an interpreter come up here who can translate to the witness?

Witness, you were summoned before this Tribunal as a witness to give evidence.

Witness Hoellenrainer: Yes.

Judge: This is a court of justice.

Witness: Yes.

Judge: And by your conduct in attempting to assault the defendant Beiglboeck in the dock, you have committed a contempt of this court.

Witness: Your Honors, please excuse my conduct. I am very excited.

Judge Beals turned to the interpreter. "Ask the witness if he has anything else to say in extenuation of his conduct."

Witness: Your Honors, please excuse me. I am so worked up. That man is a murderer. He has ruined my whole life.

Judge: Your statements afford no extenuation of your conduct. You have committed a contempt in the presence of the court, and it is the judgment of this Tribunal that you be confined in the Nuernberg prison for the period of ninety days as punishment for the contempt which you have exhibited before this Tribunal.

Witness: Would the Tribunal please forgive me? I am married and I have a small son. This man is a murderer. He gave me salt water and he performed a liver puncture on me. I am still under medical treatment. Please do not send me to prison.

Judge: That is no extenuation. The contempt before this court must be punished. People must understand that a court is not to be treated in that manner.

Will the marshal call a guard and remove the prisoner to serve the sentence which this court has inflicted for contempt. It is understood that the defendant is not to be confined at labor. He is simply to be confined in the prison, having committed a contempt in open court by attempting to assault one of the defendants in the dock."[7]

My heart fell. All I could do was lower my head so my tears could not be seen. It was impossible for me to be dispassionate at this moment. Why ninety days? Why not one or two days—just to make a point? After all the torture this witness had suffered, it seemed to me to be an outrageous elevation of process over substance.

A recess was taken.

Four days later, on July 1, 1947, the witness was brought back into the courtroom and continued his testimony, extracted as follows.[8]

Prosecutor Hardy: Witness, at the close of your testimony the other day, you were proceeding to tell the Tribunal about your activities after your arrival at the Dachau concentration camp.

Witness: Yes...

Prosecutor: After you had been physically examined and x-rayed, what happened to you?

Witness: Then we came into the so-called surgical department. We were forty men. Then a Luftwaffe doctor came and examined us. We had to take our clothes off and stand in line. Then he said, "Well, you will be given good food, such as you have never had, and then you won't get anything to eat at all, and you will have to drink sea water."

One of the prisoners whose name was Rudi Taubmann jumped up and refused. He was in an experiment, a cold-water experiment, and he didn't want to be in any more experiments. The doctor from the Luftwaffe said, "If you are not quiet, and want to rebel, I will shoot you on the spot." The doctor from the Luftwaffe always had a pistol, and then we were all quiet. For about one week we got cookies, rusks, and brown sugar. There were about twenty-one little cookies, and three or four little pieces of dextrose. Otherwise, we got nothing.

Prosecutor: Did you at any time volunteer for these experiments?

Witness: No...

Prosecutor: Did the professor or any of the other Luftwaffe physicians talk to the inmates and advise them as to the hazards of the experiment prior to the commencement of the actual experiments?

Witness: No.

Prosecutor: Now, will you, in detail, tell the Tribunal just what food the experimental subjects received prior to the experiments, during the course of the experiments, and after the experiments, and in doing so, witness, kindly talk very slowly and distinctly so that the interpreters will be able to translate you more efficiently.

Witness: Yes. At first we got potatoes, milk, and then we got these cookies and dextrose and rusks. That lasted about one week. Then we got nothing at all. Then the doctor from the Luftwaffe said, "Now you have to drink sea water on an empty stomach." That lasted about one or two weeks.

This Rudi Taubmann, as I already said, got excited and didn't want to participate, and the doctor from the Luftwaffe said, "If you get excited and mutiny, I will shoot you," and then we were all quiet. Then we began to drink sea water. I drank the worst kind that was yellowish. We drank two or three times a day, and then in the evening we drank the yellow kind. There were three kinds of water, white water, and yellow water (two kinds); and I drank the yellow kind. After a few days the people became raving mad; they foamed at the mouth. The doctor from the Luftwaffe came with a cynical laugh and said, "Now it is time to make the liver punctures." I remember one very well.

Prosecutor: Talk more slowly, witness. Thank you.

Witness: Yes. The first row on the left when you came in, the second bed, that was the first one. He went crazy and barked like a dog. He foamed at the mouth. The doctor from the Luftwaffe took him down on a stretcher with a white sheet over him, and then he stuck a needle about this long (indicating) into his right side, and there was a hypodermic needle on it, and it bled, and it was very painful. We were all quiet and excited. When that was over, the other inmates took their turn. The people were crazy from thirst and hunger, we were so hungry—but the doctor had no pity on us. He was as cold as ice. He didn't take any interest in us. Then, one Gypsy—I don't know his name any more—ate a little piece of bread once, or drank some water; I don't remember just what he did. The doctor from the Luftwaffe got very angry and mad. He took the Gypsy and tied him to a bed post and sealed his mouth.

Prosecutor: Witness, do you mean that he put adhesive tape over this Gypsy's mouth?

Witness: Yes.

Prosecutor: Go ahead, continue.

Witness: Then a Gypsy, he was lying on the right, a big strong, husky fellow, he refused to drink the water. He asked the doctor from the Luftwaffe to let him go. He said he couldn't stand the water. He was sick. The doctor from the Luftwaffe had no pity, and he said, "No, you have to drink it." The doctor from the Luftwaffe told one of his assistants to go and get a sun. Naturally, we didn't know what a sun was. Then one of his assistants came with a red tube about this long (indicating) and thrust this tube first into the Gypsy's mouth and then into his stomach.

Prosecutor: Just a moment. That tube was how long? How long would that be, a half a meter long?

Witness: About this long (indicating).

Prosecutor: That will be about a half a meter?

Witness: Yes, about a half a meter. And then the doctor from the Luftwaffe took this red tube and put it in the Gypsy's mouth and into his stomach. And then he pumped water down the tube. The Gypsy kneeled in front of him and beseeched him for mercy but that doctor had none.

Prosecutor: Witness, during the experiments was your temperature taken?

Witness: Yes.

Prosecutor: Who took your temperatures?

Witness: There were two Frenchmen, one tall thin and one short blond one; and they took the temperatures and the doctor from the Luftwaffe took the temperatures, too.

Prosecutor: When you say "the doctor from the Luftwaffe" you mean the man you referred to as the "professor." The professor and the doctor from the Luftwaffe are the same or are they two different people?

Witness: Yes.

Prosecutor: I see. Thank you. Now, who performed the liver punctures?

Witness: The doctor from the Luftwaffe carried out the liver punctures himself. Some people were given liver punctures and at the same time a puncture in the spinal cord. The doctor from the Luftwaffe did that himself. It was very painful. Something ran out at the same time at the back. It was water or something—I don't know what it was.

Prosecutor: Well, did you receive a liver puncture?

Witness: Yes.

Prosecutor: Did the professor tell you for what reason he gave you that liver puncture?

Witness: The doctor from the Luftwaffe came to me and said, "Now, Hoellenrainer, it's your turn." I was lying on the bed. I was very weak from this water and from not having anything to eat. He said, "Now, lie on your left side and take the clothes off your right side." I held onto the bedstead on top of me and the doctor from the Luftwaffe sat down next to me and pushed a long needle into me. It was very painful. I said, "Doctor, what are you doing?" The doctor said, "I have to make a liver puncture so that the salt comes out of your liver."

Prosecutor: Now, witness, can you tell us whether or not the subjects used in the experiments were Gypsies of purely German nationality or were there some Polish Gypsies, some Russian Gypsies, Czechoslovak Gypsies, and so forth?

Witness: Yes, there were about seven or eight Germans and the rest of them were all Poles and Czechs, Czech Gypsies and Polish Gypsies.

Prosecutor: Were any of the experimental subjects ever taken out of the station room to the yard outside the experimental barracks?

Witness: Yes, at the end when the experiments were all finished; and three people were carried out with white sheets over them on a stretcher. They were covered with sheets but I don't know whether they were dead or not. But we, my colleagues and I, talked about it. We never saw these three again, neither at work nor anywhere in the camp. We often talked about it and wondered where they were. We never saw them again. We thought that they were dead.

Prosecutor: Do you know where they were taken?

Witness: No, I don't know.

Prosecutor: Well, during the course of the experiments were you weighed every day?

Witness: Yes. We were weighed, too.

Prosecutor: Was that every day or every other day?

Witness: I don't remember exactly.

Prosecutor: Well, now, after the completion of the experiments in early September what happened to you? ... I am referring to the end of the experiments, after the experiments were all completed. Could you tell us what date your experiments were completed and you were transferred from the experimental station?

Witness: The experiment lasted maybe four or five weeks altogether. I don't know the date.

Prosecutor: Well, then, they were completed in early September. Is that correct?

Witness: Yes.

Prosecutor: Now, after the experiments were completed, did you then return to the camp proper or to the camp hospital?

Witness: No, to the camp, into Block 22. We couldn't walk. We all had to support each other. We were exhausted. I forgot to tell you one thing. Before we began the experiments and we had this good food for about one week, the doctor took us out into the courtyard near the hospital. The doctor from the Luftwaffe came. He had a little bottle in his hand and we all had to line up. There was some liquid in the bottle and he put a number on our chest. I had number 23. It burned a lot. Then we went back into the block. On every bed there was a number, the same number we had on our chests. One man—but I don't remember who it was—one of the inmates said, "That is what they call the death number." I was pretty scared, and the inmates said, "Yes, that is the death number so that the doctor of the Luftwaffe will know right away who is dead."

We didn't want to go on with the experiments but what choice did we have? We were just poor prisoners. Nobody bothered about us. We had to let them do with us what they wanted. We couldn't resist. I haven't got the power to relate everything. . . .

The cross-examination was done by Dr. Steinbauer, the defense counsel.

Defense counsel Steinbauer: You refused to obey your draft order?

Witness: Yes.

Defense counsel: Isn't that why you were sent to the concentration camp?

Witness: No, I was sent to the concentration camp merely because I am a Gypsy. My brothers were in the war and they came back from Russia and were sent to Sachsenhausen and were murdered there, because there weren't supposed to be any more Gypsies in the German Army.

Defense counsel: What kind of a badge did you wear in the camp?

Witness: A black one.

Defense counsel: You and your wife, too, have stated that you participated in malaria, phlegmon, typhoid, and sea water experiments?

Witness: No, only this one experiment, no malaria.

Defense counsel: Do you admit that you lied to the young doctor who talked to you?

Witness: No, I didn't lie to the doctor. I just told him the exact truth. My wife and I weren't allowed to marry. My wife had a child from me and it was cremated in Birkenau. My sister was cremated and both her children.

Defense counsel: Don't get excited. I asked you whether you told the young doctor that you were in four different experiments. All you have to say is yes or no.

Witness: I told the doctor I drank salt water.

Defense counsel: Listen, Herr Hoellenrainer, don't be evasive as Gypsies usually are. Give me a clear answer as a witness under oath. Did you tell the doctor that you participated in other experiments, yes or no?

Witness: No. I just drank salt water.

The prosecuting attorney, Mr. Hardy interjects. "Your Honor, the testimony of this doctor is not in evidence before this Tribunal. I don't understand what Dr. Steinbauer is referring to..."

Defense counsel Steinbauer: When the experiments were to begin, did the professor explain the purpose? That it was for rescuing people from shipwrecks, and that it was a sea water experiment?

Witness: Yes, of course.

Defense counsel: Did he explain that you would be very thirsty?

Witness: Yes, he did first.

Defense counsel: And that thirst was very unpleasant?

Witness: Yes...

Defense counsel: Witness, the thirst dried out the mouth?

Witness: Yes.

Defense counsel: How can you explain that these people foamed at the mouth?

Witness: They had fits and foamed at the mouth; they had fits of raving madness.

Defense counsel: I am just asking you how there can be foam on a mouth which is completely dried out?

Witness: I don't know.

Defense counsel: You don't know. Then some became mad?

Witness: Yes.

Defense counsel: You Gypsies stick together, don't you?

Witness: Yes, of course.

Defense counsel: Then you must be able to tell me who became mad.

Witness: I don't remember.

Defense counsel: You must know. If a friend of mine—I was a soldier twice—and if a friend of mine had gone mad, then I would have noticed it.

Witness: It was a tall man who was in the first row. He was the first one to start. He became raving mad and had fits and thrashed around with his hands and feet. He was a tall, slim Gypsy.

The prosecution witnesses proved that the victims in this experiment suffered excruciating torture, diarrhea, convulsions, hallucinations, foaming at the mouth, and eventually, in most cases, madness or death.

Dr. Steinbauer, defending Dr. Beiglboeck, stated, "It is well known that there is no legal definition of crimes against humanity. According to legal authors, such crimes can only be committed against persons who are persecuted for political, religious, and racial reasons."

The defendants Schroeder, Gebhardt, Sievers, Becker-Freyseng, and Beiglboeck were convicted of having special responsibility for and participation in criminal conduct involving sea water experiments.

· 12 ·

My Life in Nuremberg

BY THE TIME the court had adjourned for the first religious holidays of the trial, my initial excitement at being in Nuremberg and reporting these historic trials had diminished. I began to feel emotionally affected by all the horror that the witnesses spoke of, sometimes haltingly and tearfully. I had to accurately put these words on paper with my pen, reporting verbatim, while sometimes I had difficulty holding back my own tears.

I had been in Nuremberg almost two months, living in the small two-story house on Beulowstrasse. I remember that my bedroom was barely able to accommodate a bed, dresser, small table, and chair. I remember the thick featherbed comforter and how grateful I was to have it on freezing nights when there was no other way to stay warm. I don't remember spending any time in the small living room or dining room, and went to the kitchen only to fix cups of hot tea.

As I had nothing in common with my British and French housemates, I spent little time talking with them. The French girl seemed to have more than a few Allied boyfriends who came to visit—one by one. I kept out of their way.

I stayed away from that house as much as I could. I only slept, took my cold baths, and got dressed there. The rest of the time I worked at the Palace of Justice and joined my friends at the Grand Hotel after work.

The American soldiers who worked with us in the court reporters' office started inviting me to join their group after work at the Noncommissioned Officers Club near the Grand Hotel. There we talked, drank beer or wine, relaxed, ate dinner, and danced to jukebox music. The soldier I remember most vividly was Sergeant Joe Prantl of Phoenix. In the GI Club, I met other soldiers and women employees who worked somewhere in the many departments or divisions that were connected with the trials. I remember Vernon Dale and Dorothie Noll, John Sexton and Ruth Price.

Sergeant Dale and Dorothie Noll were eventually married. After my return to the U.S., I did not see them until the third and final Nuremberg reunion held in Washington, D.C. in 1996. Since I was only twenty-two at the trials, I was one of the youngest working at Nuremberg. In 1996, at age seventy-two, I felt like the kid there among much older reunion attendees, some in wheelchairs. But when I knew Dale and Dorothie they were also quite young. They were two of the nicest people I had met in Nuremberg. I was delighted to see them again after all the intervening years.

I loved going to the enlisted men's club with these soldiers and soon learned that rank and a social wall separated them from the officers and their club in the Grand Hotel. I had a lot of fun with the soldiers; they took me ice skating at the Red Cross ice rink and to movies at the opera house. We saw not only American movies, but also live performances by Germans of operas such as Mozart's *The Marriage of Figaro*, a rollicking comic opera of intrigues and disguises, and Rossini's comic grand opera, *The Barber of Seville.*

Piilani Ahuna, a court reporter from Hawaii, and Siegfried Ramler, an interpreter from London, had sufficient seniority to be assigned rooms in the Grand Hotel because of their time working on the trial of Hermann Goering and the twenty-one other major Nazi leaders. It seemed that everyone wanted to live at the Grand Hotel. I hoped eventually to gain sufficient seniority to get a room there. It did come later.

No. 8 Hebelstrasse

My friends, Anne Daniels of Washington, D.C., and Dorothy Fitzgerald of Cleveland, both court reporters, lived in the large, elegant three-story mansion at No. 8 Hebelstrasse and were happy there.

At the urging of Anne and Dorothy, I went to Captain Sara Kruskall and requested a move to Hebelstrasse. My request was granted. I packed my one bag and moved into a lovely room down a long hall from my friends. We still had no heat or hot water, but it was so much more elegantly comfortable—and I was beginning to get used to the cold. However, I never got used to taking an ice-cold bath, and there was no shower.

Neither Anne, Dorothy, nor I knew who the wealthy owners of No. 8 Hebelstrasse were, or where they now lived. We began not to care, the more we heard in the courtroom. Coming from a childhood of deprivation, I felt like a princess in a rich, rich castle. And I liked living with Anne and Dorothy, who were older than I by fifteen and five years, respectively.

The mansion had a high iron fence around it and a guard on the Allied payroll who occupied the little guardhouse at the gate entrance. We had an empty swimming pool and tennis courts in the back. There was a ballroom and a kitchen on the first floor. The living quarters were on the second floor and were comprised of a large (everything was large) living room, dining room, another kitchen, a music room, library, and bathrooms. The bedrooms and their bathrooms were on the third floor.

Every window—floor to ceiling—was covered in weighty, dark maroon, hunter green, or gold velvet drapes. There were no screens on the windows. We opened the windows and wooden shutters in our bedrooms when the weather permitted. This winter was one of the harshest in Germany in many years. Of course, for the Germans in their bombed-out city with no heat, the winter had to seem harsh. It did seem to be cold, dark, dreary, and snowing or raining ice much of the time.

Vivien Spitz in the back yard of her home at No. 8 Hebelstrasse

The elegant period furniture was crafted in heavy German style. The wallpaper in each room was not paper at all, but fabric with velvet textured designs in rich dark burgundy, green, or gold.

The bathrooms were large, with seven or eight private stalls, and gleaming gold or brass fixtures at every one of the decorated porcelain sinks. I think that many people must have attended lavish parties in this house before the war, as there were bathrooms sufficient to accommodate a lot of guests.

In the ballroom, the U.S. Army had a food function, called a mess, where all American and Allied military or civilian personnel housed in the surrounding area could eat breakfast. From here, for security and distance reasons, we were taken by an American army bus to the Palace of Justice. We were told not to take streetcars, on which Germans would often hang off the outside when the cars were crowded. They would not have let us get on anyway. We were the enemy and we were hated.

I had been in Nuremberg seven weeks by the time I moved into No. 8 Hebelstrasse, and the trunk with my clothes had yet to arrive. I was hearing stories from colleagues about trunks and footlockers taking three months to arrive. Some would arrive after having been opened at Bremerhaven, the port of entry, with all clothes and belongings stolen. They received trunks containing just sand and chains.

Our courtroom German monitor, Fischer, took pity on me and put me in touch with a German tailor friend who created a suit for me in the German belted style, out of off-white fabric made of wood pulp. I was happy to have a third suit and paid him handsomely in cigarettes, which was the medium of exchange when coffee did not suffice. We could buy only a very few cartons of American cigarettes per month at the post-exchange, and as I related earlier, we were limited to three bottles of liquor every month while the GIs were allowed only beer and wine. That was another difference between the commissioned and noncommissioned officers. Court reporters were considered to be in the commissioned officer category because of our education and special skill.

I do remember American Major Mills C. Hatfield, Assistant Secretary General in the courtroom, telling me in the summer of 1947 that he bought a new Volkswagen with four cartons of cigarettes, valued at $100 a carton. This I came to know as the black market, which I engaged in to a limited extent. My coworkers were buying whole sets of fine German Rosenthal porcelain and other valuable items that Germans sold for coffee and cigarettes, which they then used to buy food. I bought one Dresden Meissen figurine of a harlequin and a ballerina that stands about eleven inches tall. This rare and valuable figurine that I acquired for a few packs of cigarettes is now estimated by an antique dealer to be worth about a thousand dollars!

Without my suitcase, I had one pair of shoes and the boots I wore in the deep snow. Court reporter Ardis Ninabuck of Cincinnati, who had preceded me to Nuremberg, loaned me another pair of shoes. Luckily, we wore the same size, and her trunk had arrived full with nothing stolen. We could not go to stores to shop for clothes. There were no stores. They had all been bombed to the ground. Anything we needed in the way of clothing or anything else not found in the post-exchange had to be ordered from the United States or bought on trips to nearby countries.

We had a German housekeeper on the Allied payroll to clean this large house. She pressed clothes for us and we paid for her services with coffee or a few cigarettes. During the daytime, she hung our featherbeds out the window to air. It was strange to see white featherbeds hanging out upstairs windows in these big houses occupied by Allied personnel. We did not develop any kind of friendship with our housekeeper, and she remained distant. She had been our enemy and we were her enemy. There were frequent reports of shoes and clothing missing from my colleagues' rooms.

My steamer trunk finally arrived a little while after I moved in. Then I had my clothes, sweaters, shoes, underclothing, and jewelry. I left my jewelry on my dresser at night and sometimes during the day while at work. Once, I noticed pieces of jewelry were missing in the morning. At first it was a mystery to me—especially when just one earring had disappeared. During one night, while the shuttered window was open, I was awakened by a flapping noise and found a large bird flying around my room with an earring in its beak, trying to find its way out. I got out of bed and chased the bird around the room, vainly flailing at it with a piece of clothing. It did not drop the earring, but finally escaped through the open window carrying the jewelry in its beak.

I told Dorothy and Anne about the bird the next morning, and they laughed. Oh, yes, that is the "pack rat" bird that picks up everything shiny it can carry in its beak, literally stealing it. I kept my jewelry in a closed case after that, worried the bird might even get my watch!

For safekeeping, I kept my beautiful blue sapphire ring in its velvet case inside my jewel box on the upper shelf at the back of my closet. One day when I went to get it down to wear to a dressy evening function in the Grand Hotel's Marble Room, it was missing. And it couldn't have been either of my housemates or the birds!

Another Historical House on Habelstrasse

Across the street on Habelstrasse was another large three-story mansion in which the movie *Judgment at Nuremberg,* with Spencer Tracy, Marlene Dietrich, and Maximillian Schell, was filmed in 1961. In my time in Nuremberg, other American court reporters who worked on the trials were housed in this mansion. I went to more than a few parties in that house—parties attended by American officers, court reporters, lawyers, press reporters, and interpreters. For me, the first of these came during the December 1946 holidays.

In 1962, fourteen years after I returned to the United States, I attended the National Court Reporters Association's annual convention in Portland, Oregon. The keynote speaker was Judge James T. Brand, whom I knew in Nuremberg. He presided on Case No. 3 of the Subsequent Proceedings, the justices' case. I don't believe there was another Nuremberg reporter at the convention. After Brand's keynote speech, he said to me, "We have to find a quiet place to reminisce. How about the cocktail lounge?"

Spencer Tracy portrayed Judge Brand in the movie. The book, written by Abby Mann, described the justices' trial that finished after I returned home. I asked Judge Brand how factual and faithful to Mann's book the Hollywood production was.

He told me that Mann contacted him and told him he was writing a book about the German judges' trial, and asked could he interview him. Then, upon the judge's invitation, Mann moved into his house for two weeks. Brand told me, "Fortunately, Mann was a Scotch drinker, too!"

The result was the book *Judgment at Nuremberg,* and Brand said it was factually correct. He said he was surprised that Mann put in little anecdotes such as the story of the wife of the hanged Nazi general (played by Marlene Dietrich in the film) who came back to the house where the U.S. military had dispossessed her and asked for permission to go into the basement to retrieve some items of her husband's.

The movie is also factual, well made, and now on videotape.

Growing Numb to What Humanity Meant

Security was very tight at all housing for Allied workers. Nazi terrorists had thrown bombs into facilities in Stuttgart where Allied personnel had been housed. At the time of the Christmas adjournment, I was beginning to grow numb to what it was to be human. I had spent many hours in that courtroom, absorbing the daily horror. I was growing a little more dispassionate about what I heard and could control my emotions better but I constantly had to work on this control.

This was my first Christmas away from home, which was also true for many Allied civilians in Germany and for the freshly deployed military troops. The holiday adjournment provided a marvelous opportunity for our military to stage festivities that reprieved us from all that the courtroom presented. It gave us a chance to recuperate from our psychological wounds, to relax, and to try to regain a modicum of normalcy.

The German employees put up and decorated Christmas trees in traditional fashion with strings of colored lights and strings of cranberries and popcorn. They hung the trees with painted, carved wooden ornaments and little fabric Saint Nicholases in tiny wooden sleighs. There were angel figures and stars made of golden fabric.

By this time I was meeting and socializing with U.S. military officers in the Grand Hotel cocktail lounge, having dinner with one, two, or more and then going to the crystal-chandeliered Marble Room to dance to a live German orchestra and vocalists.

They played marvelous Viennese waltzes, polkas, and other dance music, mostly American. These were interspersed with popular German songs such as *Lili Marlene*. During the holidays, the orchestra played American holiday music, which made some of us wish we could join Bing Crosby in singing, "I'll be home for Christmas." The orchestra played "Silent Night," with Bing Crosby singing, and followed it with the German words *Stille Nacht...*, which many of us had learned in school in the U.S.

I was invited to holiday parties in private homes occupied by U.S. Army officers and fellow court employees. The Stein Castle, which housed the international press reporters and photographers, held their holiday festivities in their Press Club, and my friends and I were invited.

In 1760, Kaspar Faber established a lead pencil factory in Stein, a Nuremberg suburb. Eventually the Stein Castle was built on the estate. Large murals showed mounted knights on the backs of rearing horses, with huge pencils as lances. Long before Nuremberg, we used the Faber No. 2 pencil in classrooms.

For most of the occupying forces and civilians this was a religious holiday, especially for Jews and Christians. There were many Jewish attorneys, interpreters, court reporters, and staff working there. Not until I returned to the United States in May of 1948 did I begin to realize how difficult it must have been for those Jews to work on the trials. Many had family members exterminated in the death camps or the crematory ovens. Human beings entered these camps and became unidentified ashes carried up tall chimneys, making wreaths in the sky above and floating back onto earth, falling on everyone and everything nearby.

Coming from my little farming community of six thousand people in Woodstock, Illinois, northwest of Chicago, I really had not known who the Jews were, and I knew nothing of anti-Semitism. When I saw those Movietone newsreels in theaters that showed the atrocities in the liberated concentration and death camps, I did not know of Hitler's Final Solution—his plan to destroy all of the Jews of Europe. I did not know the effect this would have on me the rest of my life as a Christian. I was so driven to go to Nuremberg because I was half German and had been proud of my German mother and grandmother, two wonderful women. I was a very young person when I reported the Nazi doctors' trial, but because of what I learned there about anti-Semitism, my Christian conscience made it clear to me that I would have to stand up to bigotry and prejudice for the rest of my life.

The holiday break did its magic; we all felt rested and rejuvenated. We appreciated how valuable and precious life is as we returned to the courtroom of continuing horror. My mother, sister, and brother back home in Detroit were on my mind—their place in my life much more dear to me.

Nazi Terrorists Bomb the Grand Hotel Dining Room

Sometime in the late summer of 1947 my seniority made me eligible to move into the Grand Hotel, where two of my friends, Piilani Ahuna and Siegfried Ramler, had rooms. As happy as I was living in the Hebelstrasse mansion with Dorothy Fitzgerald and Anne Daniels, I wanted to be in the Grand Hotel for reasons of security and easy access to breakfast and dining facilities. It was where all of the socializing and activities seemed to center, as limited as they were for us in Germany.

I had a very nice large room on the fourth floor with an adjoining bathroom that I shared with another court reporter, Edna Malloy of Omaha, who had a connecting room on the other side. Life was very pleasant in the Grand Hotel, as I have already detailed.

One afternoon at about 5:00 p.m., while waiting for the elevator to go down to the dining room, I heard and felt an enormous explosion and vibration. I knew there was a bombing somewhere in the hotel. Rushing down three flights of stairs, as I had done several times in fire and bomb drills, I met everyone else fleeing their rooms, dashing down the stairs and out onto the street.

There we learned that two German terrorists had come out from the catacombs under the bombed-out Walled City across the street and had thrown a bomb through the large plate glass window on the street side of the hotel into the crowded dining room, filled with Allied officers and civilians. The bomb hit the wall over a table from which two people had just departed. Miraculously, no one was killed, but there were many injuries from flying glass and debris.

After this incident, our American military policemen went into the catacombs looking for these Germans. I did not learn whether they ever got them, but security around the hotel, which was already very tight, was greatly enhanced. We had all been aware that such bombings had occurred in Stuttgart and other cities where there were

Allied military and civilian personnel working and living. We were constantly reminded to be vigilant.

This frightening experience really brought home to me how hazardous living in Germany was as late as twenty-eight months after the end of the war. I no longer felt comfortable walking with friends on the nearby streets. From then on, I was always looking over my shoulder, suspicious of any Germans walking in the area, going about their business, catching streetcars, riding bicycles, or driving vehicles.

When I wrote home to my mother, I did not tell her about the bombing incident.

· 13 ·

Epidemic Jaundice (Hepatitis)

I know that these experiments were carried out, and that
some of the prisoners died as a result.

—Rudolf Brandt

THE EPIDEMIC JAUNDICE experiments were conducted from June 1943
to January 1945 on inmates at Sachsenhausen and Natzweiler concentration camps for the benefit of the German Air Force. The Nazi
doctors were investigating the causes of epidemic jaundice (hepatitis)
and possible inoculations that could be used against the condition.

After Germany attacked Russia, epidemic jaundice caused casualties of up to 60 percent in some German units.[1] Opinions at the
time differed on whether jaundice was caused by a bacteria or virus.

On June 1, 1943, Dr. Grawitz, SS physician, asked Heinrich
Himmler to make concentration camp inmates available for a viral
infection, stating that death was to be expected among the experimental subjects.[2] Himmler consented, and eight Polish Jews who had
been condemned to death at Auschwitz for participating in the Polish
Resistance Movement were subjects at Sachsenhausen. Defendant
Rudolf Brandt in his affidavit stated as follows: "Experiments had
thus far disclosed that contagious jaundice is transferred by a virus
and human beings were desired for inoculation with germs which had
been cultivated in animals… I know that these experiments were car-

ried out and that some of the prisoners died as a result. These experiments were of course well known to Karl Brandt as he was personally furthering them."[3]

Defendant Dr. Rose stated in his testimony:

> Hepatitis epidemica as such is not considered a dangerous disease by hygienists.
>
> In Germany, experiments with hepatitis virus have been carried out…and no incidents occurred. All experiments took place without ill effects. This is, of course, very limited experimental material, but material concerning hundreds of cases, which permit a more accurate judgment, has been published in England and America. Up to date, I have knowledge of about sixty experiments on human beings for hepatitis and no single incident has been reported yet.

Extract of Testimony by Dr. Karl Brandt

An excerpt from the testimony of defendant Dr. Karl Brandt, revealed on direct examination by his attorney Dr. Servatius, follows.

Defense counsel Servatius: The indictment mentions experiments with hepatitis. A letter from Grawitz to Himmler says that you furthered these experiments. Did you yourself do any clinical work on this question?

Witness Brandt: I never did any work in connection with hepatitis epidemica, for that would have been during the war, as before the war this disease was not given much importance in Germany. During the war I did not deal with this question because I was too busy with other things, and also because such a purely internal disease, although perhaps of interest to the hygienist, was relatively uninteresting to me as a surgeon.

Dr. Karl Brandt was found guilty of having special responsibility for and participation in criminal conduct involving epidemic jaundice (hepatitis) experiments. Dr. Brandt was convicted of all four counts of the indictment, whether he personally conducted any of the experiments or not. He was appointed by Hitler to be in charge of these doctors and all of their experiments, as well as the "euthanasia" (murder) program.

Near the end of the trial, Judge Sebring questioned Karl Brandt, as follows:

Judge Sebring: Witness, this question of the necessity for an experiment, is it your view that it is for the state to determine the extreme necessity for such an experiment and that thereafter those who serve the state are to be bound by that procedure? I think you can answer that "yes" or "no."

Witness Brandt: This trial shows that it will be the task of the state under all circumstances basically to clarify this question for the future.

Judge: Witness, as I understood your statements a moment ago, they were that the physician, having once become the soldier, thereafter must subordinate such medical-ethical views as he may have when they are in conflict with a military order from higher authority; is that true?

Witness: I didn't want to express it in that form. I did not mean to say that the physician, the moment he becomes a medical officer, should change his basic attitude as a physician. Such an order can in the very same way be addressed to a physician who is not a soldier. I was referring to the entire situation as it prevailed with us in Germany during the time of an authoritarian leadership. This authoritarian leadership interfered with the personality and the personal feelings of the human being. The moment an individuality is absorbed into the concept of a collective body, every demand which is put to that individuality has to be absorbed into the concept of a collective system. Therefore, the demands of society are placed above every individual human being as an entity, and this entity, the human being, is completely used in the interests of that society.[4]

· 14 ·

Sterilization

In some cases a practical experiment might be arranged by locking up a Jewess and a Jew together for a certain period and then seeing what results are achieved.

—Rudolf Brandt

THESE EXPERIMENTS WERE conducted from March 1941 to January 1945, four months before the end of the war at Auschwitz, the women's concentration camp Ravensbrueck, and other camps. By 1941 the Third Reich had adopted the policy and goal of exterminating all Jews from Germany and the countries the Nazis invaded and then occupied. However, because there was a shortage of laborers, they decided to sterilize Jews who were able to work, rather than exterminate them outright.[1]

A goal was set to develop sterilization methods that were quick. Not surprisingly, they decided to experiment on concentration camp inmates with radiation, drugs, and surgery. The purpose of the sterilization experiments was described by Rudolf Brandt in his affidavit:

Himmler was extremely interested in the development of a cheap and rapid sterilization method which could be used against enemies of Germany, such as Russians, Poles, and Jews. One hoped thereby not only to defeat the enemy but also to exterminate him. The capacity for work of the sterilized persons could be exploited by Germany, while the danger of propagation would be eliminated. As this mass sterilization was part of Himmler's racial theory, particular time and care were devoted to these sterilization experiments. Surgical sterilization was of course known in Germany and applied; this included castration. For mass application, however, this procedure was considered as too slow and too expensive. It was further desired that a procedure be found which would result in sterilization that was not immediately noticeable.[2]

Defendant Adolf Pokorny, Physician
Specialist in Skin and Venereal Diseases

Defendant Dr. Pokorny, in October 1941, advised Himmler that Dr. Madaus had produced sterility in animals with a synthetic drug produced from the caladium plant. It could be administered orally or injected.

Pokorny stated in his letter that "...the immense importance of this drug in the present fight of our people occurred to me. If, *on the basis of this research, it were possible to produce a drug, which after a relatively short time effects an imperceptible sterilization on human beings, then we would have a new powerful weapon at our disposal.* The thought alone that the three million Bolsheviks, at present German prisoners, could be sterilized so that they could be used as laborers but be prevented from reproduction, opens the most far reaching perspectives."[3]

Himmler agreed, and ordered that the intended plan of research should go forward. Then, in June 1942 it was learned that the particular caladium plant needed for the injection grew only in North America.

Prosecution Exhibit 528 is an affidavit of Dr. Karl Wilhelm Friedrich Tauboeck in which he stated that the caladium seguinum plant comes from Brazil and was used by Brazilian natives to sterilize their enemies by food or arrow wounds. Attempts to grow the plant from seed in hothouses had been successful in the earlier animal experiments, but the development of a drug was not speedy enough and the yield insufficient for large-scale experimentation.[4]

Defendant Rudolf Brandt, in his affidavit, stated, "...experiments were conducted upon concentration camp prisoners in order to test the effect of the drug produced from the caladium plant. Hothouses were used, with a certain amount of success...and the experiments were continued."[5]

At a conference on July 7 and 8, 1942, Himmler, defendant Dr. Gebhardt, Dr. Gluecks, and Dr. Clauberg discussed sterilizing Jewesses. Himmler promised that the Auschwitz concentration camp would be available for experiments on human beings to test methods of sterilizing individuals without their knowledge. Also discussed at this conference was the sterilization of men by x-rays, with the admonishment that these experiments were to be a matter of utmost secrecy.[6]

On July 10, 1942, defendant Rudolf Brandt wrote to Dr. Clauberg stating that he, Clauberg, was ordered to report to Himmler on how long it would take to sterilize a thousand Jewesses. Defendant Rudolf Brandt stated further that "in some cases a practical experiment might be arranged by locking up a Jewess and a Jew together for a certain period and then seeing what results are achieved." This was suggested as a way of testing the success of sterilization experiments without the knowledge of the participants.[7]

On June 7, 1943, on the basis of his experiments, Dr. Clauberg reported that it would be possible to sterilize from several hundred to a thousand per day, stating further that sterilization could be "performed by a single injection made from the entrance of the uterus in the course of the usual customary gynecological examination."[8]

Defendant Rudolf Brandt in his affidavit stated, "Dr. Clauberg developed further a method for the sterilization of women. This method was based upon the injection of an irritating solution into the uterus. Clauberg conducted widespread experiments on Jewish women and Gypsies in the Auschwitz concentration camp. Several thousand women were sterilized by Clauberg in Auschwitz."[9]

Sterilization by X-rays

Defendant Brack, in the spring of 1941, suggested to Himmler that Jews could be sterilized by x-rays.[10] Himmler asked Brack to determine whether the victims could be kept unaware that they had been castrated.[11]

On March 28, 1941, Brack reported to Himmler that experimental results showed that mass x-ray sterilization could be carried out without difficulty. He estimated that with twenty x-ray installations, three to four thousand victims could be sterilized daily.[12]

When Germany invaded Russia in the summer of 1941, these plans were interrupted. Then, on June 23, 1942, defendant Brack suggested to Himmler that Jews able to work could be sterilized. Jews unable to work were exterminated.[13]

On August 11, 1942, Himmler wrote to defendant Brack that further experiments to ascertain the effectiveness of x-ray sterilization should be carried out on concentration camp inmates by expert physicians.[14]

As a result, experiments on Auschwitz concentration camp inmates were carried out by Dr. Schumann.[15] After receiving severe doses of x-rays in the genital area, one of the victims was castrated by surgery to determine the effects of the x-ray.[16]

At least one hundred Poles, Russians, French, and prisoners of war were involuntary subjects. Only young, well built, healthy inmates were selected. Nearly all of these victims were eventually exterminated as they were made incapable of working by severe x-ray burns.[17]

A letter dated March 28, 1941 from defendant Brack to Himmler reported the experimental results of sterilization and x-ray castration in part:

If any persons are to be sterilized permanently, this result can only be attained by applying x-rays in a dosage high enough to produce castration with all its consequences, since high x-ray dosages destroy the internal secretion of the ovary, or of the testicles, respectively. Lower dosages would only temporarily paralyze the procreative capacity. The consequences in question are, for example, the disappearance of menstruation, climacteric phenomena, changes in capillary growth, modification of metabolism, etc. In any case, attention must be drawn to these disadvantages.

The actual dosage can be given in various ways, and the irradiation can take place quite imperceptibly. The necessary local dosage for men is 500-600 r(oentgen), for women 300-350 r. In general, an irradiation period of two minutes for men, three minutes for women, with the highest voltage, a thin filter and at a short distance, ought to be sufficient. There is, however, a disadvantage that has to be put up with; as it is impossible unnoticeably to cover the rest of the body with lead, the other tissues of the body will be injured, and radiologic malaise, the so-called "Roentgenkater," will ensue. If the x-ray intensity is too high, those parts of the skin which the rays have reached, will exhibit symptoms of burns—varying in severity in individual cases—in the course of the following days or weeks.

One practical way of proceeding would be, for instance, to let the persons to be treated approach a counter, where they could be asked to answer some questions or to fill in forms, which would take them two or three minutes. The official sitting behind the counter could operate the installation in such a way as to turn a switch which would activate the two valves simultaneously (since the irradiation has to operate from both sides). With a two-valve installation about one hundred fifty to two hundred persons could then be sterilized per day, and therefore, with twenty such installations as many as three to four thousand persons per day. In my estimation a larger daily number could not in any case be sent away for this purpose...

In summary, it may be said that, having regard to the present state of radiological technique and research, mass sterilization by means of x-rays can be carried out without difficulty. However, it seems to be impossible to do this in such a way that the persons concerned do not sooner or later realize with certainty that they have been sterilized or castrated by x-rays.

(Signed) Brack[18]

In Prosecution Exhibit 163, a letter from defendant Brack to Himmler dated June 23, 1942, stated:

Among ten millions of Jews in Europe there are, I figure, at least two to three millions of men and women who are fit enough to work. Considering the extraordinary difficulties the labor problem presents us with, I hold the view that those two to three millions should be specially selected and preserved. This can, however, only be done if at the same time they are rendered incapable to propagate. About a year ago I reported to you that agents of mine had completed the experiments necessary for this purpose. I would like to recall these facts once more. Sterilization, as normally performed on persons with hereditary diseases, is here out of the question, because it takes too long and is too expensive. Castration by x-ray however is not only relatively cheap, but can also be performed on many thousands in the shortest time. I think that at this time it is already irrelevant whether the people in question become aware of having been castrated after some weeks or months once they feel the effects...

Heil Hitler!

Yours, (Signed) Viktor Brack[19]

Defendant Viktor Brack, Chief Administrative Officer in the Fuhrer's Chancellery

Denial Testimony by Viktor Brack

Defendant Victor Brack testified that Himmler told him that because the Jews in Poland were strengthening their own position, "something had to be undertaken to stop this because through the mixing of blood in the Polish Jews with that of the Jews from Western Europe, a much greater danger for Germany was arising than even before the war, and he said it was his intention to sterilize the Jews according to reliable methods, according to a procedure which would permit mass sterilization..."

The following is an extract from the direct examination of Viktor Brack by his counsel, Dr. Froeschmann, May 7–19, 1947:

Defense counsel Froeschmann: Well, what was the effect of this communication from Himmler on you?

Witness Brack: ... In my interrogation I told the interrogator that I regarded such a plan to exterminate the Jews as unworthy of Germany and its leaders...I felt that I was under the obligation to do anything I could to prevent this. If I had raised the least objection to it openly, I would have aroused great suspicion of myself and would have aroused a false reaction in Himmler. Therefore, I had to make the best of a bad job and had to pretend that I agreed with Himmler. I pretended to be willing to clarify the question of mass sterilization through x-ray methods."[20]

On this charge defendants Gebhardt, Rudolf Brandt, and Brack were convicted.

· 15 ·

Typhus Experiments

There were cases of raving madness, delirium, people would refuse to eat, and a large percentage of them would die.

—Dr. Eugen Kogon

TYPHUS BECAME A major medical problem in the fall of 1941, after Germany attacked Russia. Because vaccines were in short supply at the time, only medical personnel in exposed positions were inoculated against typhus.

From December 1941 through March 1945 a wicked and murderous medical experimental program was initiated using concentration camp inmates at Buchenwald and Natzweiler. Its aim was to evaluate various vaccines for typhus, yellow fever, smallpox, paratyphoid A and B, cholera, and diphtheria. It was hoped that a typhus convalescent serum could be manufactured.

During the medical case it was proved that 729 inmates were subjects in the typhus experiments, of whom 154 died. Additionally, substantially all inmates called "passage persons" who had been artificially infected died (estimates were that these numbered 90 to 120).

Although defendants Handloser, Schroeder, Genzken, Rudolf Brandt, Mrugowsky, Sievers, Rose, and Hoven were convicted of criminal conduct involving typhus experiments, most of the experiments at Buchenwald were done by an infamous physician, known as

Dr. Ding (Schuler), who committed suicide after the war ended and thus was never brought to trial. Dr. Ding's professional diary survived and eventually was turned over to the U.S. Chief of Counsel for War Crimes, General Telford Taylor, and became one of the 1,471 pieces of documentary evidence prepared by the Germans. It played a major role in convicting their evil doctors.

Defendant Karl Genzken, Chief of the Medical Department of the Waffen SS

Dr. Eugen Haagen, an Air Force officer in the Medical Service and a professor at the University of Strasbourg in France under Nazi occupation, conducted typhus experiments at Natzweiler.

Early on, inmates were infected with the virus through both superficial and deep cuts in the upper arm. Others were infected by intravenous injections of fresh blood containing the typhus virus.[1] A typhus vaccine from chicken egg yolks was tested. Already available and known to be effective was the Weigl vaccine produced from the intestines of lice. However, it was expensive and complicated to manufacture. A cheaper alternative was needed.

Beginning on January 6, 1942, several vaccines were tested in several large-scale experiments at Buchenwald. Many subjects died. Usually, about forty to sixty subjects were used in a given test. In one experiment, conducted between 24 April and 1 June 1943, thirty-nine inmates were infected with typhus; twenty-one died.[2]

In the beginning, subjects were infected artificially by lacerating the skin and introducing a typhus culture from contagious lice. This changed in 1943 when subjects were injected with fresh blood containing the typhus virus intravenously or intramuscularly. Of twenty-five subjects used, nineteen died.[3]

Testimony by Dr. Eugen Kogon

These experiments can best be described by the testimony of prosecution witness Dr. Eugen Kogon, an inmate doctor, when examined by Prosecutor McHaney:[4]

Prosecutor McHaney: Now, will you please explain to the Tribunal in your own words exactly how these typhus experiments were carried out.

Witness Kogon: After 40 to 60 people, sometimes up to 120, had been detailed for a series of experiments, one-third of them were separated, and the other two-thirds were either vaccinated with a protective treatment, or it was otherwise administered to them, if it was a chemical therapeutical treatment...The infection was performed in various ways. Either typhus was transferred through fresh blood injected intravenously or intramuscularly. At the beginning, too, by scratching the skin, or by making a small incision in the arm...

A third category of the experimental persons was used to maintain the typhus cultures. Those were the so-called passage persons, amounting to three to five persons per month. They were merely infected for the purpose of ensuring a constant supply of fresh blood containing typhus. Very nearly all those persons died. I do not think I am exaggerating if I say that 95 percent of these cases were fatal.

Prosecutor: Witness, do you mean to say that they deliberately infected three to five persons a month with typhus just to have the viruses alive and available in blood?

Witness: Just for that particular purpose.

Prosecutor: Can you tell the Tribunal approximately how many of those persons died who were infected just to keep the viruses alive?

Witness: From the so-called passage persons, as I have already said, between three to five were used per month, that is, when I was working for Dr. Ding-Schuler—every month until the end of the Buchenwald concentration camp. That is to say, from April 1943 until March 1945...

Prosecutor: Now, witness, were experimental persons also infected with lice?

Witness: As far as I know, only one single experiment took place in Buchenwald where an original infection with typhus was performed with lice. The infected lice were brought from the OKH Institute in Krakow by a courier and were taken to Block 46. There they were kept in small cages which were applied to the thighs of the experimental persons, and a number of persons, I do not know how many, were infected.

Some of our comrades let a few lice escape in a room of Block 46, but they kept them under control and reported to the Kapo (inmate trusty Dietzsch) that infected lice had escaped from the cages... Dr. Hoven, following Dietzsch's advice, then ordered the destruction of these infected lice...

Prosecutor: Can you tell the Tribunal whether these experimental subjects suffered to any appreciable extent during the course of these typhus experiments?

Witness: There we must draw a strict dividing line between the general mental condition of such experimental persons and the physical condition caused by this disease. Every man in the camp knew that Block 46 was a dreadful place. Only a very few people in the camp had an exact idea of what was going on in Block 46. A dreadful horror seized anyone who was brought into any kind of connection with this block. If people were selected and taken to Block 46 through the sick bay, then they knew that the affair was a fatal one. The untold horror, which was attached to this block, made things even worse.

Apart from this, it was generally known in the camp that Kapo Arthur Dietzsch exercised iron discipline in Block 46. There the cat-o'-nine-tails really ruled supreme. Everyone, therefore, who went to Block 46 as an experimental person did not only have to expect death, and under certain circumstances a very long drawn out and frightful death, but also torture and the complete removal of the last remnants of personal freedom.

In this mental condition these experimental persons waited in the sick bays for an unknown period of time. They waited for the day or for the night when something would be done to them; they did not know what it would be, but they guessed that it would be some frightful form of death.

If they were vaccinated, then sometimes the most horrible scenes took place, because the patients were afraid the injections were lethal. Kapo Arthur Dietzsch had to restore order with iron discipline.

After a certain period, when the actual illness had set in after the infection, ordinary symptoms of typhus would appear, which, as is well known, is one of the most serious illnesses. The infection, as I have already described to you, became so powerful during the last two and a half years that the typhus almost always appeared in its most horrible form. There were cases of raving madness, delirium, people would refuse to eat, and a large percentage of them would die.

Those who experienced the disease in a milder form, perhaps because their constitutions were stronger or because the vaccine was effective, were forced continuously to observe the death struggles of the others. And all this took place in an atmosphere hardly possible to imagine. Just what happened to those people who survived the typhus was something which they did not know during the period of convalescence. Would they remain in Block 46 to be used for other purposes? Would they be used as assistants? Would they be feared as surviving witnesses of the experiments on human beings and therefore killed? All this was something which they did not know and which aggravated the conditions of these experiments.

Denial Testimony of Dr. Rose

Defendant Dr. Rose was one of the eight defendants convicted of criminal conduct involving typhus experiments; he was later hanged for his crimes. During cross-examination by Prosecutor McHaney, Rose denied several times that he had knowledge of or participated in the typhus experiments until presented with incontrovertible documentation that he had received.

Defendant Gerhard Rose, Brigadier General of the Medical Service of the Air Force

Referring to typhus experiments carried out on Natzweiler concentration camp inmates by Dr. Haagen, Mr. McHaney asked the following question:

Prosecutor McHaney: When did you first learn that Haagen was conducting experiments on concentration camp inmates?

Witness Rose: That Haagen was performing experiments on concentration camp inmates? I don't believe that even today, but I knew that he carried out vaccinations in concentration camps. I cannot remember when I first learned of it—probably in 1943...

Prosecutor: Well, did you know about this sordid occasion when Haagen had eighteen men who had been assigned to him die on transport?

Witness: I never learned anything about that at the time. I found it out from the files. I never knew that prisoners were especially taken to these concentration camps in order to be vaccinated...

After being presented with Document NO-1059, Prosecution Exhibit 490, a letter addressed to Oberstarzt Professor Dr. Rose, Inspectorate of the Medical Service of the Luftwaffe, he was asked to read it aloud:

Dear Herr Rose,
... One hundred persons from a local concentration camp were put at my disposal for immunization and subsequent infection. Unfortunately, these people were in such a poor physical condition that eighteen of them already died during transport; the remainder were likewise in such bad physical shape that they could not be used for inoculation purposes. In the meantime I have requested one hundred additional per-

sons from the SS Main Office, who should, however, be in a normal physical and nutritional condition, so that the experiments can be carried out on *material* [emphasis supplied], which at least approaches the physical condition of our soldiers.

For the time being, we will concentrate on an epidemic culture in the form of a virus, which we have received from Giroud in the meantime. This seems to be a very good culture.

With best regards,

Heil Hitler!

Prosecutor McHaney: I thought you said about two minutes ago that you didn't know of the incident where eighteen of the inmates put at Haagen's disposal had died during transport.

Witness Rose: Yes, that's true. That's what I said. I had forgotten about it. I thought that I had learned it for the first time from the records. If I had remembered it, I would, of course, not have exposed myself by denying it. But now I see this letter...

Another defense put forward was that the victims were volunteers. People do not volunteer to be killed. In one experimental series, some inmates agreed to being experimented on when assured it was harmless and were promised additional food. After the first few experiments, inmates could no longer be deceived. Thereafter, until the fall of 1943, experimental subjects were arbitrarily selected, whether habitual criminals, political prisoners, or homosexuals, including Germans, Poles, Frenchmen, and Russian prisoners of war. Nine thousand five hundred Russian prisoners of war were killed in Buchenwald. Prosecution Exhibit 470 showed that thirty "appropriate Gypsies" were also to be tested.

Prosecution witness and camp inmate Dr. Eugen Kogon testified that defendant Dr. Mrugowsky "systematically selected invalids and

The defendant Gerhard Rose in his cell, at work on his defense material

old persons, especially Frenchmen, who were in the so-called 'little camp' of Buchenwald for the purpose of withdrawing blood to be used in making blood plasma."[5]

When asked whether any of these blood donors in the little camp died from this blood-letting, Kogon replied, "The question shows that it is very difficult to gain a real concept of the 'little camp' at Buchenwald. The people died there in masses. During the night corpses were lying in the blocks naked because they were thrown out of the bunks by the other prisoners so that they would have a little more space. Even the smallest pieces of clothing were torn off by those who wanted to survive. It is impossible to determine if anybody died as the direct and immediate result of the taking of blood, because many people fell and died while walking around in the 'little camp'."[6]

The fact that concentration camp inmates who became subjects in experiments were considered guinea pigs was made clear in the testimony and documents when they were described as *material*. In

207

Prosecution Exhibit 293—a letter from the Natzweiler camp doctor, Dr. Haagen, to Dr. Hirt—Haagen wrote, "...I request, therefore, that you send me one hundred prisoners, between twenty and forty years of age, who are healthy and who are so constituted physically that they furnish comparable *material*." (Emphasis supplied.)

For the past ten years I have known a survivor of this experiment who is one of many Holocaust survivors in the Denver Jewish community. He told me that of the fifty inmates selected for the typhus experiments who originally shared his block at Buchenwald, only seventeen survived, including him. His experience has been recorded in an interview by the Steven Spielberg SHOAH Visual History Foundation.

· 16 ·

Poison Experiments

Death occurred 121, 123, and 129 minutes after entry of the projectile.

—Dr. Mrugowsky

THE EXPERIMENTS WITH poison conducted at Buchenwald and Sachsenhausen concentration camps had no scientific objective to heal or cure, but were used to time how fast death occurred and to observe the pain and agony the poisons inflicted up to the point of death. The German doctors were studying different methods of killing human beings and the length of time these methods took.

In the closing brief against defendent Dr. Mrugowsky, the prosecution stated that "Mrugowsky admitted his participation in these experiments. He defended himself on the ground that he was the legally appointed executioner in this case. Assuming the truth of this absurd statement, it cannot be held legal to torture to death prisoners of war even if they had been validly sentenced to death."[1]

The argument of the defense in its final plea for defendant Mrugowsky was that the use of poisoned Russian bullets "had increased the concern that poisoned bullets would shortly be used at the [Russian] front ... and how much time would be available in case of need to administer antidotes."[2]

In December 1943 the first group of experiments was conducted to determine the fatal dosage of poisons in the alkaloid group—organic basic substances found in plants. The poison was administered to four Russian prisoners of war in their food, without their knowledge. German doctors stood behind a curtain to watch their reactions. All four survived, but were strangled on hooks on the wall in a crematorium of the concentration camp so autopsies could be performed.

Testimony of Dr. Eugen Kogon

The following was extracted from the testimony of camp inmate Dr. Eugen Kogon, a prosecution witness. He was questioned by Prosecutor McHaney.

Prosecutor McHaney: Do you know anything about experiments with poisons in the Buchenwald concentration camp?

Witness Kogon: I know of two such cases. The one case was about the turn of the year 1943-44 or in the late fall of 1943, and the second case was probably in the summer of 1944. In each case Russian prisoners of war were used for these experiments. In the first case various preparations of the so-called alkaloid series were put into noodle soup and administered to four of these prisoners of war who were in Block 46. They, of course, had no idea what was going on. Two of these prisoners became so sick that they vomited, one was unconscious, the fourth showed no symptoms at all. Thereupon, all four were strangled in the crematorium. They were dissected and the contents of their stomachs and other effects were determined...

Prosecutor: Witness, before continuing with the second experiment, I wonder if you could tell the Tribunal the reason why this poison experiment which you have just mentioned was carried out?

Witness: ...In order to determine the fatal dosage of poisons of this type, the SS court ordered an experiment on four Russian prisoners of war. This is the experiment which I have just described in Block 46...at any rate, they went to the crematorium, not to Block 46. The Russian prisoners of war, again, four of them, had been taken there into the cellar with the forty-six hooks on the walls on which the people were strangled. These four Russians were given this poison.

Defendant Joachim Mrugowsky,
Chief Hygienist of the Reich Physician SS

Prosecution Exhibit 290 is a report from Mrugowsky, dated September 12, 1944, describing experiments on five inmates shot with bullets that contained crystallized poison:

> The experimental subjects, in a lying position, were each shot in the upper part of the left thigh. The thighs of two of them were cleanly shot through. Even afterwards, no effect of the poison was to be observed. These two experimental subjects were therefore exempted...
>
> The symptoms of the condemned three showed a surprising similarity. At first no peculiarities appeared. After twenty to twenty-five minutes a motor agitation [movement] and a

slight ptyalism [excretion of saliva] set in, but stopped again. After forty to forty-five minutes a stronger salivation set in. The poisoned persons swallowed repeatedly, but later the flow of saliva became so strong that it could not even be overcome by swallowing. Foamy saliva flowed from their mouths. Then choking and vomiting set in.

After fifty-eight minutes the pulse of two of them could no longer be felt...One of the poisoned persons tried to vomit. To do so he introduced four fingers of his hand up to the knuckles into his throat, but nevertheless could not vomit. His face was flushed.

The other two experimental subjects had already early shown a pale face. The other symptoms were the same. The motor unrest increased so much that the persons flung themselves up and down, rolled their eyes and made meaningless motions with their hands and arms. Finally the agitation subsided, the pupils dilated to the maximum, and the condemned lay motionless. ...Death occurred 121, 123, and 129 minutes after entry of the projectile.

It took up to two hours and nine minutes to kill these people.

Although defendants Genzken, Gebhardt, Mrugowsky, and Poppendick were charged with criminal conduct in this experiment, only Mrugowsky was convicted.

· 17 ·

Incendiary Bomb Experiments

... four experimental subjects from Block 46, who had survived other experiments, had this phosphorus liquid applied
to their forearms. The whole mass was then ignited ...

—inmate doctor Eugen Kogon

DR. DING-SCHULER CONDUCTED the incendiary bomb experiments at
Buchenwald. The purpose of these experiments was to test the effectiveness of a preparation of liquid carbon tetrachloride solvent,
referred to as R-17, and other skin ointments or liquids for combating
wartime injuries and burns caused by incendiary bombs that were
dropped on the battlefield. If successful, these ointments were to be
dispensed at air raid precaution dispensaries for all potential victims
of these bombs.

Between November 19 and 25, 1943, Dr. Ding selected "five
experimental persons [who] were deliberately burned with ignited
phosphorus which was taken from an incendiary bomb. The resulting
burns were very severe, the victims suffered excruciating pain and permanent injury."[1]

Prosecution Exhibit 288 is a report on the findings of January 2,
1944 on a Skin Ointment—R 17—for Phosphorus Burns, from which
the following extract is taken:

19 November. The mixture, which had been applied to a smooth spot of skin on the forearm, was removed with a 2 percent solution of copper sulphate. There appeared a black-ish-brownish, strongly viscous mass with a metallic sheen which, when rubbed off, spread over the entire experimentation area. After an initial formation of black smoke (phosphorus fumes) and a strong glow, the phosphorescence, because of the formation of a copper-phosphate coating, ceased almost immediately.[2]

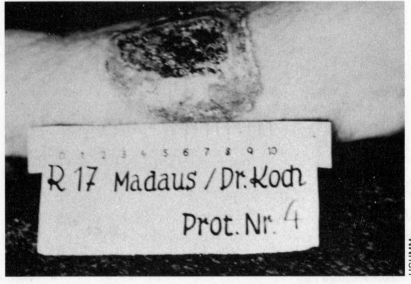

Phosphorus burn inflicted on an inmate of the Buchenwald concentration camp. Document NO-579. Prosecution exhibit 288.

On November 25 a phosphorus mixture was applied to the skin of an inmate and immediately ignited. After burning for twenty seconds, it was extinguished with water and wiped off with the liquid carbon tetrachloride solvent, R-17.

In another experiment on November 25 the mixture was applied to a skin area and immediately ignited. It burned for fifty-five seconds until it went out by itself, then was wiped off with R-17.

Other tests were done in which burning was allowed for thirty seconds, forty seconds, and sixty seconds. In each case the fire went out by itself.

On November 25 the phosphorus mixture was applied to a piece of cloth covering the skin and then ignited. "Sixty-seven seconds elapsed before it had burned itself out. The piece of cloth, except for a small remainder, was carbonized."[3]

In each of these cases, after treatment with carbon tetrachloride and other healing ointments—including a cod liver oil ointment— swelling, blisters, and scabs occurred. It took up to six weeks for healing to occur in these experiments.

Testimony of Dr. Eugen Kogon

The following is an extract from the testimony of prosecution witness Eugen Kogon under direct examination by Mr. McHaney.

Answering a question that Mr. McHaney had asked, Kogon replied:

Witness Kogon: By way of Obersturmbannfuehrer Dr. Koch and the higher police leader of the Dresden sector, the contents of phosphorus incendiary bombs were sent to Buchenwald, and four experimental subjects from Block 46, who had survived other experiments, had this phosphorus liquid applied to their forearms. The whole mass was then ignited and was then treated in various manners.

Prosecutor McHaney: Witness, did you see any of the experimental subjects who were burned with this phosphorus?

Witness: I personally saw all the experimental subjects because this experiment was carried out in the private room of Dr. Ding in Block 50 and in the library of the Hygiene Institute in Block 50. The reason for this was that the experiment in Block 46 among the experimental subjects that were located there, and who were destined for other purposes, would have caused far too much excitement.

Prosecutor: Were these burns very severe?

Witness: As far as I can recall they were very severe in three out of the four cases.

Prosecutor: Did the experimental subjects suffer any pain?

Witness: Kapo Arthur Dietzsch had suggested that the subjects should be given an anesthetic as soon as they came into Block 50, so that violent scenes could be avoided, and in Block 50, which was completely different from Block 46, having persons handcuffed, as was the common practice in Block 46, was to be avoided...

Prosecutor: Do you know whether the injuries which they received are permanent?

Witness: In the case of some of the wounds, it is completely impossible that they will ever become completely healed; very deep scars must have remained because the wounds were big and were as deep as two or two and a half centimeters.

Prosecutor: Do you know whether any of the experimental subjects died?

Witness: Four persons were returned to Block 46, and I do not know anything about the future fate which awaited them there. I especially do not know if they were used for further experiments.

Prosecutor: Do you know the nationality of the experimental persons used?

Witness: No. However, all four wore the green triangle to signify that they were habitual criminals, and they were Germans.

Defendant Dr. Mrugowsky in his testimony stated:

When, after a considerable time I still had not heard from the Reich Physician whether the drug R-17 was to be made known to the air-raid precaution dispensaries, I asked the Reich Physician about it at a meeting. He then declared that the drug would not be introduced, as it only possessed phosphorus-dissolving properties, but did not directly contribute to the healing of the burns.[4]

Although defendants Genzken, Gebhardt, Mrugowsky, and Poppendick were charged with special responsibility for and participation in criminal conduct involving incendiary bomb experiments, all were acquitted.

Phlegmon, Polygal, and Phenol Experiments

The total number of traitors killed was about 150, of whom 60 were killed by phenol injections, either by myself or under my supervision in the camp hospital, and the rest were killed by various means, such as beatings, by the inmates.

—defendant Dr. Hoven

THE THREE TYPES of experiments described in this chapter—phlegmon, polygal, and phenol—were not specifically described in paragraph six of the indictment. The prosecution, however, introduced evidence calculated to show that inhumane acts and atrocities as generally alleged in paragraph six were committed in the course of these experiments.

Phlegmon (Inflammation and Infection) Experiments

Simulating battlefield injuries and surgery, experiments with inflammation and infection were conducted in the fall of 1942 at Dachau and Auschwitz. The concentration camp inmates were artificially infected with pus, a procedure that inflicted horrible pain. Half received biochemical treatments, and half were treated with sulfanil-amide. The seriously ill cases refused to take the biochemical tablets because they were required to take them every five minutes all day and all night long, a torturous treatment regimen.

One set of studies used twenty German inmates, of whom seven died. In a second series, forty clergymen of various nationalities were infected, and twelve died.[1]

Testimony of Heinrich W. Stoehr

Prosecution witness Heinrich W. Stoehr, an inmate nurse at Dachau concentration camp, testified on December 17, 1946.

Prosecutor Hardy: Witness, did you ever hear of the sepsis [infection] or phlegmon [inflammation] experiments at the Dachau concentration camp?

Witness Stoehr: Yes these experiments were conducted at my station.

Prosecutor: Witness, will you kindly explain to the Tribunal in what manner these phlegmon experiments were conducted. That is, the details of the experiments? What did they do to the victim?

Witness: Mainly, phlegmon was treated. It was very general in the camp. That is to say, phlegmon was the typical camp disease. The biochemical treatment was carried out in the following manner: Three similar cases were observed. One of these cases was given *allopathic treatment,*[2] another biochemical, and the third one received only ordinary surgical treatment. That is, the third one received no drugs whatsoever, and the wound was treated in an ordinary way with bandages, and so on. These were the directives of the physicians who were there. We saw on many occasions that the patient was cured much faster who received no drugs or injections.

Experiments of that kind were conducted for many weeks, and if I may as a layman make a judgment, I must say that the physicians, according to my observations, were not satisfied with these experiments.

In addition, I have to emphasize that not only wounds were treated according to these methods, but internal diseases, too. They tried to find out whether biochemical treatment was suitable for treating the thirst for water, which was so frequent in the camp. We saw that the biochemical drugs had no influence whatsoever as to the cause of this illness.

During the fall, this Dr. Schuetz told the camp doctor, who was named Babo, to infect a number of people with pus. We nurses were told nothing about that, and we did not know the purpose. These experiments were conducted on a group of men, and they extended over a period of approximately six to seven weeks.

First, a group of Germans were infected with pus. We nurses had no idea of the cause of the illness, and we gave the patients the drugs that were ordered by the physicians. I emphasize again that half of these people received allopathic and the other half biochemical treatment.

As nurses, we could observe the following facts: the patients who received allopathic treatment were cured much quicker, that is, if they had any power of resistance to their illness, but the patients who had to take those pathological tablets, if I remember correctly, died with the exception of one person. There were approximately ten persons who, at that time, were infected.

The second group consisted of forty clergymen of all nationalities and brothers of religious fraternities. These patients were selected from the block where the clergymen were housed. They were selected by the Chief Physician Dr. Walda and were sent to the operational room of the concentration camp Dachau. They were operated on by Dr. Schuetz and Dr. Kieselwecker, and these experiments were conducted on them. A number of nurses, and also the personnel of the operating room, and I myself, saw how the injections were made. We were standing in the anteroom of the operating room.

Prosecutor: Witness, will you explain to the Tribunal what the word "phlegmon" means?

Witness: Phlegmon, as far as a layman can answer that question, means an inflammation of the tissues, and in the camp of Dachau phlegmons were very numerous because the people there were mostly sent to the hospital too late. Typical camp phlegmons, as far as I know, are caused by germs. Persons got phlegmons who suffered from lack of water.

Prosecutor: Witness, did you say that inmates were used for experiments in which they were injected with pus?

Witness: Yes.

Prosecutor: Did you see these injections of pus being administered?

Witness: Yes.

Prosecutor: How were the inmates to be used for these experiments selected? In what manner did they select the inmates to be used for these experiments, which dealt with the injection of pus? In other words, how were they selected? What type of prisoners? What were their nationalities, etc.?

Witness: They were forty persons coming from the so-called clergymen block.

Prosecutor: Were these inmates used for these experiments with injection of pus healthy inmates?

Witness: Completely healthy and strong men.

Prosecutor: You have told us that they had one group, the first group, of ten Germans. How many died in that group?

Witness: I believe that the first group consisted of ten people of whom, as far as I remember, seven died.

Prosecutor: Now, you have told us of a second group of forty clergymen. How many died in that group?

Witness: I have seen a list of the survivors, and according to that list, twelve clergymen or rather brothers must have died.

Prosecutor: Were the victims used in these experiments treated by medical doctors after they had been injected with pus?

Witness: The operation was done by physicians.

Prosecutor: Well, after they had been infected with pus, what kind of treatment was given to them?

Witness: After the injection, Sturmbannfuehrer Schuetz gave instructions to the nurses that one-half of them should receive allopathic and the other half biological treatment. I emphasize that the group which received allopathic treatment had special drugs, the so-called sulfanilamide drugs. We had the impression that the physicians wanted to prove that the biological drugs were not suitable to cure such a severe disease.

Prosecutor: Then you say, witness, that 50 percent were treated with sulfanilamide and the other 50 percent with biological medicants?

Witness: Yes.

Prosecutor: Now, after these injections with pus, did abscesses develop on the inmate?

Witness: The greater part of those who were treated biologically, or rather, all of them, developed abscesses and very deep abscesses. Some of the persons who received allopathic and prophylactic treatment with sulfanilamide had no abscesses.

Prosecutor: Did the inmates who endured this treatment suffer pain?

Witness: Yes.

Prosecutor: Severe pain?

Witness: As far as I know, the pain was very severe.

On this charge defendants Poppendick, Oberheuser, and Fischer were acquitted. Defendant Gebhardt claimed, "I did not have any previous knowledge of these experiments," when questioned by his counsel. However, he was found guilty on counts 2 (war crimes), 3 (crimes against humanity), and 4 (membership in the SS) of the indictment charging his involvement with not only the phlegmon experiments, but all twelve experiments already described. He was sentenced to death by hanging.

Polygal (Blood Coagulant) Experiments

Polygal (blood coagulant) experiments were not specifically described in the indictment with the first twelve major experiments. Carried out by the infamous Dr. Sigmund Rascher on Dachau concentration camp inmates who were shot with bullets, these murderous experiments were conducted to test the effectiveness of polygal, which acts as a quick blood coagulant.

Affidavit of Dr. Fritz Friedrich Karl Rascher

Prosecution Exhibit 462 is an affidavit of Dr. Fritz Friedrich Karl Rascher, the uncle of Dr. Sigmund Rascher, taken on December 31, 1946. In it, the prosecution argued that in August 1943 Dr. Fritz Rascher visited his nephew Dr. Sigmund Rascher in Dachau, and while Sigmund was away from his office, Dr. Fritz Rascher saw a report that he described as follows:

It refers to a report about the shooting (execution) of four people for the purpose of experimenting with the hemostatic preparation "polygal 10." As far as I remember they were a Russian commissar and a Cretin; I do not remember who the other two were. The Russian was shot in the right shoulder from above by an SS man who stood on a chair. The bullet emerged near the spleen. It was described how the Russian twitched convulsively, then sat down on a chair and died after about twenty minutes.

In the dissection protocol the rupture of the pulmonary vessels and the aorta was described. It was further described that the ruptures were tamponed [plugged] by hard blood clots. That could have been the only explanation for the comparatively long span of life after the shot. After reading this first protocol I was so shocked that I did not read the others.

At the end of 1943 or beginning of 1944 I received a letter from my nephew, in which he informed me that he and his wife had been arrested because of illegal adoption (and registration) of a child.

Since this occurrence in 1943 or 1944 I have not heard from either Dr. Sigmund Rascher or his wife. Only in 1946 I learned from various people that my nephew had been shot in Dachau before the arrival of the Americans and that his wife had been hanged at Ravensbrueck or Berlin on orders of Himmler."[3]

Prosecution Exhibit 247 described the administration of polygal after amputation of the thigh of a forty-year-old male "patient" by

Dachau concentration camp physician Dr. Kahr: "As regards the effectiveness of polygal, one can say that it was absolutely evident how little the tissues bled. ... The effectiveness of "polygal" must in this case be described as complete."[4]

It is interesting to note that this inmate victim was described by the Dachau physician as a *patient*, since the experimental subject was usually referred to as a *Versuchsperson, experimental person, subject,* or *material.*

Prosecution Exhibit 221 is an affidavit of Oswald Pohl. He said:

Sievers told me the following: Ahnenerbe, of which Sievers was manager, was developing a drug in Dachau, by order of Himmler, which had as its result the quick coagulation of blood. He said that it was very important for fighting units because it prevented their bleeding to death. The experiments in Dachau, during which one inmate was shot at, have proved these results."[5]

On this charge only Sievers was convicted. On counts 2 (war crimes), 3 (crimes against humanity), and 4 (membership in the SS) of the indictment, Sievers was found guilty and sentenced to death by hanging.

Phenol (Gas Oedema) Experiments

This was the third group of experiments not specifically set forth in the indictment but that were prosecuted because of evidence that brought out the commission of inhumane acts and atrocities.

The purpose of this experiment was to test the tolerance of serum containing phenol on gas-gangrene-wounded soldiers. The effort was made in concentration camps and in the army to discover protective means to combat gas gangrene.

Phenol is a strong corrosive poison and its watery solution, carbolic acid, is used as an antiseptic. Phenol injections also became a medical method of direct mass killing in the euthanasia program, with no scientific objective to heal or cure, but rather to "heal" the health of the German *Volk* by eradicating all "subhuman elements." These were loosely categorized as the Jews, Gypsies, and Slavs—"life unworthy of life"—the visibly sick or diseased, retarded, feeble-minded, epileptics, the mentally ill, blind, and deformed—and the "undesirables"—criminals, homosexuals, alcoholics, and other categories.

Defendant Dr. Mrugowsky testified in March 1947 that "no infection can be taken so seriously in the surgical field as the infection by gas gangrene, since the mortality cases of these injuries were very high."[6]

Prosecution Exhibit 473 is a report from Grawitz to Himmler on gas gangrene experiments, dated September 7, 1942, which includes a report by defendant Dr. Gebhardt on his clinical surgical experiments at the women's concentration camp, Ravensbrueck. He appointed defendant Dr. Fischer as a coworker, who got cooperation from defendant Dr. Mrugowsky and defendant Dr. Oberheuser.

After the doctors cut into muscle tissue, they implanted bacterial cultures on the damaged tissue. In the first series of experiments, the prisoners were inoculated with staphylococci and streptococci. Then wood shavings were added.

Affidavit of Defendant Dr. Hoven

In Prosecution Exhibit 281, defendant Dr. Hoven testified on October 24, 1946, as chief physician at Buchenwald:

> In some instances I supervised the killing of these unworthy inmates by injections of phenol at the request of the inmates. These killings took place in the camp hospital, and I was assisted by several inmates. On one occasion Dr. Ding came to the hospital to witness such killings with phenol and said that I was not doing it correctly, therefore, he performed some of the injections himself. At that time three inmates were killed with phenol injections, and they died within a minute.
>
> The total number of traitors killed was about 150, of whom 60 were killed by phenol injections, either by myself or

under my supervision in the camp hospital, and the rest were killed by various means, such as beatings, by the inmates.[7]

The beatings that Dr. Hoven referred to occurred because some prisoners received preferential treatment. Inmates who were given key positions in the camp, usually because they had been imprisoned for something other than "political" reasons, were often able to get better living conditions. This caused jealousy on the part of the less-favored prisoners, which led to retaliation, including killings. Such behavior was common in the concentration camps. Hoven uses the word "traitor" to imply that the experimental subjects were political prisoners.

Defendant Waldemar Hoven,
Chief Doctor, Buchenwald concentration camp

Testimony of Dr. Ding-Schuler

Prosecution Exhibit 283 is a sworn statement by Dr. Erwin Schuler—the infamous "Dr. Ding." As a witness of euthanasia with undiluted raw phenol at Buchenwald, he stated:

One by one, four or five prisoners were led in. The upper part of the body was naked so that their nationality patch (on their clothing) could not be distinguished. The condition of their bodies was bad and their age was advanced. I do not remember a diagnosis as to why euthanasia was to take place, but probably I did not ask about it either.

They sat down quietly on a chair, that is, without any sign of excitement, near a light. A male nurse blocked the vein in the arm, and Dr. Hoven quickly injected the phenol. They died in an immediate total convulsion during the actual injection without any sign of other pain. The time between the beginning of the injection and death I estimate at about one-half second. The rest of the dose was injected as a precautionary measure, although part of the injection would have been enough for the fatal result. (I estimate five cc.)

The dead were carried into an adjoining room by the nurses—I estimate the time of my presence at ten minutes.[8]

For euthanasia by phenol, defendants Mrugowsky and Hoven were convicted; Handloser was acquitted.

In the euthanasia program to be described later, during the pure killing process, whole wards of people were killed by phenol injections. The number killed in this manner totaled over twenty thousand.

· 19 ·

Jewish Skeleton Collection

Following the subsequently induced death of the Jew, whose head should not be damaged, the delegate will separate the head from the body and will forward it to its proper point of destination in a hermetically sealed tin can, especially produced for this purpose and filled with a conserving fluid.

–Dr. Hirt

DEFENDANTS RUDOLF BRANDT and Wolfram Sievers were charged in the indictment and convicted of possibly the most revolting crimes—murdering civilians and members of the armed forces who were from nations at war with Germany. More specifically, they were charged with the murder of 112 Jews to complete a skeleton collection for the Reich University at Strasbourg, France, during its Nazi occupation. This murderous action took place in the Natzweiler camp.

Prosecution Exhibit 175 is a report by Dr. Hirt sent by Sievers in February 1942 to Rudolf Brandt in which Hirt stated:

We have a nearly complete collection of skulls of all races and peoples at our disposal. Only very few specimens of skulls of the Jewish race, however, are available with the result that it is impossible to arrive at precise conclusions from examining them. The war in the East [with Russia] now presents us with the opportunity to overcome this deficiency.

By procuring the skulls of the Jewish-Bolshevik Commissars, who represent the prototype of the *repulsive, but characteristic subhuman,*[1] we have the chance now to obtain a palpable, scientific document.

The best practical method for obtaining and collecting this skull material could be handled by directing the Wehrmacht [army] to turn over alive all captured Jewish-Bolshevik Commissars to the Field Police.

The special deputy who will be in charge of securing the "material" has the job of taking a series of previously established photographs, anthropological measurements, and in addition has to determine, as far as possible, the background, date of birth, and other personal data of the prisoner. Following the subsequently induced death of the Jew, whose head should not be damaged, the delegate will separate the head from the body and will forward it to its proper point of destination in a hermetically sealed tin can, especially produced for this purpose and filled with a conserving fluid.

Having arrived at the laboratory, the comparison tests and anatomical research on the skull, as well as determination of the race membership of pathological features of the skull form, the form and size of the brain, etc., can proceed. The basis of these studies will be the photos, measurements, and other data supplied on the head, and finally the tests of the skull itself.[2]

Thereafter Himmler, Sievers, and Rudolf Brandt decided to procure the skulls from Auschwitz concentration camp inmates instead of from Jews killed in battle in Russia. Sievers wrote in June 1943, "Altogether 115 persons were worked on, seventy-nine were Jews, thirty were Jewesses, two were Poles, and four were Asiatics."[3]

The corpses of these Jews were sent to Strasbourg. After a year, the Allied armies were nearing Strasbourg where this monstrous exhibit of the culture of the master race reposed. Sievers was so alarmed about the advancing Allied armies that he sent a telegram to Rudolf Brandt in September 1944 that read, "Professor Dr. Hirt has assembled a skeleton collection which has never been in existence before. Because of the vast amount of scientific research that is connected with this project, the job of reducing the corpses to skeletons has not yet been completed...The collection can be defleshed and rendered unrecognizable."[4]

Defendant Wolfram Sievers,
Reich Manager of the Ahnenerbe Society

Dr. Hirt then ordered two assistants to cut up the eighty-six corpses and have them cremated, but the job was too enormous for only two men. The evidence of these deliberate murders and ghastly defleshing could not be destroyed completely. "The pictures of these corpses and of the gas chambers in the Natzweiler concentration camp, where the victims of the Jewish skeleton collection were murdered, taken by the French authorities after the liberation of Strasbourg, tell the grim story of this mass murder more vividly than witnesses and documents ever could."[5]

· 20 ·

Euthanasia

The dead were still standing like stone statues, there having
been no room for them to fall or bend over.

—Waffen *SS* member Kurt Gerstein

HITLER GAVE DEFENDANT Dr. Karl Brandt, on September 1, 1939, the
responsibility to execute a euthanasia program by "enlarging the
authority of certain physicians to be designated by name in such a
manner that persons who, according to human judgment, are incurable can, upon a most careful diagnosis of their condition of sickness,
be accorded a mercy death."[1] This included anyone who might arbitrarily be designated "incurable."

A special department was established to kill children with mental
and physical deficiencies. Previous consultation with parents or relatives about the killing of these children did not take place. That the
child was going to be killed was categorized as *Top Secret*. Half-
Jewish, healthy children were among the estimated five thousand who
were killed.

Concentration camp inmates no longer able to work were selected for extermination by gas. Prosecution Exhibit 411 covered Jews
who were termed "habitual criminals," "shirkers," or those who
"defiled the race." They were selected for extermination. German and
Polish Jews, Polish and Russian nationals, and other non-German

nationals were euthanized.[2] Murdering concentration camp inmates pursuant to euthanasia began as early as autumn 1939.

The Reich Ministry of the Interior sent questionnaires to every German mental institution to be completed for each inmate of the institution and sent back to the Reich Ministry. Questionnaires had a space provided for "race," defined as German or of German blood, Jew, mixed breed Grades 1 or 2, or Negro (mixed breed).[3] Three experts examined the questionnaires and sent their individual medical opinions to the Reich Labor Association. Adult Gypsies were killed.[4] Dr. Brandt exempted the war-wounded and persons who became insane as a result of air attacks. The patients judged to be subject to euthanasia were sent to collecting points and then to euthanasia stations.

Patients in nursing homes, asylums, and hospitals who were aged, insane, or who had arteriosclerosis, tuberculosis, cancer, or other disabling illnesses were termed "useless eaters." People who no longer had any value to the state were to be accorded a "mercy death" by starvation.[5]

"It was pointed out that during the war healthy people had to give up their lives while these severely ill people continued to live, and would continue to live, unless euthanasia was carried out."[6] With a shortage of food and nursing personnel, it was considered justified to eliminate these people.

The position of defendant Karl Brandt in his closing brief to the court was, "The aim of euthanasia was to solve an old medical problem."[7] The elimination of "useless eaters" was the principal rationale of the whole program.

An affidavit from Rueggeberg (Karl Brandt Exhibit 16), reported a radio interview by London radio commentator Robert Graham with Pastor Bodelschwingh, chief of the mental institutions of Bethel, in the summer of 1945 after the war. Bodelschwingh declared that one should not consider Karl Brandt a criminal, but, ironically, an *idealist*.

Hitler had directed Adolf Eichmann to exterminate Jews unable to work in the East. A special section in the Gestapo, headed by Adolf Eichmann, was formed pursuant to the plans made in the summer of

1941 for the Final Solution of the Jewish Question in Europe. According to Eichmann, "the policy pursued resulted in the killing of six million Jews, of which four million were killed in the extermination institutions."[8]

"The doctors who performed euthanasia were warned that they would be severely punished if they sabotaged the work."[9] To avoid unrest among the population, "the whole program of euthanasia was to be kept secret."[10] It was estimated by the Czechoslovak War Crimes Commission that at least 275,000 aged, insane, and incurable people, and those unfriendly to the Nazi regime were killed in nursing homes, hospitals, and asylums.

Defendants Karl Brandt and Brack admitted that about fifty to sixty thousand people were killed in the euthanasia program in Germany and Austria alone.

Since the end of World War II in 1945, "German and Austrian courts have repeatedly held that the killing of persons of *any* nationality under the guise of euthanasia was in violation of the German Criminal Code and punishable as murder."[11]

Witnesses Walter Schmidt and Dr. Mennecke, who testified before the Tribunal, were convicted by a German court for their participation in the euthanasia program and sentenced to life imprisonment and death, respectively.[12] "Thus, it is established that euthanasia was murder according to German law."[13]

The Court of Assizes in Berlin, at the session on March 25, 1946, found the defendants Hilde Wernicke and Helene Wieczorek guilty of murder and sentenced them to death. This was ten months after the war ended.

Protest by the Bishop of Limburg

Prosecution Exhibit 246 is a letter, dated August 13, 1941, from Dr. Hilfrich, Bishop of Limburg, to the Reich Minister of Justice in Berlin protesting against the killing of mentally ill people. The bishop, realizing that this slaughter would be the downfall of the Third Reich, wrote:

About eight kilometers from Limburg in the little town of Hadamar, on a hill overlooking the town, there is an institution which had formerly served various purposes and of late had been used as a nursing home. This institution was renovated and furnished as a place in which, by consensus of opinion, the above mentioned euthanasia has been systematically practiced for months—approximately since February 1941...

Several times a week buses arrive in Hadamar with a considerable number of such victims. School children of the vicinity know this vehicle and say "There comes the murder-box again." After the arrival of the vehicle, the citizens of Hadamar watch the smoke rise out of the chimney and are tortured with the ever present thought of depending on the direction of the wind.

The effect of the principles at work here are that children call each other names and say, "You're crazy; you'll be sent to the baking oven in Hadamar." Those who do not want to marry, or find no opportunity, say, "Marry, never! Bring children into the world so they can be put into the bottling machine! When the feeble-minded have been finished off, the next useless eaters whose turn will come are the old people."

All God-fearing men consider this destruction of helpless beings a crass injustice. And if anybody says that Germany cannot win the war, if there is yet a just God, these expressions are not the result of a lack of love for the Fatherland but of a deep concern for our people...High authority as a moral concept has suffered a severe shock as a result of these happenings... I beg you most humbly, Herr Reich Minister, in the sense of the report of the Episcopate of 16 July of this year, to prevent further transgressions of the Fifth Commandment of God.

Prosecution Exhibit 428

The following is an extract taken from the field interrogation of Waffen SS member Kurt Gerstein, on April 26, 1945, describing the mass gassing of Jews and other "undesirables." The deposition of Kurt Gerstein began:

Hearing of the massacres of idiots and insane people at Grafeneck, Hadamar, etc., shocked and greatly affected me, having such a case in my family. I had but one desire—to gain an insight into this whole machinery and then to shout it to the whole world! With the help of two references written by the two Gestapo employees who had dealt with my case, it was not difficult for me to enter the Waffen SS...

In January, 1942, I was appointed chief of the technical branch dealing with strong poison gases for disinfection. On June 8, 1942, SS Sturmbannfuehrer Guenther of the RSHA entered my office. He was in plain clothes and I did not know him. He ordered me to get a hundred kilograms of prussic acid and to accompany him to a place which was only known to the driver of the truck. We left for the potassium factory near Collin (Prague). Once the truck was loaded, we left for Lublin (Poland). We took with us Professor Pfannenstiel, Professor for Hygiene at the University of Marburg on the Lahn. At Lublin, we were received by SS Gruppenfuehrer Globocnik. He told us, "This is one of the most secret matters there are, even the most secret. Whoever talks of this shall be shot immediately. Yesterday, two talkative men died." Then he explained to us that at the present moment—August 17, 1942—there were four installations: 1. Belcec, on the Lublin-Lvov road, in the sector of the Russian demarcation line. Maximum fifteen thousand persons a day. Seen! 2. Sobiber, I do not know exactly where it is located. Not seen. Twenty thousand persons per day. 3. Treblinka, 120 kilometers NNE of Warsaw. Twenty-five thousand persons per day. Seen! 4. Maidanek, near Lublin. Seen—in the state of preparation.

Globocnik then said, "You will have to handle the sterilization of very large quantities of clothes, ten or twenty times the amount of the clothing and textile collection, which is only arranged in order to conceal the source of these Jewish,

Polish, Czech, and other clothes. Your other duties will be to change the method of our gas chambers (which are run at the present time with the exhaust gases of an old Diesel engine), using more poisonous material, having a quicker effect: prussic acid. But the Führer and Himmler, who were here on August 15, the day before yesterday, ordered that I personally should accompany all those who are to see the installations."

Then Professor Pfannenstiel asked, "What does the Führer say?" Then Globocnik, now Chief of Police and SS, from the Adriatic Riviera to Trieste, answered: "Quicker, quicker! Carry out the whole program!" And then Dr. Herbert Linden, Ministerial-director in the Ministry of the Interior said: "But would it not be better to burn the bodies instead of burying them? A future generation might think differently of these matters!" Globocnik replied, "But, gentlemen, if after us such a cowardly and rotten generation should arise that it does not understand our work which is so good and so necessary, then, gentlemen, all National Socialism will have been for nothing. On the contrary, bronze plaques should be put up with the inscription that it was we, we who had the courage to achieve this gigantic task. And Hitler said, 'Yes, my good Globocnik, that is the word, that is my opinion, too.'"

The next day we left for Belcec, a small special station of two platforms against a hill of yellow sand, immediately to the north of the Lublin-Lvov road and railway. To the south, near the road were some service houses with a signboard, "Belcec, Service Center of the Waffen SS." Globocnik introduced me to SS Hauptsturmfuehrer Obermeyer from Pirmasens, who with great restraint, showed me the installations. No dead were to be seen that day but the smell of the whole region, even from the main road, was pestilential. Next to the small station there was a large barrack marked "Cloakroom," and a door marked "Valuables." Next to that, a chamber with a hundred barber's chairs. Then came a corridor, 150 meters long, in the open air and with barbed wire on both sides. There was a signboard "To the baths and inhalations!" Before us we saw a house, like a bathhouse, with concrete troughs to the right and left containing geraniums or other flowers. After climbing a small staircase, we came to three garage-like rooms on each side, 4 x 5 meters in size and 1.90 meters high. At the back were invisible wooden doors. On the roof was a Star of David made out of copper. At the entrance to the building was the inscription, "Heckenholt Foundation." That was all I noticed on that particular afternoon.

Next morning, a few minutes before seven, I was informed that in ten minutes the first train would arrive. And indeed, a few minutes later the first train came in from Lemberg (Lvov); forty-five cars containing 6,700 persons, 1,450 of whom were already dead on arrival. Behind the little barbed-wire openings were children, yellow, half scared to death, women, and men. The train stopped; 200 Ukrainians, forced to do this work, opened the doors and drove all the people out of the coaches with leather whips. Then, through a huge loudspeaker, instructions were given to them to undress completely and to hand over false teeth and glasses—some in the barracks, others right in the open air. Shoes were to be tied together with a little piece of string handed to everyone by a small Jewish boy of four years of age; all valuables and money were to be handed in at the window marked "Valuables," without receipt. Then the women and girls were to go to the hairdresser who cut off their hair in one or two strokes, after which it vanished into huge potato bags "to be used for special submarine equipment, door mats, etc.," as the SS. Unterscharfuehrer on duty told me.

Then the march began. To the right and left, barbed wire; behind, two dozen Ukrainians with guns. Led by a young girl of striking beauty, they approached. With Police Captain Wirth, I stood right in front of the death chambers. Completely naked, they marched by, men, women, girls, children, babies, even one-legged persons, all of them naked. In one corner, a strong SS man told the poor devils in a strong deep voice, "Nothing whatever will happen to you. All you have to do is to breathe deeply; it strengthens the lungs. This inhalation is a necessary measure against contagious diseases; it is a very good disinfectant!" Asked what was to become of them, he answered, "Well, of course the men will have to work, building streets and houses. But the women do not have to. If they wish, they can help in the house or the kitchen." Once more, a little bit of hope for some of these poor people, enough to make them march on without resistance to the death chambers.

Most of them, though, knew everything; the smell had given them a clear indication of their fate. And then they walked up the little staircase—and behold the picture: mothers with babies at their breasts, naked, lots of children of all ages, naked too; they hesitate, but they enter the gas chambers, most of them without a word, pushed by the others behind them, chased by the whips of the SS men. A Jewess of about forty years of age, with eyes like torches, calls down the blood of her children on the heads of their murderers. Five lashes in her face, dealt by the whip of Police Captain Wirth himself, drive her into the gas chamber. Many of them say their prayers; others ask, "Who will give us the water for our death?" Within the chambers, the SS press the people closely together; Captain Wirth had ordered "Fill them up full." Naked men stand on the feet of the others. Seven to eight hundred crushed together on twenty-five square meters, in forty-five cubic meters! The doors are closed!

Meanwhile the rest of the transport, all naked, waited. Somebody said to me, "Naked, in winter! Enough to kill them!" The answer was, "Well, that's just what they are here for!" And at that moment I understood why it was called the Heckenholt Foundation. Heckenholt was the man in charge of the Diesel engine, the exhaust gases of which were to kill these poor devils. SS Unterscharfuehrer Heckenholt tried to set the Diesel engine going, but it would not start! Captain Wirth came along. It was obvious that he was afraid because

I was a witness of this breakdown. Yes, indeed, I saw everything and waited. Everything was registered by my stop
watch. Fifty minutes—seventy minutes—the Diesel engine
did not start! The people waited in their gas chambers—in
vain. One could hear them cry. "Just as in a synagogue,' says
SS Sturmbannfuehrer Professor Dr. Pfannenstiel, Professor
for Public Health at the University of Marburg/Lahn, holding
his ear close to the wooden door! Captain Wirth, furious,
dealt the Ukrainian who was helping Heckenholt eleven or
twelve lashes in the face with his whip. After two hours and
forty-nine minutes—as registered by my stopwatch—the
Diesel engine started. Up to that moment the people in the
four chambers already filled were still alive—four times 750
persons in four times forty-five cubic meters! Another twenty-
five minutes went by. Many of the people, it is true, were dead
by that time. One could see that through the little window as
the electric lamp revealed for a moment the inside of the
chamber. After twenty-eight minutes only a few were alive.
After thirty-two minutes all were dead!

From the other side, Jewish workers opened the wooden
doors. In return for their terrible job, they had been promised
their freedom and a small percentage of the valuables and the
money found. The dead were still standing like stone statues,
there having been no room for them to fall or bend over.
Though dead, the families could still be recognized, their
hands still clasped. It was difficult to separate them in order to
clear the chamber for the next load. The bodies were thrown
out blue, wet with sweat and urine, the legs covered with
excrement and menstrual blood. Everywhere among the others were the bodies of babies and children.

But there is no time! Two dozen workers were busy check-
ing the mouths, opening them with iron hooks—"Gold on the
left, no gold on the right!" Others checked anus and genitals
to look for money, diamonds, gold, etc. Dentists with chisels
tore out gold teeth, bridges, or caps.

Dachau concentration camp

Crematorium at Dachau, containing bones of inmates

Inmates at Dachua concentration camp

Corpses of inmates killed at Dachau

Photos by Edwin Gorak

In the center of everything was Captain Wirth. He was on familiar ground here. He handed me a large tin full of teeth and said: "Estimate for yourself the weight of gold! This is only from yesterday and the day before! And you would not believe what we find here every day! Dollars, diamonds, gold! But look for yourself!"

Then he led me to a jeweler who was in charge of all these valuables. After that they took me to one of the managers of the big store, Kaufhaus des Westens, in Berlin, and to a little man whom they made play the violin. Both were chiefs of the Jewish worker units. "He is a captain of the Royal and Imperial Austrian Army, and has the German Iron Cross First Class," I was told by Hauptsturmbannfuehrer Obermeyer.

The bodies were then thrown into large ditches about 100 x 20 x 12 meters located near the gas chambers. After a few days the bodies would swell up and the whole contents of the ditch would rise 2 to 3 meters high because of the gases which developed inside the bodies. After a few more days the swelling would stop and the bodies would collapse. The next day the ditches were filled again, and covered with 10 centimeters of sand. A little later, I heard, they constructed grills out of rails and burned the bodies on them with Diesel oil and gasoline in order to make them disappear.

At Belcec and Treblinka nobody bothered to take anything approaching an exact count of the persons killed. Actually, not only Jews, but also many Poles and Czechs, who, in the opinion of the Nazis, were of bad stock, were killed. Most of them died anonymously.

Commissions of so-called doctors, who were actually nothing but young SS men in white coats, rode in limousines through the towns and villages of Poland and Czechoslovakia to select the old, tubercular, and sick people and have them done away with shortly afterwards in the gas chambers. They were the Poles and Czechs of category no. III, who did not deserve to live because they were unable to work.

Police Captain Wirth asked me not to propose any other kind of gas chamber in Berlin, but to leave everything the way it was. I lied—as I did in each case all the time—and said that the prussic acid had already deteriorated in shipping and had become very dangerous, that I was therefore obliged to bury it. This was done right away.

The next day, Captain Wirth's car took us to Treblinka, about seventy-five miles NNE of Warsaw. The installations of this death center scarcely differed from those at Belcec, but they were even larger. There were eight gas chambers and whole mountains of clothes and underwear about thirty-five to forty meters high. Then a banquet was given in our "honor," attended by all the employees of the institution.

The Obersturmbannfuhrer, Professor Pfannenstiel, Hygiene Professor at the University of Marburg/Lahn, made a speech. "Your task is a great duty, a duty useful and necessary." To me alone he talked of this institution in terms of "beauty of the task;" "humane cause;" and speaking to all of them he said, "Looking at the bodies of these Jews, one understands the greatness of your good work!"[14]

· 21 ·

Medical Ethics

WORLD-RENOWNED DR. ANDREW C. IVY was nominated by the American Medical Association to the Secretary of War of the U.S. to be a medical consultant and expert witness for the prosecution. His testimony served as a guide for the judges in setting down the ten points of the Nuremberg code for permissible medical experiments on human beings.

An extract from his testimony under cross-examination by defense counsel Dr. Servatius is as follows:

Defense counsel Servatius: Witness, take the following case. You are in a city in which the plague is raging. You, as a doctor, have a drug that you could use to combat the plague. However, you must test it on somebody. The commander, or let us say the mayor of the city, comes to you and says, "Here is a criminal condemned to death. Save us by carrying out the experiment on this man." Would you refuse to do so, or would you do it?

Witness Ivy: I would refuse to do so, because I do not believe that duress of that sort warrants the breaking of ethical and moral principles. That is why the Hague Convention and Geneva

Convention were formulated, to make war, a barbaric enterprise, a little more humane.

Defense counsel: Do you believe that the population of a city would have any understanding for your action?

Witness: They have understanding for the importance of the maintenance of the principles of medical ethics which apply over a long period of years, rather than a short period of years. Physicians and medical scientists should do nothing with the idea of temporarily doing good which, when carried out repeatedly over a period of time, would debase and jeopardize a method for doing good. If a medical scientist breaks the code of medical ethics and says, "Kill the person," in order to do what he thinks may be good, in the course of time that will grow and will cause a loss of faith of the public in the medical profession, and hence destroy the capacity of the medical profession to do its good for society. The reason that we must be very careful in the use of human beings as subjects in medical experiments is in order not to debase and jeopardize this method for doing great good by causing the public to react against it.

Defense counsel: Witness, do you not believe that your ideal attitude here is more or less that of a single person standing against the body of public opinion?

Witness: No, I do not. That is why I read out the principles of medical ethics yesterday, and that is why the American Medical Association has agreed essentially to those principles. That is why the principles, the ethical principles for the use of human beings in medical experiments, have been quite uniform throughout the world in the past.

Defense counsel: Then you do not believe that the urgency, the necessity of this city would make a revision of this attitude necessary?

Witness: No, not if they were in danger of killing people in the course of testing out the new drug or remedy. There is no justification in killing five people in order to save the lives of five hundred.

Defense counsel: Then you are of the opinion that the life of the one prisoner must be preserved even if the whole city perishes?

Witness: In order to maintain intact the method of doing good, yes.

Defense counsel: From the point of view of the politician, do you consider it good if he allows the city to perish in the interests of preserving this principle and preserving the life of the one prisoner?

Witness: The politician, unless he knows medicine and medical ethics, has no reason to make a decision on that point.

Defense counsel: But as a politician he must make a decision about what is to happen. Shall he coerce the doctor to carry out the experiment, or shall he protect the doctor from the rage of the multitude?

Witness: You can't answer that question. I should say this, that there is no state or no politician under the sun that could force me to perform a medical experiment which I thought was morally unjustified.

Defense counsel: You then, despite the order, would not carry out the order, and would prefer to be executed as a martyr?

Witness: That is correct, and I know there are thousands of people in the United States who would have to do likewise.[1]

The following is an extract from the testimony of Dr. Ivy on direct examination by Mr. Hardy of the prosecution:

Prosecutor Hardy: Now, Professor Ivy, before adjournment you were beginning to discuss medical ethics in the United States. Do you have there also the principles and rules as set forth by the American Medical Association to be followed?

Witness: Yes.

Prosecutor: What was the basis on which the American Medical Association adopted those rules?

Witness: I submitted to them a report of certain experiments which had been performed on human subjects along with my conclusions as to what the principles of ethics should be for use of human beings as subjects in medical experiments. I asked the association to give me a statement regarding the principles of medical ethics and what the American Medical Association had to say regarding the use of human beings as subjects in medical experiments.

Prosecutor: Well now, you have, first of all, a basic requirement for experimentation on human beings, "(1) the voluntary consent of the individual upon whom the experiment is to be performed must be obtained."

Witness: Yes.

Prosecutor: "(2) The danger of each experiment must be previously investigated by animal experimentation," and "(3) the experiment must be performed under proper medical protection and management."

Now, does that purport to be the principles upon which all physicians and scientists guide themselves before they resort to medical experimentation on human beings in the United States?

Witness: Yes. They represent the basic principles approved by the American Medical Association for the use of human beings as subjects in medical experiments.

Judge Sebring interjects, "How do the principles which you have just enunciated comport with the principles of the medical profession over the civilized world generally?"

Witness: They are identical, according to my information. It was with that idea in mind that I cited the principles which were mentioned in this circular letter from the Reich Minister of the Interior dated February 28, 1931, to indicate that the ethical principles for the use of human beings as subjects in medical experiments in Germany in 1931 [before Hitler came to power in 1933] were similar to those which I have enunciated and which have been approved by the House of Delegates of the American Medical Association.

Prosecutor: To your knowledge have any experiments been conducted in the United States wherein these requirements which you set forth were not met?

Witness: Not to my knowledge.

Prosecutor: Dr. Ivy, in medical science and research is the use of human subjects necessary?

Witness: Yes, in a number of instances.

Prosecutor: Is it frequently necessary and does it perform great good to humanity?

Witness: Yes. That is right.

Prosecutor: Do you have an opinion that the state, for instance, the United States of America, could assume the responsibility of a physician to his patient or experimental subject, or is that responsibility solely the moral responsibility of the physician or scientist?

Witness: I do not believe the state can assume the moral responsibility that a physician has for his patient or experimental subject.

Prosecutor: On what do you base your opinion? What is the reason for that opinion?

Witness: I base that opinion on the principles of ethics and morals contained in the Oath of Hippocrates. I think it should be obvious that a state cannot follow a physician around in his daily administration to see that the moral responsibility inherent therein is properly carried out. This moral responsibility that controls or should control the conduct of a physician should be inculcated into the minds of physicians just as moral responsibility of other sorts, and those principles are clearly depicted or enunciated in the Oath of Hippocrates with which every physician should be acquainted.

Prosecutor: Is the Oath of Hippocrates the Golden Rule in the United States and to your knowledge throughout the world?

Witness: According to my knowledge it represents the Golden Rule of the medical profession. It states how one doctor would like to be treated by another doctor in case he were ill. And in that way how a doctor should treat his patient or experimental subjects. He should treat them as though he were serving as a subject.

Prosecutor: Several of the defendants have pointed out in this case that the Oath of Hippocrates is obsolete today. Do you follow that opinion?

Witness: I do not. The moral imperative of the Oath of Hippocrates I believe is necessary for the survival of the scientific and technical philosophy of medicine.[2]

Permissible Medical Experiments

During the court's detailed judgment, it set forth guidelines for permissible medical experiments, known as *The Nuremberg Code*. This document reads as follows:

The great weight of the evidence before us is to the effect that certain types of medical experiments on human beings, when kept within reasonably well-defined bounds, conform to the ethics of the medical profession generally. The protagonists of the practice of human experimentation justify their views on the basis that such experiments yield results for the good of society that are unprocurable by other methods or means of study. All agree, however, that certain basic principles must be observed in order to satisfy moral, ethical, and legal concepts:

1. The voluntary consent of the human subject is absolutely essential.

This means that the person involved should have legal capacity to give consent; should be so situated as to be able to exercise free power of choice, without the intervention of any element of force, fraud, deceit, duress, overreaching, or other

ulterior form of constraint or coercion; and should have sufficient knowledge and comprehension of the elements of the
subject matter involved as to enable him to make an understanding and enlightened decision. This latter element
requires that before the acceptance of any affirmative decision
by the experimental subject there should be made known to
him the nature, duration, and purpose of the experiment; the
method and means by which it is to be conducted; all incon-
veniences and hazards reasonably to be expected; and the
effects upon his health or person which may possibly come
from his participation in the experiment.

The duty and responsibility for ascertaining the quality of
the consent rests upon each individual who initiates, directs,
or engages in the experiment. It is a personal duty and responsibility, which may not be delegated to another with impunity.

2. The experiment should be such as to yield fruitful
results for the good of society, unprocurable by other methods
or means of study, and not random and unnecessary in
nature.

3. The experiment should be so designed and based on the
results of animal experimentation and a knowledge of the natural history of the disease or other problem under study that
the anticipated results will justify the performance of the
experiment.

4. The experiment should be so conducted as to avoid all
unnecessary physical and mental suffering and injury.

5. No experiment should be conducted where there is an
a priori reason to believe that death or disabling injury will
occur; except, perhaps, in those experiments where the experimental physicians also serve as subjects.

6. The degree of risk to be taken should never exceed that
determined by the humanitarian importance of the problem
to be solved by the experiment.

7. Proper preparations should be made and adequate facilities provided to protect the experimental subject against even
remote possibilities of injury, disability, or death.

8. The experiment should be conducted only by scientifically qualified persons. The highest degree of skill and care should be required through all stages of the experiment of those who conduct or engage in the experiment.

9. During the course of the experiment the human subject should be at liberty to bring the experiment to an end if he has reached the physical or mental state where continuation of the experiment seems to him to be impossible.

10. During the course of the experiment the scientist in charge must be prepared to terminate the experiment at any stage, if he has probable cause to believe, in the exercise of the good faith, superior skill and careful judgment required of him that a continuation of the experiment is likely to result in injury, disability, or death to the experimental subject.[3]

Statement of IMT Chief Prosecutor, Robert H. Jackson

In the International Military Tribunal trial of the major Nazi leaders, United States Chief Prosecutor Robert H. Jackson, in his opening statement, said:

The former high station of these defendants, the notoriety of their acts, and the adaptability of their conduct to provoke retaliation make it hard to distinguish between the demand for a just and measured retribution, and the unthinking cry for vengeance which arises from the anguish of war. It is our task, so far as humanly possible, to draw the line between the two.

We must never forget that the record on which we judge these defendants today is the record on which history will judge us tomorrow.[4]

It is this record, which I and the other court reporters made, that is the basis of most of what I have related in this book. It is my hope that this record will not be forgotten by history.

· 22 ·

Judgments and Sentences
in the Medical Case

MILITARY TRIBUNAL 1 was established on October 25, 1946, under General Orders No. 68, issued by command of the United States Military Government for Germany. Several military tribunals were constituted in the U.S. Zone of Occupation pursuant to Military Government Ordinance No. 7 to try offenses recognized as crimes by Law No. 10 of the Control Council for Germany.

The indictment was filed on October 25, 1946, and served on each defendant in German on November 5, 1946. The defendants were arraigned on November 21, 1946, each pleading not guilty to the charges filed.

The prosecution started its presentation of evidence on December 9, 1946. Its case-in-chief took 25 court days. Then the defendants presented their evidence, taking 107 court days. All evidence was concluded by July 3, 1947.

Final arguments on both sides began July 14, 1947, and the personal statements of the defendants were heard on July 19, 1947, which was the last day of the trial.

The trial was conducted in both English and German, consuming 139 trial days. Thirty-two witnesses testified for the prosecution and fifty-three witnesses, including the twenty-three defendants, testified for the defense. Prosecution exhibits totaled 570 affidavits, reports, and documents; defense totaled 901, for a grand total of 1,471 pieces of documentary evidence.

Each defendant was represented by counsel of his own choosing. Each counsel had the right to cross-examine prosecution witnesses and to offer all evidence of probative value under Ordinance No. 7. No consultation with client was allowed while court was in session.

The entire record is available in the Library of Congress, the National Archives, universities, and other places.

Extracts from Final Statements of Defendants

Karl Brandt

It is immaterial for the experiment whether it is done with or against the will of the person concerned...The meaning is the motive—devotion to the community...ethics of every form are decided by an order or obedience.

Siegfried Handloser

If there is anything which could console me for the mental suffering of the last months, it is the consciousness of knowing that before this court, before the German people, and before the people of the world, it has been made clear that the serious general charges of the prosecution against the Medical Corps of the German Armed Forces have been proved to be without any foundation.

Paul Rostock

Throughout my life I have never worked for one form of a state or another, or for any political party in Germany, but simply and solely for my patients and for medical science.

Oskar Schroeder

What can I, as a defendant, bring against these argu-ments?...Not the craving for glory and honor was the purport of my life's work, but the firm intention to put my entire capacity, my full knowledge, into the service of my beloved Fatherland; to help the soldier, as a physician, to heal the wounds caused by wartime and peacetime service, both as a physician for the individual, as well as a medical officer for the mass of troops which were in my care.

Karl Genzken

If my fatherly concern for my twenty-five hundred doctors and thirty thousand men of the Medical Service of the Waffen SS was mentioned here in this courtroom, it is nevertheless my duty to speak from this place on behalf of those men who, in the majority, were decent and brave doctors and medical attendants. I am proud to have been their leader, a leader of those who sacrificed their lives and blood with unceasing fer-vor to help me in building up the organization of the Medical Service of the Waffen SS, and to overcome the tremendous losses among the ranks of our comrades at the front...

My request and my wish is that our former opponents should realize the honest idealism of these victims, do justice to it, and give them back belief in justice.

Karl Gebhardt

It was only because I was the competent responsible surgical expert that I was informed about the imminent experiments on human beings in my field of surgery, which had been ordered by the state authorities. After the order had been given, it was no longer a question of stopping these experi-ments, but the problem was the method of their execution...

I hope that hitherto I have always faced criticism, even from foreign countries, without any secrecy, but also without any feeling of guilt for my activities as an expert.

I believe that this pile of rubble, Germany, with its wasted biological material, cannot afford to let these fine young doctors perish in camps and in other inactivity.

Kurt Blome

I feel myself free of the guilt of ever having committed or furthered crimes against humanity.

Joachim Mrugowsky

My life, my actions, and my aims were clean. That is why now that at the end of this trial I can declare myself free of personal guilt.

Rudolf Brandt

In accordance with the truth I repeat what I have said in the witness stand, that I had a general knowledge of experiments on human beings; I can no longer say when and on what particular opportunity I gained that knowledge. But this fact alone does not deserve death, because I never had the feeling that I had participated in such crimes by my activity in the personal Referat [administrative office].

Helmut Poppendick

What I knew about medical experiments in the SS was, in my opinion, as little connected with criminal matters as those experiments of which I knew from my clinical experience before 1933...

Before this trial all of these matters were no problems for me. I did not know of any transgressions. Moreover, I was always convinced that anything which came to my knowledge about experiments on human beings in clinics of the state before 1933, and within the scope of the SS in later years, were conscientious efforts of serious scientists to the good of mankind.

The ethical foundation of these matters also seemed to be there until this trial. Therefore, after sincere examination of my conscience, I cannot find any feelings of guilt and expect with a clear and peaceful conscience the verdict of the Tribunal.

Wolfram Sievers

That in true recognition of the consequences which might be daily expected for myself and my family I devoted myself to resistance, continued in it undaunted, and never abandoned it, is now the only reason why I find myself in this dock. For that reason, I look forward to the judgment of this Tribunal with confidence, due to my conviction that I have lived for a good cause and acted on it, on behalf of something which—then as today—filled me with true belief.

Gerhard Rose

A subject of the personal charges against myself is my attitude toward experiments on human beings ordered by the state and carried out by other German scientists in the field of typhus and malaria. Works of that nature have nothing to do with politics or with ideology, but they serve the good of humanity, and the same problems and necessities can be seen independently of any political ideology everywhere, where the same dangers of epidemics have to be combated.

Siegfried Ruff

After detailed inquiry into my conscience, I still today hold the belief that I never sinned against my duty as a man and as a doctor.

Viktor Brack

For all those years I had no reason to have any misgivings with regard to Hitler's personality. Therefore, I also believed in the legality of the euthanasia decree as it emanated directly from the head of the state. The state officials and doctors, competent for me at that time, told me that euthanasia had always been an endeavor of mankind and was morally as well as medically justified. Therefore, I never doubted the legal character of the euthanasia decree.

Wolfgang Romberg

I have seen how the Tribunal itself, by a precise questioning, clarified the facts, and to the statements made by my defense counsel I have nothing to add, because they are the truth.

Herman Becker-Freyseng

For all the irrelevant, spiteful talk with which outside circles believed they had to twist around the objectivity of these proceedings like thorn bushes, the verdict of this Tribunal must be and will be the appropriate answer. I look forward to it with the firm conviction that I never failed in my duty to mankind as a physician and scientist, and as a soldier to my Fatherland.

Georg August Weltz

I have nothing to add to the statement made by my defense counsel. I thank Dr. Wille for his efforts made in my defense.

Konrad Schaefer

May it please the Tribunal, since I consider myself entirely innocent, I have nothing more to add. I ask to be acquitted, if possible, even before the verdict.

Waldemar Hoven

I have nothing to add to Dr. Gawlik's plea of yesterday. I would at this point like to thank my defense counsel for the considerable help he has given me.

*Defendant Konrad Schaefer, Staff Doctor,
Institute for Aviation Medicine*

Wilhelm Beiglboeck

I was never directed by any sentiment other than that of a human being and of a physician. The experiments as they were actually conducted never went beyond what can be justified by the physician. I consider myself free of guilt as a physician and as a human being.

Adolf Pokorny

With this hope I am looking forward to your judgment, and in that connection I am thinking of my children who, for years now, have lived under the protection of an allied power, and who will not believe that their father, after everything that he has suffered, could possibly have acted as an enemy to human rights.

Herta Oberheuser

In administering therapeutical care, following established medical principles, as a woman in a difficult position, I did the best I could.

Fritz Fischer

In my life I have never followed egotistical aims, and I was never motivated by base instincts. For that reason, I feel free of any guilt inside me. I have acted as a soldier, and as a soldier I am ready to bear the consequences. However, that I was born a German, that is something about which I do not want to complain.[1]

Sentences—July 20, 1947

The indictment under which the Nazi doctors were tried was comprised of four counts:

Count 1 - common design or conspiracy

Count 2 - war crimes

Count 3 - crimes against humanity constituting murders, brutalities, cruelties, tortures, atrocities, and inhumane acts

Count 4 - membership in a criminal organization declared so by the International Military Tribunal, commonly known as the SS

Four doctors—Karl Brandt, Karl Gebhardt, Joachim Mrugowski, and Waldemar Hoven—were found and adjudged guilty and sentenced to death by hanging. They were convicted of charges 2, 3, and 4.

Three assistants—Rudolf Brandt, Wolfram Sievers, and Viktor Brack—were found and adjudged guilty and sentenced to death by hanging. Like the four doctors above, they were convicted of charges 2, 3, and 4.

Dr. Siegfried Handloser, Dr. Oskar Schroeder, and Dr. Gerhard Rose were found and adjudged guilty of charges 2 and 3. Each was sentenced to life in prison.

Dr. Karl Genzken and Dr. Fritz Fischer were found and adjudged guilty of charges 2, 3, and 4 and were sentenced to life in prison.

Dr. Helmut Poppendick was found and adjudged guilty of charge 4 and sentenced to ten years in prison.

Dr. Hermann Becker-Freyseng and Dr. Herta Oberheuser were found and adjudged guilty of charges 2 and 3. Each was sentenced to twenty years in prison.

Dr. Wilhelm Beiglboeck was found and adjudged guilty of charges 2 and 3. He was sentenced to fifteen years in prison.

Doctors Paul Rostock, Konrad Schaefer, Kurt Blome, Siegfried Ruff, Hans Wolfgang Romberg, Georg August Weltz, and Adolf Pokorny were found and adjudged not guilty of the charges in the indictment. All were released from custody upon adjournment of the Tribunal.[2]

Petitions and Executions

Article XV of Ordinance No. 7 of the United States Military Government for Germany provides for judgments to be final and not subject to review.[3]

Article XVII provides the Military Governor with the power to mitigate, reduce, or otherwise alter any sentence imposed, but he may not increase the severity thereof. All sixteen defendants found guilty petitioned for clemency to the Military Governor of the U.S. Zone of Occupation.

Each of the condemned defendants, except Dr. Poppendick, petitioned the United States Supreme Court for a writ of *habeas corpus* and for a writ of prohibition against the proceeding or an order nullifying the trial and setting the defendants at liberty.

With the exception of Dr. Becker-Freyseng, all defendants filed appeals with the U.S. Secretary of War.

All sentences were affirmed by the U.S. Military Governor on November 22, 1947.

The U.S. Supreme Court denied writs of *habeas corpus* on February 16, 1948. The executions were carried out on June 2, 1948, at Landsberg Prison in Bavaria.

At his execution on June 2, 1948, Karl Brandt stated, "It is no shame to stand on this scaffold. I served my Fatherland as others before me."

Before Joachim Mrugowsky's execution, he stated, "I die as a German officer sentenced by a brutal enemy and conscious I never committed the crimes charged against me."

There was not one scintilla of remorse shown by any of these defendants. I was stunned at the evil, expressionless, hard faces of these doctors and assistants during the trial. They often expressed resentment when testifying, spewing defensive justifications and denying responsibility.

With the executions, Case No. 1, The Medical Case of the Nuremberg War Crimes Trials, had ended.

I would spend the rest of my life trying to recover from what I had heard and written in what was called a "Record That Will Never Forget."

The medical case of the Nazi doctors is the story of the mass violation of basic human rights and the dignity of life, of indifference to evil, of people who knew and kept silent, and of heads of state who looked the other way. Too many church leaders did not speak out against what was happening because of fear for their personal safety or security. Many of the courageous clergy who did speak out were rounded up and sent to concentration camp Dachau, northwest of Munich. This was the collection site for over 2,770 Catholic priests and members of religious orders; and Protestant, Orthodox, and Moslem clergyman. Eight hundred sixty-eight Polish priests died, three hundred in medical experiments or by torture.[4]

Although cultural animosity toward Jews was common, Western European bishops who harbored no ill will toward Jews tried to rescue them. "Many bishops believed that in the face of Nazi ruthlessness, Catholics could accomplish more by sheltering a few Jews than by a public protest against their mass slaughter. . . . A number of bishops would very likely have spoken out if Pope Pius himself had done so or had encouraged them to do so."[5]

I was neither a witness nor a victim, but I was a verbatim court reporter of the words that came from the mouths of the witnesses and victims at Nuremberg. I thought about this the first time I heard Peter, Paul, and Mary sing the Bob Dylan song *Blowin' in the Wind*: "How many times can a man turn his head and pretend that he just doesn't see?"

My answer was given by a famous German pastor of the Confessing Church, Martin Niemoeller. He said:

> In Germany they came first for the Communists, and I didn't speak up because I wasn't a Communist. Then they came for the Jews, and I didn't speak up because I wasn't a Jew. Then they came for the trade unionists, and I didn't speak up because I wasn't a trade unionist. Then they came for the Catholics, and I didn't speak up because I was a Protestant. Then they came for me, and by that time no one was left to speak up.[6]

On April 12, 1945, General Dwight D. Eisenhower, Supreme Commander of the Allied Forces in Europe, wrote the following words in a letter to Chief of Staff General George C. Marshall, describing his first visit to Ohrdruf slave labor camp, one of the camps liberated by U.S. forces:

> The things I saw beggar description...The visual evidence and the verbal testimony of starvation, cruelty, and bestiality were so overpowering as to leave me a bit sick.
>
> In one room, where there were piled up twenty or thirty naked men killed by starvation, George Patton would not even enter. He said he would get sick if he did so.
>
> I made the visit deliberately, in order to be in a position to give firsthand evidence of these things if ever, in the future, there develops a tendency to charge these allegations merely to "propaganda."[7]

That is precisely what is happening in the world today with the insidious spread of Holocaust denial.

How could this horror story have happened in a modern, civilized society? What created this fertile field for sowing the seeds of extermination? Fredrick Abrams, M.D., Director of the Clinical Ethics Consultation Group in Colorado, engages these questions in the foreword to this book. These questions are one reason I decided to write this book for the general public, to warn against bigotry and hatred and the evil indifference breeds.

· 23 ·

Going Home

MY ONE YEAR contract with the U.S. Department of War was up on November 1, 1947. I made it known to my military and civilian superiors that I wanted to go home. I had not been able to cope well with the horror I had heard from survivors and witnesses, or what I had seen in the captured German film clips and photographs that were admitted as exhibits into evidence.

I was not the only employee who wanted to escape and get home. For the first time I could understand why so many reporters, attorneys, interpreters, linguists, and staff left after the end of their tour of duty on the major Nazi leaders' trial.

The military could not assign me a seat on a plane or passage on a ship back to the United States from anywhere in Europe because of a Russian Communist threat brewing in Berlin.

At the end of World War II, Germany had been partitioned into four sectors that were occupied and governed by the four victorious powers until such time as Germany could be stabilized under a democratic government. Then the occupying forces could leave.

The city of Berlin had also been divided. It became obvious that the Russians wanted to squeeze the Allies out of Berlin. This created a looming threat that stopped anyone from leaving, because the United States started sending American dependents—adults and children—from Berlin back to the United States. These evacuations took all available transport space. Thus, what was called the Berlin Crisis began.

Because there was nothing I could do about this delay, I went back to work in the courtroom, working on other trials. There were still eleven other cases in trial or to be tried, with two or three going on simultaneously. The thirteen trials that began on November 20, 1945, went on until June 1949.

All of us were now working and living with anxiety and uncertainty about what the Russians were doing in Berlin and planning on doing elsewhere.

We got through Thanksgiving and the holidays, which helped take our minds off of the uncertainty. I continually checked to see if there was any possibility of my leaving on a military plane or ship, in vain.

On the weekend of February 17, 1948, about a dozen reporters and a few GI staff members in our office, plus a couple of interpreters and members of the press, obtained orders to go by U.S. Army bus to Prague, Czechoslovakia, for the weekend. Prague was my favorite city. Its welcoming, friendly people and beautiful nightclubs and dining rooms, which were located below street level, put us in another world away from that courtroom. With the street above dark and stores closed, one could never guess there was such a beautiful, peaceful, quiet scene below ground. Classical music groups wandered about the dining room playing wonderful music. The dinner hour began about 10:00 p.m. We never got back to our hotel rooms until 2:00 in the morning. Nothing could have prepared us for what was to come within a week.

When we returned to Nuremberg that Sunday, some of us planned on going back to Prague at the end of the week. I kept about three hundred dollars worth of Czech money and did not get it exchanged. I still have that money. That next weekend I had a cold and could not go. My friends made the trip to experience a frightening, historic weekend.

In Nuremberg, we got the news that the Czech Communists had seized the ministries and the government during the night. When my colleagues awoke the next morning in Prague, there were machine guns on every corner. They were arrested, held, and questioned for twenty-four hours. When the U.S. military intervened, my colleagues were released and returned to Nuremberg on the Army bus. How I wished I had been there!

On February 29, 1948, Communist Party leaders in Czechoslovakia, led by Prime Minister Klement Gottwald, seized full control of the country.[1]

The Communists closed the border between Czechoslovakia and Germany, and we could no longer go to Prague. We watched the agony and despair of the Czech diplomats and employees who worked with us on the remaining trials. Some chose not to return home to their families because it would require living under Communist rule. They became displaced persons.

This Communist coup in Czechoslovakia caused security in Nuremberg to be increased. We were apprehensive about what was going to happen next in Berlin.

That question was answered on April 24 when the Berlin Soviets set up a blockade, trying to force the Allies out of Berlin. The Soviets imposed restrictions on the movement of trains and vehicles through the Soviet zone to Allied outposts in Berlin. Supplies to the Allies were cut off. All actions deepened the developing Cold War atmosphere.

Although the air routes to Berlin were not shut down, Soviet fighter planes buzzed American air transports when airlifting food and supplies to the Allies and German people in Berlin. On June 25, the Russians tightened the blockade around the Allied sectors in Berlin. Barges from Hamburg were intercepted, coal shipments were stopped, and the supply of electricity to the Allies was reduced.

The Allies, in response, outlawed food shipments to the Soviets and interrupted coal and steel shipments. By February 28, 1949, in its eighth month of the Allied airlift, a total of one million tons of cargo was flown into West Berlin via this "air bridge," which provided food and fuel for two and a half million people in West Berlin. The blockade ended on May 12, 1949, after negotiations in New York, under the auspices of the United Nations. The Allies spent two million dollars for the airlift and fifty-five people died in plane accidents.[2]

During this time, I tried repeatedly to get U.S. military transport home—as did others. The threat of another conflict, this time with Russia, was looming. Rumors were floating in Nuremberg: "The Russians are coming!"

I decided to try to find my own way out of Europe and pay my way. I traveled to Paris and Brussels, only to learn there was not a seat available on a ship or plane out of Europe. I went on waiting lists with travel offices in these cities. Finally, I was called and told there was passage on the S.S. United States, sailing from Le Havre, France. I bought my own ticket for four hundred dollars—a lot of money in 1948, even for passage across the ocean. (I later sent a bill to the U.S. Government and was paid!)

I obtained my military release orders and got to Paris and Le Havre. I boarded the ship and sailed toward home in the first week of May 1948, arriving eleven days later in New York. The ship was loaded with hundreds of Czechs—many of them Jews who were now refugees. I was to view the most emotional scene of my life when they all fell on their knees on deck, sobbing, as the S.S. United States steamed into New York Harbor and the Statue of Liberty came into view!

Culture Shock

It was 1948. I had just returned to the United States from a bombed, war-torn, spiritless country. I had lived for nineteen months in accommodations with no heat or hot water and no safe drinking water without chlorine, and under strict military restrictions. The United States was still trying other categories of Nazi criminals at Nuremberg. The trials would last for more than a year after my return.

The German population hated us, refusing to believe that the trials and film, photographs, and documents presented in evidence were not faked in a grand sham. They were invited to come and sit in the courtroom in a special visitors' section to hear and see what their leaders had done to their country and people. Most did not come, and they did not believe in the proceedings.

I stayed in New York with friends for a short time. In America, there were few signs that a long, terrible war had ended only three years before in 1945. Few people seemed aware that war crimes trials were continuing. I was disheartened by the shift in priorities from my life in Germany to life in America.

The city was flooded with people on the streets, busily dodging noisy traffic, and horns were constantly blowing. Bright, flashing neon signs assaulted me everywhere. They beckoned me to enter movie houses, shows, stores, restaurants, hotels, and all manner of businesses, large and small. Everything was the opposite of the sparse, restricted living I had just left. It almost made me want to turn around and go back to somewhere—anywhere—quiet and peaceful, to think about where I had been and where I was going.

Nightmares

At this time I began having terrible nightmares. I was always trying to escape from a concentration camp through a tunnel under the barbed wire fence, with four or five small children in tow. I tried to keep them from making noise because they would be heard by the Nazi guard with his bayoneted rifle, marching back and forth overhead. The dark shroud of the night brought these nightmares frequently. In a deep sleep, my heart would pound so loud I feared the Nazi guard could hear it. And then I would remember the children— what about them? They were so good, so quiet. How hard their little hearts were pounding! I was carrying a small lamp of some kind, looking for a light at the end of that tunnel.

With these nightmares that started soon after my return to the U.S., I realized how badly I had been affected by the horror of the words I had reported day after day, month after month. I had just returned from hearing the story of what was to have been Hitler's "Final Solution of the Jewish Question," which had been revealed in the Nuremberg War Crimes Trials. So many bad things happened to innocent people just for being who they were. This was coordinated evil and hatred on an unprecedented scale perpetrated by a modern, civilized society of my heritage. German society had produced such brilliant writers, composers, and scientists as Goethe, Kant, Bach,

Beethoven, Wagner (a favorite of Hitler), Bessel, Roentgen, and Einstein.

Adolf Hitler was not criminally insane; he was criminally sane. Our humanity is linked to the six million Jews and millions of non-Jews who comprised the eleven million victims of the Holocaust. One cannot easily comprehend that figure until one sees a copy of the orders at the Treblinka death camp in Poland for the extermination of fourteen thousand per day, for example.

The nightmares that started in 1948 were always the same. They invaded my sleep for over three years—until about 1951. I had to get on with life. Married to a U.S. Army military police officer who had been in charge of several major Nazi leaders on trial, I continued my life as a military wife and court reporter at military bases, reporting courts-martial. We eventually had two sons and, in 1956, moved to Denver. I obtained an officialship in the District Court where I worked until 1972.

Appointment as Reporter in the U.S. House of Representatives

In 1969, I was first approached by the Chief Reporter, Charles Drescher, in the United States Senate, about receiving an appointment as an Official Reporter of Debates. This would make me the first woman reporter in the Senate. During the next three years I took short leaves of absence from my Denver court with my judge's blessing. I traveled to Washington, D.C. to report the debates with other Senate reporters and started training to be a parliamentary reporter.

During the first week of June 1972 I was in my district courtroom in the Denver City and County Building working on a jury trial. The court clerk came into the courtroom and put a note on Judge Robert Kingsley's desk. One attorney was questioning a witness. The judge stopped the proceedings and said, "Ladies and Gentlemen, we will have to take a short recess at this time. The Speaker of the United States House of Representatives, Carl Albert, is on the telephone and has asked to speak to Vivien."

We were all very surprised by this announcement. I certainly was. It had taken three years for a reporter's position to open up, and then it was in the House, not the Senate. Yes, I told Speaker Albert I was interested in the job. He asked me if I could be in Washington by noon the next day to be sworn in and then return to Denver to give adequate notice.

I moved to McLean, Virginia, in June 1972 and became one of the eight parliamentary reporters of the nation's business. The major product of this work is *The Congressional Record*. We were two women and six men on the team.

The years passed by. During this time I had been concerned that the non-Jewish world did not seem to talk much about the Holocaust or educate about it. It seemed only the Jews commemorated it during those thirty years after it happened. I could never understand why. I thanked God that they commemorated it every year in their synagogues, schools, and community centers. They were never going to let this stain on history be forgotten or be removed. But where were the rest of us—the Christians? We should have been commemorating not only the death of six million Jews in this German state-sponsored mass genocide, but also the five million non-Jewish victims of the Holocaust. This was still wearing on my mind.

Hans Frank, Governor General of Poland, one of the major Nazi leaders tried and convicted in the International Military Tribunal trial, commenting on Hitler's planned Thousand-Year Reich, just before he was hanged at Nuremberg stated, "A thousand years will pass and the guilt of Germany will not be erased."[3]

Holocaust Television Series

Two important events occurred during 1978. The first of these was that a miniseries entitled *Holocaust* was produced and shown on national television. It was shown over four evenings. Several congressmen asked me to watch it and then discuss it with them. I watched the first night, which showed the flaming of a synagogue packed with Jewish men, women, and children standing crushed against each other. Then the horror of my nightmare returned—the same nightmare from thirty years earlier in which I was trying to escape with little children through a dark tunnel. The Nazi guard, with his bayoneted rifle, marched back and forth along the barbed-wire fence overhead. Was I ever going to find the light at the end of this tunnel? I could not watch the other three nights of *Holocaust* on television. Friends, colleagues, and representatives in Congress—both Jewish and Gentile—told me they were shocked by what they saw and heard in this miniseries.

Jimmy Carter shaking Vivien Spitz's hand before delivering a speech to Congress that she reported.

The President's Commission on the Holocaust

The second important event occurred on November 1, 1978, while I was still working in Congress. President Jimmy Carter, by executive order, established the President's Commission on the Holocaust, appointing the famous Buchenwald concentration camp survivor, Elie Wiesel, as chairman.

On April 2, 1979, President Carter, by proclamation, designated April 28 and 29, 1979, as "Days of Remembrance of Victims of the Holocaust," asking the people of the United States "to observe this solemn anniversary of the liberation of Dachau by U.S. Armed Forces on April 28 and 29 of 1945."[4]

On April 24, 1979, the first National Civic Holocaust Commemoration Ceremony to observe "Days of Remembrance" by the Congress of the United States was held in the Rotunda of the Capitol in Washington, D.C. Both President Carter and Elie Wiesel gave moving speeches. Because I had been a court reporter at the Nuremberg War Crimes Trials and was then a parliamentary Reporter of Debates in Congress, I was invited to attend. I felt fortunate to be present.

Days of Remembrance

On September 23, 1980, as the Chief Reporter of Debates, I reported H. R. 8081, a bill to establish the United States Holocaust Memorial Council. The council consisted of sixty voting members appointed by the President, chaired by Elie Wiesel, and would provide for appropriate ways for the nation to commemorate the Days of Remembrance as an annual civic commemoration of the Holocaust. The council was charged with encouraging and sponsoring appropriate observances of such Days of Remembrance throughout the United States. In addition, it would plan, construct, and oversee the operation of a permanent living memorial museum to the victims of the Holocaust. The bill also established an educational foundation and a Committee of Conscience to help provide early warning threats of genocide against any people throughout the world. Finally, it provided that one week each year be designated as Days of Remembrance to be marked by a national civic commemoration throughout the United States.

At last! All has come to pass. Colorado Governor Richard Lamm, in 1982, held Colorado's first civic ceremony of Days of Remembrance in commemoration of all victims of the Holocaust.

Meeting Hitler's Court Reporter

Our Nation's Bicentennial Year, 1976, occurred twenty-eight years after I returned from Nuremberg. The National Shorthand Reporters Association held its national convention in Washington, D.C., to celebrate its seventy-fifth year and our nation's two hundredth birthday. Since I was already working in Congress, I was asked by my association to chair this convention for approximately nine hundred U.S. and international court reporters. Special invitations had been extended to reporters from fourteen foreign countries, including Germany. Reporters from all countries came, some sponsored by their governments.

During the July before the convention, while I was working in Congress, the German Bundestag parliamentary reporter Heinz Lorenz suddenly appeared in my office, looking for me. He introduced himself, spoke excellent English, and was friendly and outgoing. I was somewhat startled. We remembered having met four years before in 1972 when the convention was held in Denver. Because I chaired that convention committee and had to get back to my new position in Congress, we did not spend any time talking to each other. I did have some trepidation about meeting any German reporters.

Although I understood Lorenz had been told that I had reported the Nuremberg trials, he did not mention it. Nor did I. We never discussed it. I have often wondered why I did not ask him what he did during the war in one of our frequent casual and friendly get-togethers in 1976. Was he in the German Army? The German Air Force? Or German Navy? Did he work for the Nazi hierarchy as a reporter?

I could never have brought myself to ask if he had been a Nazi Storm Trooper or whether he had worked at a concentration camp. I was afraid of his answer. After all, my association and I had invited him to be our guest, along with his reporting colleague, Mrs. Gisela Meyer, and a few other German reporters who attended. For my own peace of mind, I had put this horror story behind me long ago.

After I gave him an impressive tour of the United States House of Representatives and the Senate, we discussed differences in our parliamentary systems of government and the various shorthand methods, manual and machine, used to report debates. At his request, I arranged for him to address our reporters' convention on these very topics.

Heinz and Gisela were eventually married and came back to the United States to attend our national court reporters conventions twice more. I was always glad to see them, as were my colleagues. We enjoyed discussing many facets of life and our mutual reporting concerns—but never the Nuremberg trials or life in Nazi Germany during the war years.

It was not until after his death in the late 1980s that his widow Gisela revealed that Heinz had been one of Hitler's court reporters during the war. Heinz was a journalist as well. She told us that he had been the last reporter in the Berlin bunker to leave on April 29, 1945, the day before Hitler's suicide.

When my colleagues and I learned this, we were stunned. I wished I had known so I could have discussed it with him. Gisela told us he was afraid that if we knew, especially since I had reported the Nuremberg doctors' trial, that we would ostracize him.

In April 1988, shortly after Lorenz's death, German court reporter Gerhard Herrgessell wrote an article entitled, "Reporting at Hitler's Headquarters," published in the *National Shorthand Reporter* magazine, and reprinted by permission from *Neue Stenographische Praxis*. Herrgessell wrote that he, Lorenz, and another reporter named Dr. Haagen were the three reporters in the Berlin bunker with Hitler at the end of the war. Several hundred members of Hitler's staff were there. It was their duty to report the final conferences before Hitler's planned suicide on April 30, 1945. Herrgesssell and Haagen left on April 22-23, leaving Heinz Lorenz to report the three final conferences. The last one was on April 29.

Herrgessell states Lorenz was able to escape the bunker as the Tiergarten and Chancellery overhead were being bombed by the Russians. Many of those trying to escape the bunker were killed by the bombing. Lorenz escaped through the Russian lines to the British, who interned him.

Gisela, his widow, reported that he had sewn his shorthand notes into the inner lining of his civilian suit, but during his internment they were discovered, and he was forced to transcribe them in the Eselheide prison detention camp. The British Secret Service sent these transcripts to England. Gisela said German and foreign press people contacted Lorenz for interviews to reveal what was in the notes, but he always declined. Years later the German magazine *Der Spiegel* obtained a copy from "private possession," and they were published in its January 10, 1966, issue. Hitler's last tactical conferences became public, as reported by Lorenz in the Berlin bunker.

I had read William L. Shirer's *The Rise and Fall of the Third Reich* shortly after its publication in 1960. After learning of Heinz Lorenz's role in Hitler's Third Reich, as a shorthand reporter and journalist appointed to the Propaganda Ministry, I pulled Shirer's book from my shelves and went to the last chapter, "The Last Days," to read again the bunker scene. The following is from that chapter:

Hitler called this his "Political Testament." Divided into two parts, the first appealed to posterity, blaming the Jews for the millions of battlefield deaths and the bombed cities. In the second part of his Testament, he dealt with succession after his death, expelling former Reich Marshal Hermann Goering from the party and withdrawing from him "all the rights that were conferred on him by the decree of June 20, 1941. In his place I appoint Admiral Doenitz as President of the Reich and Supreme Commander of the Armed Forces." He then dictated his personal will.

Daylight was breaking over Berlin, but the sun was obscured by the smoke of battle. In the electric light of the bunker much remained to be done. The first consideration was how to get the Führer's last will and testament out through the nearby Russian lines so that it could be delivered to Grand Admiral Karl Doenitz and others, and preserved for posterity.

Three messengers were chosen to take copies of the precious documents out: Major Willi Johannmeier, Hitler's military adjutant; Wilhelm Zander, an S.S. officer and adviser to Bormann, and Heinz Lorenz, the Propaganda Ministry official who had brought the shattering news of Himmler's treachery the night before.[5]

Johannmeier was to deliver his copy of the papers to Field Marshal Ferdinand Schoerner. Zander and Lorenz were to deliver their copies to Doenitz. The three men left the bunker at noon on April 29, 1945, the day before Hitler's suicide.

They were separated during their escape through Russian lines and Lorenz got to the British, who arrested and interned him. He never wrote about his experiences during his Nazi life and post-war life in Germany. And therein lies another whole story we may never know.

April 17, 1947 interrogation of Admiral Karl Doenitz at the Palace of Justice, after he had been sentenced to ten years in prison. This photograph was taken moments after Doenitz, reacting to the unwelcome presence of the photographer, called his interrogators "American swine." (l to r) Admiral Karl Doenitz, interpreter Fritz Kauffman (partially obscured), interpreter Fred Tridell, Judge Michael A. Musmanno, court reporter Vivien Spitz.

· 24 ·

Confronted by Holocaust Denial

YEARS HAD PASSED since my nightmares had ended for the second time, following the 1978 television miniseries *Holocaust*. After 1978, I stuffed all of my memories of the horror of the Nazi doctors' trial into a cocoon in the attic of my mind, determined to go on with my life.

That cocoon burst wide open in 1987 when I read in *The Denver Post* that a German language arts teacher at a high school in my Denver suburb of Aurora referred to the Holocaust as the "Holohoax" to her students![1] The extermination of eleven million Jews and non-Jews by the Nazis during World War II, as historically documented, was a Holohoax?

The Denver Post reported that after this teacher used the term Holohoax she was demoted as head of the language arts department. She appealed, but the school district refused to accept an arbitrator's ruling in July 1988 that she be reinstated to her job. Then she filed a lawsuit against the Aurora Public School District in May 1990, claiming the district took away her academic freedom. She argued that she was teaching students critical thinking by using the word Holohoax. She claimed breach of contract and censorship, destroying her academic freedom.

The Denver Post reported that she stated, "I merely expressed my opinion that not everyone agrees on the facts of the Holocaust." Her lawsuit claimed the district was forcing her to teach "only the majority view," thus chilling her "right to exercise academic freedom and free speech."[2]

Her quoted words were, "Some say Holocaust, some say Holohoax."[3]

One Denver Auschwitz death camp survivor, a friend of mine, said, "My blood curls that somebody should deny historical facts. I believe in freedom of speech, but I do not believe in freedom of teaching lies."

Wounds Reopened

Holohoax! I was so livid, fired up with passion, that I hauled out transcripts, material, and original press photographs that I had brought from Nuremberg and stored away in boxes all these years. I put together the lecture and presentation that I have now given for more than fifteen years. I show thirty slides of mostly captured German film of the Nazi doctors' atrocities. My talk is based upon basic human rights and the dignity of life, the difference between good and evil, and what can happen when we stand silently by and do nothing when the snake of evil slithers into our lives.

From 1987 to 2004 I have spoken in over thirty-nine states, Canada, and Singapore to more than forty thousand people in law schools, bar associations, colleges, universities, hospitals, synagogues, Catholic and Protestant churches, middle and high schools, court reporter associations, service and veterans organizations, professional groups, and groups of Holocaust survivors and concentration camp liberators. I never had an agent and never promoted myself. Through word of mouth, from one group to the next, a mission has found me.

The Holocaust Awareness Institute

In 1987, I was invited to join the board of The Holocaust Awareness Institute of the University of Denver's Center for Judaic Studies and became a member of their speakers' bureau.

In 1990 I was interviewed on twenty-three national radio talk shows across the country from New York to Los Angeles. I have been interviewed on television and for national newspapers many times.

Meeting Elie Wiesel

On May 7, 1990, Elie Wiesel—a famous Buchenwald survivor, Nobel Laureate, author, and lecturer—spoke at the University of Denver on "Are We a Moral Society?" As a member of the Holocaust Awareness Institute's board, I received an invitation. Elie Wiesel's first powerful book, *Night,* had left such an impression of horror with me that I wanted to meet this man, this survivor. On a previous occasion, as the only court reporter in Congress who had worked on the Nuremberg trials, I had been invited to be present on April 24, 1979, at the National Civic Holocaust Commemoration Ceremony in the Rotunda of the United States Capitol in Washington, D.C., when President Carter honored Wiesel as Chairman of the President's Commission on the Holocaust.

A friend of mine, Paulie Brody, one of the sponsors of the University of Denver event, invited me to the V.I.P. reception for Elie Wiesel after his lecture. She and I waited behind the people standing in line to meet and briefly chat with him. When we got up to him, she introduced me, saying, "Elie, I want you to meet the youngest court reporter at the Nuremberg War Crimes Trials, Vivien Spitz."

I reached out to shake his hand. He took my hand and hung on to it, staring deeply into my eyes, saying just, "Oh! Oh! Oh!" There was such a depth of sadness in his eyes that I will never forget. Then I told him about having been present in the Rotunda on April 24, 1979, at the Holocaust remembrance event honoring him, at which he had his little boy. This brought a chuckle from him, saying he had quite a time keeping his son from wriggling around. Then we had a brief, very meaningful conversation.

Interview by the Steven Spielberg SHOAH Foundation

In December 1995 a Denver suburban high school teacher of Holocaust studies, Gary Lubell, called me to make a videotaped interview for the Steven Spielberg SHOAH Visual History Foundation in Los Angeles. He had gone to Los Angeles to be trained as an interviewer of Holocaust survivors and witnesses for Spielberg's world-wide program aimed at preserving testimonies. I had spoken several times to students at Lubell's invitation. On one occasion I spoke to teachers of Holocaust courses for their continuing education credit, which Gary Lubell arranged.

I was not a survivor of the Holocaust, but I was categorized as a Witness to History by the Spielberg Foundation. I was honored to have been considered a witness deserving of having my testimony preserved. The videotapes comprising three volumes are in the SHOAH Foundation in Los Angeles.

On April 29, 2004, I received a personalized letter from Steven Spielberg thanking me for my willingness to recall, retell, and record testimony. The year 2004 marked the tenth anniversary of the interviewing of Holocaust survivors by the SHOAH Visual History Foundation and the success of this massive archive, now totaling over fifty-two thousand recorded testimonies of survivors, witnesses, and liberators worldwide.

Confronted by Holocaust Denial Again

In July 1997 I gave a luncheon presentation to the Colorado El Paso County Bar Association of lawyers and judges at the Antlers Hotel in Colorado Springs. Prior to the start of the luncheon, I was going over the program with the bar president when another attorney came up to us and said someone was out in the hall handing out propaganda to those registering. At that moment, a man came bounding up to us with a big smile on his face, handed me a three-page document, and asked me if I was familiar with their Institute for Historical Review. The Institute for Historical Review is based in Newport Beach, California, a short distance from Long Beach.

I looked at the title and said, "I am very familiar with your institute, but you do not have the correct title at the top. It should be 'Institute for Historical Revision and Holocaust Denial.'" He then became very hostile and challenged me to debate him on the Nuremberg trials and the Holocaust. Stunned, I said, "I will not only *not* debate you, but I will not dignify with an answer any question you put to me. I have nothing further to say to you."

An attorney whose parents had been cremated in the ovens of Auschwitz notified hotel security and security agents entered the room. This man who challenged me went to a table at the back of the room and, as soon as I finished my presentation, got up and left quickly.

I have his document in my files; it consists of three pages of sixty-six numbered items questioning the documented authenticity of the Holocaust and the Nuremberg War Crimes Trials. The first question is: "What proof exists that the Nazis practiced genocide or deliberately killed six million Jews?"

The Institute for Historical Review is documented in chapter 8 of the excellent book *Denying the Holocaust—The Growing Assault on Truth and Memory* by Professor Deborah Lipstadt of Emory University in Atlanta.

More Challenges

On February 6, 1999, I gave a presentation at the Long Beach Hilton Hotel for a professional organization. Great advance publicity was given to me in the *Los Angeles Times*. As a result, the Hilton reported receiving phone calls from people claiming to be historians, asking for the time and place in the hotel where I would be speaking. When the hotel advised them this was a private professional association that had arranged for me to speak, and that the event was not open to the public, they demanded that they be allowed to attend. Demanded!

The Hilton asked the president of the association to call me in Denver and ask me to register under an assumed name when I arrived, saying they were staffing additional security. I arrived in Long Beach on Friday afternoon, registered under an assumed name, and spoke Saturday afternoon to a group of over two hundred people from all over California. Then I held the question-and-answer session.

Suddenly the doors to the hall flew open on my right, and an armed security guard with a gun on his hip approached me on the podium and said urgently and quietly, "I have to take you off of the podium right now!"

I could hear commotion in the hall and knew something was going on. I don't believe the people in the room who were asking me questions after my speech knew there was a problem.

Without saying a word to the audience, I went immediately with the security officer out the door behind the podium to the elevator just across the hall. The guard took me to the basement and through the hotel kitchen to a front elevator. From there, we went up to my room on the tenth floor. I told the officer I was going to have dinner with court reporter friends. He said, "Don't leave this room without calling me."

The officer told me that the people in the hall were demanding to get in. The Hilton had asked them to leave, and they refused.

More Holocaust Denial

In August of 1999, the Los Angeles CNN TV producer Michael Cary and reporter Anne McDermott called me in Denver to arrange a meeting in my home within the next few days. They had seen the publicity in the *Los Angeles Times*. They flew to Denver, bringing along their videographer. They came to my home and interviewed me on camera for ninety minutes. The piece aired worldwide on August 18 and for several subsequent days, reported by Anne McDermott.

Within one week, I received a telephone call from an English-speaking news bureau reporter from Tehran, in the Islamic Republic of Iran, asking me if I would be willing to give a taped interview with someone who claimed the Holocaust never happened and that it was a hoax. I gave this man a short, curt speech, telling him I would not debate this subject with any Holocaust denier.

Within a few days I received a call from a news bureau in Vienna, Austria. This more welcome call resulted in a thirty-minute interview that was interpreted simultaneously into German, Albanian, Serbian, Bosnian, and Croatian for their audience. It was an excellent interview.

Appearance on Broadway
with Tony Randall

In April 2001 the now deceased screen and stage actor Tony Randall produced Abby Mann's *Judgment at Nuremberg* on the Broadway stage in New York. He was president of the National Actors Theatre in New York at the time. Mann's book was about the trial of the four top Nazi jurists who relinquished their judicial independence and allowed the legal system to become politicized in the name of nationalism during Hitler's era. This was Case No. III, The Justices Case, of the Subsequent Proceedings of the thirteen Nuremberg War Crimes Trials.

Henry Korn, a New York attorney who had had me speak at his Larchmont Synagogue in 2000, called me in Denver. He said Tony Randall asked him if there was anyone still alive who actually reported the Nuremberg trials. Korn said, "I know just the person."

I had booked another presentation at the Larchmont synagogue a week before Tony Randall wanted me to appear. Dr. Marlene Warshawski Yahalom, New York Education Director of the American Society for Yad Vashem, arranged for me to appear at the performance on Sunday, April 22, 2001, at the Longacre Theatre on Broadway, where I met Tony Randall. Professor Harry Reicher, a leading expert on international law, was on the program with me, and we were both written up in the playbill.

The audience was invited to stay after the performance to hear each of us make short presentations and answer questions. The performance was a masterful production to a full theatre.

After the show, chairs were lined up in a row on the stage. The professor and I were in the center. All actors were seated next to us on stage, including the stars Maximilian Schell and George Grizzard.

Tony Randall monitored the questions. By the time I finished answering the insightful questions, I had given a condensed version of my speech. The questions would have continued, but time had to be called.

Then I was invited by Tony Randall to join the actors for the cast party at the New York Actors Club. He gave me a personal tour of the rooms housing the oil paintings of several famous Broadway stars, from Helen Hayes and the Barrymores to the present. Several of the actors came to me after dinner to chat about my experiences in Nuremberg. It was a night to remember. After I returned to Denver, they sent me a large cardboard sign from the front of the theatre, signed, "To Vivien—Tony Randall." All of the actors signed this poster as well.

Afterword

IN LIGHT OF ongoing war crimes trials in The Hague and elsewhere, and future war crimes trials to be conducted in Iraq and other countries in this world of continuing genocides and slaughter, the violation of basic human rights and the dignity of life and indifference to evil goes on. Terrorism continues.

George Santayana's warning, "Those who can not remember the past are condemned to repeat it"[1] is not being heeded. The past is prologue to the future.

The past has become the present because nations have chosen not to remember. All nations must learn and teach the lessons of the past, to build a more humane world with liberty, peace, and justice. There cannot be peace and justice without liberty.

My eyes were opened to a truth just beyond my young life's experiences. I could not comprehend the depth of evil to which ordinary Germans could sink. As a court reporter, today with over forty years of experience, I have never been confronted with defendants accused of greater crimes than those at Nuremberg.

I was incredulous that ordinary Germans did not aid and abet their military and did not know about the camps and crematoria, as they claimed.

In 1966, twenty years after the end of the major Nazi leaders' International Military Tribunal trial, a play entitled *Investigation of*

Auschwitz was produced in Berlin by Germans. In the play, one of the characters states, "Each secretary, each telegraph operator through whose hands passed the orders for deportation *knew*. Each man occupied in each of the thousands of administrative positions involved in The Final Solution *knew*. Each conductor, each worker whose job it was to load men and women on the trains *knew*, and each one in his place *knew* exactly what needed to be done for the functioning of the Reich."

In a press interview in July 2004 a Maryland news reporter asked me, "What were your impressions of the doctors in the dock? Was their evil evident? Or did they look like Everyman—people who might be your neighbors, or shoppers in the grocery store, or fellow drivers on the street?"

To answer this question, you can look at the head shots of each of the twenty-three defendants in this book. Look into their eyes, as I did in that courtroom. Is their evil evident? Do they look like ordinary Germans? Do they look like Everyman?

I have written about glimpses behind the courtroom doors not found in the impersonal official record of the Nazi doctors' trial, which I helped prepare. Those who did not work on these unique trials but who have written about them will never know what it meant to hear the voices, watch the victims and witnesses as they spoke, and make a record of such violence. The devastating brutality I describe is not gratuitous and is not fictionalized. How vicious can we, the human species, possibly be in our hearts?

When we are born in the United States, we are born with blessings we just take for granted. We will not be arrested, bludgeoned, tortured, and exterminated solely because of our race, religion, or political activity. Born into freedom, with free will in the human story, we innately know the difference between right and wrong. We must each wage a personal war against obedience to unethical, immoral, and illegal evil authority. We owe our responsibility and accountability to humankind.

In genocides there are four categories of human beings: the perpetrator, the victim, the silent bystander, and the rescuer. What is the guilt of the silent bystander? Do we ordinary people have the courage to be rescuers, at the risk of personal safety, and sometimes the loss of life? We have proven that we can be rescuers.

Among the many heroic rescuers during the Nazi era were the Christians who put their own lives at risk by hiding the Jewish children turned over to them by the childrens' parents, who were then gathered for transport to the concentration and death camps.

I stand in awe of the indomitable human spirit exhibited by those in the Denver community and around the country whom I have come to know who survived the medical experiments and labor and death camps.

As an international speaker on The Nazi Doctors Case of the Nuremberg War Crimes Trials, my mission has been to educate by informing and to make people think. We must not forget the past of the violent twentieth century—the war and genocide—which is now continuing into the twenty-first century. We must not allow malignant evil to go unchallenged and unchecked.

This stain on humanity's history raises provocative questions in this new century. Will a whole generation nurtured on television violence, film violence, and video game violence be far less likely to be guardians of good and become more indifferent to evil than our common ancestors were in Nazi Germany?

At the first war crimes trial of the major Nazi leaders before the International Military Tribunal, Mr. Justice Robert H. Jackson stated, "The wrongs which we seek to condemn and punish have been so calculated, so malignant, and so devastating, that civilization cannot tolerate their being ignored because it cannot survive their being repeated."[2]

Appendix
Statistics on the Medical Case

- Military Tribunal One, The Medical Case, was convened 139 times.

- The indictment was filed October 25, 1946.

- The indictment was served November 5, 1946.

- The arraignment was November 21, 1946.

- The prosecution's opening statement was December 9, 1946.

- The defense's opening statement was January 29, 1947.

- The prosecution's closing statement was July 14, 1947.

- The defense's closing statement was July 14-18, 1947.

- The prosecution's case-in-chief took twenty-five court days.

- The defense's case-in-chief took 107 court days.

- The prosecution offered 570 written exhibits.

- The defense offered 901 written exhibits.

- The prosecution had thirty-two witnesses.

- The defense had thirty witnesses and all defendants.

- The prosecution introduced forty-nine affidavits.

- The defense introduced 535 affidavits.

- Judgment was entered on August 19, 1947.

- Sentences were handed down on August 20, 1947, sentencing four doctors and three medical assistants to death by hanging, five to life imprisonment, two to twenty years, one to fifteen years, and one to ten years. Seven were found not guilty and released.

- Affirmation of sentences by Military Commander of the United States Zone of Occupation was on November 25, 1947.

- The order of the United States Supreme Court denying writs of habeas corpus was entered on February 16, 1948.

- Sentences were carried out on June 2, 1948.

Notes

Introduction

1 *The Value of the Human Being—Medicine in Germany 1918-1945*, Arztekemmer Berlin, Edition Hentrich, 1991.

Chapter 2, The Nuremburg War Crimes Trials

1 International Military Tribunal, Major Nazi leaders' trial transcript, Preface, US Government Printing Office, pp. xxiv, xv.

Chapter 4, Case No. 1, the Medical Case

1 Nuremberg Military Tribunals, *The Medical Case*, Vol. 1, US Government Printing Office, p. 18. This is the condensed transcript of the trial.

2 Ibid., p. 27.

3 Ibid., p. 58.

4 Ibid., p. 62.

5 Major Nazi leaders' trial transcript, Vol. 1, p. 247; International Military Tribunal judgment, cited in *The Medical Case* transcript, Vol. 1, p. 67.

6 *The Medical Case*, Vol. 1, p. 71

7 These documents were set forth in detail under *Organization of the German Medical Services*, Vol. 1, pp. 81—91, Document NO-080, Prosecution Exhibit 5; Document NO-081, Prosecution Exhibit 6; Document NO-082, Prosecution Exhibit 7; Document NO-227, Prosecution Exhibit 11; Document NO-303, Prosecution Exhibit 32; Document NO-422, Prosecution Exhibit 33; Document NO-894, Prosecution Exhibit 38; and Document NO-645, Prosecution Exhibit 3.

Chapter 5, High Altitude Experiments

1 *The Medical Case*, Vol. 1, p. 104, NO–476, Prosecution Exhibit 40.

2 Ibid., p. 104. Photo document NO-610, Prosecution Exhibit 41, shows inmates in simulated altitude experiments conducted in the low-pressure chamber.

3 Ibid., p. 100, Prosecution Exhibit 51.

4 Ibid., p. 146.

5 Ibid., p. 154.

6 Ibid., p. 105.

7 Ibid., p. 899, NO-610, Prosecution Exhibit 41.

8 Ibid., p. 161, NO-402, Prosecution Exhibit 66.

9 Ibid., p. 113.

10 Ibid., p. 177.

11 Ibid., p. 183.

12   Ibid., p. 186.

13   Ibid., p. 157.

Chapter 6, Freezing Experiments

1   *The Medical Case*, p. 199, Prosecution Exhibit 88.

2   Ibid., p. 245, Prosecution Exhibit 92.

3   Original mimeographed Medical Case transcript, p. 874.

4   Ibid., p. 879.

5   Ibid., p. 881.

6   Ibid., p. 882.

7   *The Medical Case*, Vol. 1, p. 245, Prosecution Exhibit 94.

8   Ibid., p. 245, Prosecution Exhibit 94.

Chapter 7, Malaria Experiments

1   *The Medical Case*, Vol. 1, p. 297-98.

2   Ibid., p. 295.

3   Orig. mimeographed transcript, p. 875.

4   Ibid., p. 876.

5   Ibid., p. 876.

6   Ibid., p. 878.

7   *The Medical Case*, Vol. 1, p. 294.

Chapter 8, Bone, Muscle, and Nerve Experiments

1   *The Medical Case*, Vol. 1, p. 392.

2   Ibid., p. 393.

3   Orig. mimeographed transcript, p.1447.

4   Ibid., p. 4235.

5   NO-865, Prosecution Exhibit 230.

6   *The Medical Case*, Vol. 1, p. 399.

7   Ibid., p. 409; Orig. mimeographed transcript, 20 December 1946, pp. 815–832.

8   Testimony in mimeographed transcript, 20 December 1946, pp. 832–838.

9   Prosecution Exhibit 230, Document NO-875.

10   *The Medical Case*, Vol. 1, p. 400.

Chapter 9, Mustard Gas Experiments

1   *The Medical Case,* Vol. 1, p. 44.

2   Prosecution Exhibit 446.

3   Orig. mimeographed transcript pp. 1052–53.

4   Ibid., pp. 1034–5.

5   Orig. mimeographed transcript, p. 2383.

6   Prosecution Exhibit 263.

Chapter 10, Sulfanilamide Experiments

1   Orig. mimeographed transcript, pp. 4010–14.

2   Prosecution Exhibit 473, NO-2734.

3   Prosecution Exhibit 206, NO-228.

4   Ibid.

5   Orig. mimeographed transcript, pp. 1438, 1449, 797, 845, 863.

6   Ibid., pp. 795, 824, 863.

7   Ibid., p. 1462.

8   Orig. mimeographed transcript, p. 857.

9   Prosecution Exhibit 228.

10   Orig. mimeographed transcript, p. 790.

11   Ibid., p. 822.

12   *The Medical Case*, Vol. 1, p. 372.

13   Prosecution Exhibit 234.

14   Orig. mimeographed transcript, pp. 838–847.

15   Ibid., pp. 3334, 3338.

16   *The Medical Case*, Vol. 1, p. 397.

17   Ibid., p. 831.

Chapter 11, Sea Water Experiments

1   *Reich Law Gazette 1*, p. 268; Vol. 1, p. 442.

2   Orig. mimeographed transcript, p. 10201.

3   *The Medical Case*, Vol. 1, p. 419.

4   Ibid., p. 420.

5   Orig. mimeographed transcript, p. 9387.

6   *Reich Law Gazette 1*, p. 1334; Vol. 1, p. 442.

7   *The Medical Case*, Vol. 1, pp. 457–458.

8   Ibid., p. 458.

Chapter 13, Epidemic Jaundice (Hepatitis)

1   *The Medical Case*, Vol. 1, p. 495, Prosecution Exhibit 187.

2   Ibid.

3   *The Medical Case*, Vol. 1, p. 503, Prosecution Exhibit 186.

4   *The Medical Case*, Vol. 2, p. 29.

Chapter 14, Sterilization

1   Prosecution Exhibit 163, NO-205.

2   *The Medical Case*, Vol. 1, p. 699, Prosecution Exhibit 141, NO-440.

3   *The Medical Case*, Vol. 1, p. 696.

4   Prosecution Exhibit 148.

5   *The Medical Case*, Vol. 1, p. 696, Prosecution Exhibit 141.

6   Prosecution Exhibit 170.

7   Prosecution Exhibit 171.

8   Prosecution Exhibit 173.

9   Prosecution Exhibit 141.

10   Prosecution Exhibit 160.

11   Orig. mimeographed transcript, p. 7484.

12   Prosecution Exhibit 161.

13   Prosecution Exhibit 163.

14   Prosecution Exhibit 164.

15   Prosecution Exhibit 166.

16   Orig. mimeographed transcript, p. 541.

17   Ibid., p. 543, 557.

18   Prosecution Exhibit 161.

19   *The Medical Case*, Vol. 1, p. 722.

20   Orig. mimeographed transcript, pp. 7413–7772.

Chapter 15, Typhus Experiments

1   *The Medical Case*, Vol. 1, p. 509, Ding Diary, NO-265.

2   *The Medical Case*, Vol. 1, pp. 510, 511, Prosecution Exhibit 286, NO-582.

3   *The Medical Case*, Vol. 1, p. 517, Prosecution Exhibit 287.

4   *The Medical Case*, Vol. 1, pp. 583-586, Orig. mimeographed transcript, pp. 1151–1883, Jan. 6–9, 1947.

5   *The Medical Case*, Vol. 1, p. 518; Orig. mimeographed transcript, pp. 1194–96.

6   *The Medical Case*, Vol. 1, p. 518.

Chapter 16, Poison Experiments

1   *The Medical Case*, Vol. 1, p. 632.

2   Ibid., p. 634.

Chapter 17, Incendiary Bomb Experiments

1   *The Medical Case*, Vol. 1, p. 640.

2   Ibid., p. 644.

3   Ibid., p. 645.

4   Ibid., p. 653.

Chapter 18, Phlegmon, Polygal, and Phenol Experiments

1   *The Medical Case*, Vol. 1 p. 657, Prosecution Exhibit 249.

2   Allopathy is a system of therapeutics in which diseases are treated by producing a condition incompatible with or antagonistic to the condition to be cured or alleviated. *–Dorland's Medical Dictionary*, Twenty-fifth Edition.

3   *The Medical Case*, Vol. 1, p. 678.

4   Ibid., p. 681.

5   Ibid., p. 682.

6   Ibid., p. 688.

7   Ibid., p. 686.

8   Ibid., pp. 687-688.

Chapter 19, Jewish Skeleton Collection

1   Emphasis supplied.

2   *The Medical Case*, Vol. 1, p. 739.

3   Ibid., p. 751.

4   Ibid., pp. 739-759; Vol. 2, p. 262.

5   *The Medical Case*, Vol. 1 p. 741, NO-483, Prosecution Exhibit 184; NO-807, Prosecution Exhibit 185.

Chapter 20, Euthanasia

1   *The Medical Case*, Vol. 1, p. 795, Prosecution Exhibit 330.

2   *The Medical Case*, Vol. 1, p. 798, Prosecution Exhibit 366.

3   Ibid., Prosecution Exhibit 357.

4   *The Medical Case*, Vol. 1, p. 799, Prosecution Exhibit 371.

5   Ibid., Prosecution Exhibits. 370, 372, 399.

6   *The Medical Case*, Vol. 1, p. 801.

7   Ibid., p. 813.

8   Prosecution Exhibit 505.

9   Orig. mimeographed transcript, p. 1894.

10   Ibid. p. 1923.

11   *The Medical Case*, Vol. 1, p. 806.

12   Ibid.

13   A law legalizing murder, euphemistically called "euthanasia," was never passed in Germany.

14   *The Medical Case,* Vol. 1, pp. 865–870.

Chapter 21, Medical Ethics

1   *The Medical Case*, Vol. 2, pp. 42-43.

2   Ibid., pp. 82-86. Complete testimony is recorded in mimeographed transcript, 12, 13, 14, 16 June 1947, pp. 9029-9324.

3   *The Medical Case*, Vol. 2, pp. 181-183.

4   Major Nazi leaders' trial transcript, p. 33.

Chapter 22, Judgments and Sentences in the Medical Case

1   *The Medical Case*, Vol. 2, pp. 130-170.

2   Ibid., pp. 298-300.

3   Ibid., p. 301.

4   "The Priests of Dachau," William J. O'Malley, S. J., *America*, Nov. 14, 1987.

5   *The Catholic Church and the Holocaust,* 1930-1965, Michael Phayer, Indiana University Press, 2000.

6   *Bartlett's Familiar Quotations*, Martin Niemoeller, 1892-1984, Dachau 1944.

7   United States Holocaust Memorial Museum.

Chapter 23, Going Home

1   Clifton Daniel, ed., *Chronicle of the 20th Century*, Chronicle Publications, Inc., New York, 1987, p. 637.

2   Ibid, pp. 641–662.

3   *The Anatomy of the Nuremberg Trials,* Telford Taylor, Alfred A. Knopf, N. Y., 1992, p. 539.

4   *The Congressional Record,* September 23, 1980, p. H9426

5   *The Rise and Fall of the Third Reich*, William L. Shirer, Simon & Schuster, 1960, Chapter 31, "The Last Days."

Chapter 24, Confronted by Holocaust Denial

1   *The Denver Post*, Dec. 3, 1990.

2   Ibid.

3   Ibid.

Afterword

1   *The Life of Reason,* George Santayana, 1905.

2   Major Nazi Leaders' trial transcript, opening statement, p. 33;
     also *The Anatomy of the Nuremberg Trials*, Telford Taylor,
     Knopf, 1992, p. 167.

Bibliography

General Reference Works

International Military Tribunal: *In the Matter of the United States of America, the French Republic, the United Kingdom of Great Britain and Northern Ireland, and the Union of Soviet Socialist Republics versus Hermann Wilhelm Goering, et al.*, United States Government Printing Office, November 1945 to October 1946.

Nuremberg Military Tribunals: *The United States of America versus Karl Brandt, et al., Case No. 1 (The Medical Case)*, vols. 1 and 2, United States Government Printing Office, October 1946 to June 1948.

Daniel, Clifton, Editor, *Chronicle of the 20th Century*, Chronicle Publications, Inc., New York, 1987, pp. 414-593.

Field Enterprises Educational Corporation, "Czechoslovakia," *The World Book Encyclopedia*, 1963 ed., vol. 3, p. 971.

Books

Annas, George J., *Nazi Doctors and the Nuremberg Code: Human Rights in Human Experimentation*, Oxford University Press, 1992.

Berenbaum, Michael, *The World Must Know*, United States Holocaust Memorial Museum, 1993.

Goldhagen, Daniel Jonah, *Hitler's Willing Executioners: Ordinary Germans and the Holocaust*, Alfred A. Knopf, New York, 1996.

Greene, Joshua M. *Justice at Dachau*, Broadway Books, New York, 2003.

Lifton, Robert Jay, *The Nazi Doctors,* Basic Books, Inc., New York, 1986.

Lipstadt, Deborah E., *Denying the Holocaust: The Growing Assault on Truth and Memory*, The Free Press, New York, 1993.

Phayer, Michael, *The Catholic Church and the Holocaust*, 1930-1965, Indiana University Press, 2000.

Pross, Christian, and Goetz, Aly, *The Value of the Human Being: Medicine in Germany 1918-1945*, Arztekammer Berlin, Edition Hentrich, 1991.

Schmidt, Ulf, *Justice at Nuremberg: Leo Alexander and the Nazi Doctors' Trial*, Palgrave Macmillan, 2004.

Taylor, Telford, *The Anatomy of the Nuremberg Trials*, Alfred A. Knopf, New York, 1992.

Shirer, William L. *The Rise and Fall of the Third Reich*, Simon & Shuster, New York, 1960.

Magazine Articles

Alexander, Leo, M. D., "Medical Science Under Dictatorship," *The New England Journal of Medicine*, vol. 241, No. 2, pp. 39-47 (July 1949).

Berger, Robert L., M. D., "Nazi Science—The Dachau Hypothermia Experiments," *The New England Journal of Medicine*," vol. 322, No. 20, pp. 1435-1440 (May 1990).

O'Malley, William J., S. J., "The Priests of Dachau," *America*, vol. 157, No. 14 (November 1987).

The Congressional Record, April 2, 1979.

Newspaper Article

The Denver Post, December 3, 1990.

Acknowledgments

I PUT OFF writing this book for fifty years after reporting the Nazi doctors' case of the Nuremberg War Crimes Trials. As a front seat witness to the survivors' stories, I was badly affected all of my life. I wanted to put the horror behind me.

The shock of my first confrontation with Holocaust denial in 1987 made me realize I had to start speaking out about the truth to combat this insidious claim that the Holocaust was a "Holohoax." I have now reached over forty thousand people in this and other countries. I did not have a book in mind at that time. However, at every event, including dozens of TV and radio talk shows and press interviews, I was asked if I had a book. After being seriously confronted in 1997 and 1999 by Holocaust deniers at presentations, I started writing.

I am especially grateful to all of the following who encouraged, guided, pushed, and facilitated me along this painful path.

Dr. William Silvers, Clinical Professor at the University of Colorado Medical Sciences Center, worked with me on the Holocaust Awareness Institute of the University of Denver Center for Judaic Studies in the late 1980s. To the present, he has me lecturing at hospital grand rounds in Colorado on the Nazi doctors' trial and lessons to be learned. Dr. Fredrick R. Abrams, a renowned ethicist, graciously provided the foreword. Dr. Michel Reynders, a rescuer, wrote his story for my dedication page.

Theresa and Paul Messinger arranged many speaking forums for me. We worked together for twelve years on the Anne Frank Art and Writing Competition while Theresa was State Chairman.

Brigadier General J. R. Albi, USAF (Ret.), arranged in 1993 for the first of many lectures to the officers and cadets at the United States Air Force Academy.

Professor Frances Pilch, Ph.D. has continued my lectures at the academy and has provided other forums for the past several years.

Marlene Warshawski Yahalom, Ph.D., Education Director of the American Society of Yad Vashem, arranged for speaking engagements in New York.

New York attorney Henry Korn scheduled me to speak in several venues for two successive years. He also arranged, at the late Tony Randall's request, for my appearance on the Broadway stage after Randall's 2001 production of *Judgment at Nuremberg.*

Dean John Cech of the Rocky Mountain College in Billings, Montana arranged for a joint lecture to the college and Montana State University. President Arthur H. DeRosier Jr. of Rocky Mountain College presented me with their 2001 Distinguished Service Award.

Judge Leslie G. Johnson, Director of the Mississippi Judicial College in Jackson, arranged several presentations to Mississippi court reporters. Professor Janice K. Bounds of the University of Mississippi continued booking me.

The National Court Reporters Association has given me the honored position of keynote speaker to court reporters numbering in the thousands at New York, Boston, and Phoenix conventions over 16 years. Academy of Professional Reporters Fellow Gary Cramer of Chatsworth, California sponsored NCRA's Humanitarian Award to me in 2000, the first in that organization's 106 years. The Colorado Court Reporters Association has had me present to them several times.

National Court Reporters Association past president William C. Oliver, Ph.D. arranged for me to speak at Northwood University in Dallas for two successive years, to other Dallas forums, and in Little Rock, Arkansas.

Academy of Professional Reporters Fellow H. Allen Benowitz of Miami arranged for presentations over several years, resulting in the Greater Miami Jewish Federation's honoring me with a Humanitarian Award in 1996. I am indebted to all of the reporters in state and Canadian associations who had me speak to them.

Cantor Birdie Becker of B'nai B'rith of Colorado arranged for me to speak in an interfaith program and schools and to the Western Region B'nai B'rith convention. I thank all of the Rabbis in synagogues in Colorado, across this nation, and in Singapore who honored me for speaking to their congregations. I very much appreciate Denver Congregation Beth Joseph and the America-Israel Friendship League for their Humanitarian Awards. My thanks go also to Protestant and Catholic pastors for having me speak in their churches. I am grateful to the Most Reverend Charles J. Chaput, Archbishop of Denver, for having me speak as a Catholic in a Catholic-Jewish dialogue seminar.

Professor Michael Phayer, Ph.D., prolific author and Fulbright Fellow, arranged for me to speak at Milwaukee's Jesuit Marquette University. This was remarkable because a Catholic university commemorated Kristallnacht (The Night of Broken Glass) in Germany on November 9, 1938, which began the state-sponsored, planned and organized destruction of Europe's Jews.

Professor Dan Clayton, Ph.D. of Regis University in Denver arranged for lectures to staff, students, and the general public in their continuing World War II seminars over the past four years.

I am indebted to one Metro Denver educator especially, Gary Lubell of the Cherry Creek School District, who with great sensitivity and caring interviewed me in 1995 for the Steven Spielberg SHOAH Visual History Foundation and who had me lecture to teachers and students in his district several times.

In my two visits to the United States Holocaust Memorial Museum in 1996 and 1998, Archivist Henry Mayer and Photo Archivist Sharon Müeller, and in 2004 Maren Read, generously provided me with very helpful information and obtained material and photographs I needed for this book. The Denver Public Library Government Documents Archivist was very helpful in making

Volumes I and II of *The Nuremberg Medical Case* available to me. In 1998, Dan Pegadorn and Paul K. McCutcheon provided me with *Jane's All the World's Aircraft 1945/1946* from the archives of the National Air and Space Museum in Washington, D. C. so that I could gain detailed information about the Douglas C-54 Skymaster U. S. Air Force troop transport and the Douglas C-47 Skytrain Transport, planes on which I flew to Nuremberg, Germany.

I am very appreciative of the patience and guidance given by publisher Connie Shaw and her staff of Sentient Publications in Boulder, who expertly made corrections and suggestions and smoothed out my text to make it flow much better than I could have done. I thank my friend Lynn Donaldson, Ph.D. for initially reading my manuscript and making useful suggestions and changes.

I am so grateful to my two sons, John and Peter Spitz, who continually urged and pushed me to finish my book between speaking engagements. John extolled it to anyone who would listen, and Peter arranged for me to speak at the Singapore Synagogue by calling and telling the Rabbi, "My mother is a national speaker on the Nuremberg Trials. Do you want to hear her? She is coming to visit."

I am thankful to photographer Edwin F. Gorak with the Forty-fifth Division, Battery B, of the U. S. Army who provided me with many World War II photographs he took during the liberation of Dachau on April 29, 1945, by General Felix L. Sparks.

Responsibility for any errors or shortcomings in this work is mine alone. I wrote the truth about what I saw and heard, learned and felt.

About the Author

Lifetouch Directories

VIVIEN SPITZ IS a fellow of the Academy of Professional Reporters of the National Court Reporters Association, and was an official reporter of debates and chief reporter in the United States House of Representatives from 1972 to 1982. During this time she reported Presidents Nixon, Ford, Carter, and Reagan on their state of the union addresses to the nation. She reported as well all foreign heads of state who addressed Congress, including King Juan Carlos of Spain, President Anwar Sadat of Egypt, and Prime Minister Itzhak Rabin of Israel. She reported President Carter's establishment in 1978 of the President's Commission on the Holocaust, appointing Elie Wiesel as chairman.

By contract with the United States War Department, Mrs. Spitz reported the Nuremberg War Crimes Trials in Germany from 1946 to 1948, including the Nazi doctors' case. Since 1987 she has made presentations on this case to over forty thousand people in the United States, Canada, and Singapore, using graphic slides of captured German film that show experiments the doctors conducted on concentration camp victims without their consent. Her message is about basic human rights and the dignity of life, the difference between good and evil, and indifference to evil.

In recognition of her presentations to refute the claims that the Holocaust never happened, she has received several national Human Relations Awards, and in 2000 she received the thirty-thousand-member National Court Reporters Association's first Humanitarian Award.

She is a member of the University of Denver Holocaust Awareness Institute's Speakers Bureau, and in 2002 was honored as a "Righteous Gentile" by the Institute. In 1978 and 1993 she was listed in the *World Who's Who of Women* at Cambridge, England; in 1981 in Marquis' *Who's Who of American Women*.

Vivien Spitz lives in Houston, Texas.

Sentient Publications, LLC publishes books on cultural creativity, experimental education, transformative spirituality, holistic health, new science, ecology, and other topics, approached from an integral viewpoint. Our authors are intensely interested in exploring the nature of life from fresh perspectives, addressing life's great questions, and fostering the full expression of the human potential. Sentient Publications' books arise from the spirit of inquiry and the richness of the inherent dialogue between writer and reader.

Our Culture Tools series is designed to give social catalyzers and cultural entrepreneurs the essential information, technology, and inspiration to forge a sustainable, creative, and compassionate world.

We are very interested in hearing from our readers. To direct suggestions or comments to us, or to be added to our mailing list, please contact:

SENTIENT PUBLICATIONS, LLC
1113 Spruce Street
Boulder, CO 80302
303-443-2188
contact@sentientpublications.com
www.sentientpublications.com